Nebraska Symposium on Motivation

Volume 69

Series Editor
Lisa Crockett, Department of Psychology
University of Nebraska-Lincoln
Lincoln, NE, USA

The Nebraska Symposium on Motivation has been sponsored by the Department of Psychology at the University of Nebraska-Lincoln since 1953. Each year the Symposium invites leading scholars from around the world on a topic of current interest in psychology for a conference at the University followed by publication of an edited volume.

2019 2-year Impact Factor: 1.643 2019 5-year Impact Factor: 1.464

Jeffrey R. Stevens
Editor

Canine Cognition
and the Human Bond

Editor
Jeffrey R. Stevens
Department of Psychology
and Center for Brain, Biology & Behavior
University of Nebraska-Lincoln
Lincoln, NE, USA

ISSN 0146-7875
Nebraska Symposium on Motivation
ISBN 978-3-031-29788-5   ISBN 978-3-031-29789-2   (eBook)
https://doi.org/10.1007/978-3-031-29789-2

© The Editor(s) (if applicable) and The Author(s), under exclusive license to Springer Nature Switzerland AG 2023, Corrected Publication 2023
This work is subject to copyright. All rights are solely and exclusively licensed by the Publisher, whether the whole or part of the material is concerned, specifically the rights of translation, reprinting, reuse of illustrations, recitation, broadcasting, reproduction on microfilms or in any other physical way, and transmission or information storage and retrieval, electronic adaptation, computer software, or by similar or dissimilar methodology now known or hereafter developed.
The use of general descriptive names, registered names, trademarks, service marks, etc. in this publication does not imply, even in the absence of a specific statement, that such names are exempt from the relevant protective laws and regulations and therefore free for general use.
The publisher, the authors, and the editors are safe to assume that the advice and information in this book are believed to be true and accurate at the date of publication. Neither the publisher nor the authors or the editors give a warranty, expressed or implied, with respect to the material contained herein or for any errors or omissions that may have been made. The publisher remains neutral with regard to jurisdictional claims in published maps and institutional affiliations.

This Springer imprint is published by the registered company Springer Nature Switzerland AG
The registered company address is: Gewerbestrasse 11, 6330 Cham, Switzerland

Series Preface

We are pleased to offer this volume from the 69th Nebraska Symposium on Motivation. This year, the volume editor is Jeffrey R. Stevens. In addition to overseeing the development of this book, the volume editor coordinated the 69th Symposium, including selecting and inviting the contributors. I would like to express my appreciation to Professor Stevens for a stimulating meeting and an excellent series of papers on canine cognition and the emotional bond between humans and dogs.

Historically, the symposium series has been supported by funds from the Office of the Chancellor of the University of Nebraska-Lincoln and by funds given in memory of Professor Harry K. Wolfe to the University of Nebraska Foundation by the late Professor Cora L. Friedline. This year's symposium was supported by funding from Chancellor Ronnie Green.

This symposium volume, like those in the recent past, is dedicated in memory of Professor Wolfe, who brought psychology to the University of Nebraska. After studying with Professor Wilhelm Wundt in Germany, Professor Wolfe returned to his native state to establish the first undergraduate laboratory in psychology in the nation. As a student at the University of Nebraska, Professor Friedline studied psychology under Professor Wolfe.

Lincoln, NE, USA   Lisa Crockett

Contents

1. **Of Dogs and Bonds** 1
   Jeffrey R. Stevens

2. **Biological and Hormonal Approaches to the Evolution of Human-Canine Relationships** 11
   Gwendolyn Wirobski, Martina Lazzaroni, Sarah Marshall-Pescini, and Friederike Range

3. **Measuring the Dog Side of the Dog-Human Bond** 37
   Jordan G. Smith and Jeffrey S. Katz

4. **A Dog's Life in the Human Jungle** 63
   Anindita Bhadra and Rohan Sarkar

5. **Effects of University-Based AAIs: Conceptual Models Guiding Research on Active Treatment Components of AAIs on Stress-Related Outcomes** 91
   Patricia Pendry and Alexa M. Carr

6. **Canine-Assisted Interventions: Insights from the B.A.R.K. Program and Future Research Directions** 117
   John-Tyler Binfet

Correction to: Canine Cognition and the Human Bond C1

Index 135

The original version of this book was revised. A correction is available at https://doi.org/10.1007/978-3-031-29789-2

Contributors

Anindita Bhadra Department of Biological Sciences, Indian Institute of Science Education and Research Kolkata, Mohanpur, West Bengal, India

John-Tyler Binfet Okanagan School of Education, University of British Columbia, Kelowna, BC, Canada

Alexa M. Carr Department of Human Development, Washington State University, Pullman, WA, USA

Jeffrey S. Katz Department of Psychological Sciences, Auburn University, Auburn, AL, USA

Martina Lazzaroni Domestication Lab, Konrad Lorenz Institute of Ethology, Department of Interdisciplinary Life Sciences, University of Veterinary Medicine Vienna, Vienna, Austria

Sarah Marshall-Pescini Domestication Lab, Konrad Lorenz Institute of Ethology, Department of Interdisciplinary Life Sciences, University of Veterinary Medicine Vienna, Vienna, Austria

Patricia Pendry Department of Human Development, Washington State University, Pullman, WA, USA

Friederike Range Domestication Lab, Konrad Lorenz Institute of Ethology, Department of Interdisciplinary Life Sciences, University of Veterinary Medicine Vienna, Vienna, Austria

Rohan Sarkar Department of Biological Sciences, Indian Institute of Science Education and Research Kolkata, Mohanpur, West Bengal, India

Jordan G. Smith Department of Psychological Sciences, Auburn University, Auburn, AL, USA

Jeffrey R. Stevens Department of Psychology and Center for Brain, Biology & Behavior, University of Nebraska-Lincoln, Lincoln, NE, USA

Gwendolyn Wirobski Domestication Lab, Konrad Lorenz Institute of Ethology, Department of Interdisciplinary Life Sciences, University of Veterinary Medicine Vienna, Vienna, Austria

Chapter 1
Of Dogs and Bonds

Jeffrey R. Stevens

In four of Charles Darwin's classic works (Darwin, 1859, 1868, 1871, 1872), the domestic dog (*Canis familiaris* or *Canis lupus familiaris*)[1] featured prominently, offering key examples to illustrate his ideas about evolution, domestication, comparative behavior and cognition, and emotional expression. Darwin held a clear fondness for dogs, and when replying to letters detailing the "sagacity" of dogs, he remarked "I can believe almost anything about them" (Darwin, 2014). Despite the early interest in their behavior and cognition by a number of leading scientists, dogs were rarely subject to serious investigation as a study species for 150 years. In 2000, the number of studies on dog behavior and cognition began increasing rapidly, as more behavioral researchers worldwide began to work with them (Aria et al., 2021; Bensky et al., 2013). This research covers both the social and nonsocial domains of behavior and cognition (Bensky et al., 2013; Miklósi, 2015). In the social domain, researchers study how dogs interact with social agents (both conspecifics and heterospecifics) in areas such as play, social relationships, perspective taking, cooperation, communication, and social learning. In the nonsocial domain, researchers study how dogs interact with their physical environment by investigating perception, learning, memory, categorization, physical reasoning, numerical cognition, and spatial cognition. Combined, this work has highlighted dogs as an ideal study

---

[1] Different authors use different species concepts to classify domestic dogs. Those who employ the biological species concept refer to dogs as *Canis lupus familiaris*, while those who employ the ecological species concept use *Canis familiaris* (Miklósi, 2015). For consistency throughout the book, we will use *Canis familiaris*.

J. R. Stevens (✉)
Department of Psychology and Center for Brain, Biology & Behavior, University of Nebraska-Lincoln, Lincoln, NE, USA

© The Author(s), under exclusive license to Springer Nature Switzerland AG 2023
J. R. Stevens (ed.), *Canine Cognition and the Human Bond*, Nebraska Symposium on Motivation 69, https://doi.org/10.1007/978-3-031-29789-2_1

system for understanding the evolution of behavior and cognition, domestication and co-evolution, applied animal science, and even human health (ManyDogs Project et al., 2023).

Many species exhibit fascinating aspects of behavior and cognition. But what sets dogs apart is their relationship with humans. No other species has been invited into our homes, farms, schools, hospitals, libraries, and airports to the degree that dogs have. They have an exaggerated presence in the media we consume, from beloved cartoon characters such as Peanut's Snoopy to a pudgy little pug setting the morning mood for millions of people on social media (Graziano, 2022). Further, many people identify as "pet parents" and treat their dogs as they would their children (Volsche, 2021). Mirroring the dog cognition trends, we have recently witnessed a sharp increase in studies of canine-human interaction, exploring the motivational, emotional, cognitive, physiological, and neural mechanisms of dogs on human psychology and well-being. Despite increase in both dog cognition and canine-human interaction, there is not as much cross talk between these fields as one might hope for. Here, we bring these research fields together to take seriously the questions of why dogs play such an important role in our hearts and minds and why the canine-human bond is so strong.

1.1 What Is a Dog?

To understand the canine-human bond, we must understand the dog's origin story. Like many origin stories, the dog's is controversial and fraught with uncertainty. For our purposes, we will keep things fairly simple. Dogs diverged from a common ancestor with wolves (*Canis lupus*) between 15,000 and 30,000 years ago. While the fossil record supports the more recent divergence, genetic approaches indicate earlier divergence (Miklósi, 2015). In addition to uncertainty surrounding *when* exactly dogs originated, there is uncertainty *where* dogs originated. Genetic evidence points toward Asia, but it is not clear if they originated in east Asia or west Asia/Middle East/Europe (Miklósi, 2015). To add a final layer of uncertainty, there are multiple competing hypotheses about *how* dogs diverged, that is, what environmental circumstances provided the pressure for divergence. The two primary hypotheses boil down to whether humans played a more passive or active role in domesticating dogs (see Wirobski et al., this volume).

Despite this ambiguity about when, where, and how dogs originated, the key point is that dogs have lived and co-evolved with humans for thousands of years, resulting in a close relationship between us. Being the first domesticated animals has given dogs the opportunity to evolve traits that make them well suited to living with us. There are many shared traits between dogs and their closest living relative the wolf. However, of particular interest are behavioral and cognitive traits exhibited uniquely by dogs. Comparisons between dogs and wolves can offer insights

1 Of Dogs and Bonds

Fig. 1.1 Dogs have specific muscles to generate "puppy-dog eyes." Wolves do not have these muscles. (Photo credit: Bharathi Kannan on Unsplash; licensed for free use)

into these similarities and differences, but they face challenges, including maintaining equivalent rearing and socialization practices between the two species (see Wirobski et al., this volume) as well as assessing the genetics of the wolf populations to ensure they are not wolf-dog hybrids. With these safeguards in place, we can begin to explore possible species differences that are attributable to domestication.

These aspects of social cognition may be important in facilitating a strong connection with humans. But dogs have taken this a step further by potentially evolving traits that not only facilitate a relationship with humans but actually exploit existing cognitive systems in humans to manipulate us. For example, oxytocin is a neuropeptide hormone associated with social bonding between parents and infants (Feldman et al., 2007) and between romantic partners (Algoe et al., 2017). Eye contact between mothers and infants is associated with changes in oxytocin levels (Kim et al., 2014). Likewise, owners gazing into the eyes of their dogs results in an oxytocin boost in both owner and dog (Nagasawa et al., 2015). So dogs may be co-opting an existing physiological system in humans associated with bonding. They may have even taken a step further to evolve morphology that hijacks our emotions by evolving specific muscles around their eyes that result in "puppy-dog eyes" (Fig. 1.1; Kaminski et al., 2019).

1.2 Role of the Dog

Over the thousands of years of co-evolution with humans, dogs have filled various roles in human society, with the number of roles increasing more recently.

1.2.1 Free-Ranging Dogs

Of course, the original "role" of the dog was not so much a role but an association, with dogs just hanging out around human settlements. Currently, there are estimated to be 900 million dogs worldwide (Gompper, 2013). Incredibly, about 80% of these dogs are free-ranging dogs (Fig. 1.2a)—also called village dogs, street dogs, or feral dogs (Lord et al., 2013). While in North America and Europe free-ranging dogs are relatively rare, they are quite common throughout the Global South. This fact likely explains why the vast majority of research on dog behavior omits this critical and ubiquitous population of dogs. Fortunately, a number of researchers are attempting to remedy this oversight (see Bhadra and Sarkar, this volume).

1.2.2 Companion Dogs

Arguably the most common role of dogs considered by people is that of a pet or companion animal. Dogs live with us in our homes or on our property, where we provide them food and shelter and they provide us with companionship (Fig. 1.2b).

Fig. 1.2 Examples of (**a**) free-ranging dogs, (**b**) companion dogs, (**c**) working dogs, and (**d**) assistance dogs. (Photo credits: (a) Anoir Chafik on Unsplash, (b) Anna Dudkova on Unsplash, (c) William Milliot on Unsplash, and (d) PersianDutchNetwork on Wikipedia Commons; all licensed for free use or under CC BY-SA 3.0)

This can range from farm dogs who may live in barns or dog houses to the highly pampered "fur babies" doted on by pet parents (Blouin, 2013). Thus, the role of companion dogs ranges from property protector to cherished member of the family, potentially substituting for human children (Volsche, 2021).

In many countries worldwide, the number of companion dogs is increasing. In the United States, for instance, the percentage of households with dogs increased from 38% in 2016 to 45% in 2020 (American Veterinary Medical Association, 2022). The recent COVID-19 pandemic in particular drove up interest in dog adoptions as people were looking for more companionship in difficult times (Ho et al., 2021). Mirroring the increase in interest in dogs by the general public, research on canine behavioral science has grown rapidly in the last two decades (Aria et al., 2021), with the vast majority of studies using pet dogs as their study sample (Bensky et al., 2013).

1.2.3 Working Dogs

One of the early roles that dogs likely provided humans was protection from predators and competitors. Since then, we have selected dogs to fill a number of working roles for us (Fig. 1.2c). In fact, many breeds of dog were specifically created to fill different working roles. Some of the more breed-specific working roles include livestock guarding, herding, hunting, and sled pulling (Lord et al., 2016). Dogs have been bred to serve in these roles for hundreds or thousands of years. More recently, we have trained and sometimes bred dogs for roles that focus on their amazing olfactory abilities. We have created a number of different roles for detection dogs, including search and rescue and the detection of explosives, cadavers, drugs, disease, and threatened or invasive species (Bray et al., 2021; Helton, 2009). Given the agricultural, military, law enforcement, medical, and conservation applications of these dogs, increasing research interest is being directed toward these dogs to improve their breeding, selection, training, performance, and welfare.

1.2.4 Assistance Dogs

Though assistance dogs are actually a subcategory of working dogs, I separate them out due to their unique influences on our physical and mental health and well-being (Fig. 1.2d). While many dog owners may feel that their well-being is improved by having a dog, general benefits to owning a dog (the so-called pet effect) are not well supported by larger-scale research (Herzog, 2011). This is in part because dogs can provide costs as well as benefits to people. Assistance dogs are working dogs that perform some form of assistance or support for people (McMichael & Singletary, 2021). The more specific nature of the assistance can in fact provide direct benefits to people.

There are several types of assistance dogs. *Service dogs* refer to a dog trained "to perform specific tasks or do specific work for the benefit of an individual with a recognized disability" (Americans with Disabilities Act), which include physical, sensory, or psychiatric assistance. Service dogs are highly trained and work with a specific individual. *Therapy dogs*, in contrast, do not perform specific tasks beyond allowing other individuals beside their owners to pet and interact with them. This can occur in formal setting such as mental health therapy offices or more informally through visits to facilities such as retirement homes and hospitals. Therapy dogs are trained to interact with people other than their owners. *Facility dogs* are similar to therapy dogs but, instead of being brought in specifically for short-term interactions, they are regularly present in a facility such as a school, retirement home, or hospital. *Emotional support dogs* are dogs that provide physical, psychological, and/or emotional support through companionship (McMichael & Singletary, 2021). There are no training requirements for emotional support animals, and they interact only with their owner in that capacity. With the increasing numbers of assistance animals in society, research interest in them is rapidly growing.

1.3 Canine Cognition and the Human Bond

With the roles of dogs increasing in our society, understanding the relationship between dogs and people becomes ever more important. The aim of the 69th Annual Nebraska Symposium on Motivation and this volume was to bring together researchers from psychology, biology, neuroscience, anthropology, and social work to delve deeper into the canine-human bond. The advantage of this approach is that it engages experts in dog cognition with experts in canine-human interaction. Only by studying both ends of the leash can we truly understand our unique connection with dogs.

In Chap. 2, the volume begins with Wirobski, Lazzaroni, Marshall-Pescini, and Range setting the stage for understanding canine-human relationships by reviewing what we know about dog origins and domestication. This chapter begins by summarizing a number of different hypotheses about the origins of dogs and their history of domestication. The authors then argue that behavioral data alone may not be sufficient to distinguish between these hypotheses. Instead, integrating hormonal data with behavior may best test these hypotheses. Specifically, aspects of the hypothalamo-pituitary-adrenal axis and the oxytocinergic system can provide insights into dog origins and the human-canine relationship. The authors then describe a set of studies comparing wolves, comparably raised dogs, pet dogs, and free-ranging dogs. These studies investigated differences in dog and wolf motivations to interact with humans, as well as effects of human interactions and social contact on dog and wolf behavior and hormone levels. While wolves share some behavioral and hormonal responses with dogs, they differ in some situations. Investigating the role of life experience and hormonal mechanisms can go a long way to help us understand the canine-human bond.

1 Of Dogs and Bonds　　　7

In Chap. 3, Smith and Katz explore the behavioral and neuroscientific evidence for the dog-human bond. They begin by reviewing the state of knowledge for key measures of socio-cognitive abilities of dogs, focusing on the object-choice task and the unsolvable task. They then dive into how canine researchers have adapted measures of human attachment to measure attachment between dogs and humans. With this background in place, the authors review the current state of the field of canine neuroscience, a burgeoning research area that noninvasively measures brain activity in awake and unrestrained (but highly trained!) dogs in a scanner. Critically, researchers can use functional magnetic resonance imaging (fMRI) to measure neural activity in dogs as they receive visual, olfactory, or auditory stimuli. This nascent research area has already yielded critical insights into dog behavior and cognition as well as intriguing parallels with human neuroscience. The authors end by applying a neural model of human attachment to dogs, providing a theoretical framework for better understanding the canine-human bond.

In Chap. 4, Bhadra and Sarkar describe a research program focused on understanding free-ranging dogs. Despite decades of studying so many other species, we have only just recently begun recording the natural history of domestic dogs in their natural environment—the streets, neighborhoods, and countryside adjoining human settlement. The authors describe groundbreaking, foundational natural history information about free-ranging dogs in India. They begin by cataloging births and deaths of free-ranging dog pups and recording the seasonality of birth, along with the mortality rate across ages of the pups. The authors then describe characteristics and qualities of dens that mothers choose with respect to how they exploit aspects of the human environment. Once pups are born, the next phase of maternal care is nursing the pups, which is tied directly to key theories of parental investment and parent-offspring conflict. Though mothers provide most of the parental care for their pups, the authors describe the extent to which allo-mothers and putative fathers contribute to pup care, including nursing, play, and protection. Finally, the authors end with a series of studies exploring how free-ranging dogs interact with humans by investigating (1) how they detect high-quality food found in human garbage, (2) how they understand and use human communication cues, and (3) how they trade-off food vs. social rewards (petting) from humans. In short, this chapter introduces us to the way that most domestic dogs on the planet interact with humans—not those dogs kept as pets but those that experience both the spoils and perils of interacting with humans on their own terms.

In Chap. 5, Pendry and Carr demonstrate direct effects of dogs on human well-being. They first introduce the field of anthrozoology—which studies human-animal interactions—and the different forms of animal-assisted interventions. In particular, they focus on animal visitation programs in which animal-handler teams visit university campuses to allow students to briefly interact with the animals. The authors frame the issue in a transactional model that describes how stress and human-animal interactions influence the stress system, which in turn influences physical and mental health. With this in mind, they describe a series of studies in which university students experience animal visitation programs or control conditions to assess the effect of animal interactions on self-reports of well-being, as well as physiological measures such as cortisol. Critically, they carve up the study populations based on individual differences such as experience with depressive symptomatology, mental health conditions, and/or academic deficiency to examine how useful the programs are to certain subpopulations. Combined, these studies use rigorous methods to directly assess not only whether these animal-assisted interventions work but also for whom and under what circumstances they may work.

In Chap. 6, Binfet reflects on what he has learned over the last 10 years of implementing a dog-focused animal visitation program at the University of British Columbia, Okanagan campus. His *Building Academic Retention through K9s* or B.A.R.K. program has helped thousands of university students cope with the stresses of college life. Building a program like this involves selecting and training a large numbers of dog-handler teams, and this chapter starts by describing key characteristics of both therapy dogs and their handlers, keeping in mind the welfare of the dogs in addition to the efficacy of the interventions. Binfet then describes a number of studies conducted as a part of the program. The first investigated the importance of touch as a part of the animal interaction by comparing measures of well-being across groups who petted/touched the dog, only viewed the dogs, or only interacted with a handler. Born out of the COVID-19 pandemic, another study investigated the efficacy of virtual interactions with dogs by comparing groups who had live vs. pre-recorded virtual encounters with dogs or handlers. Finally, the chapter ends with a look toward future research questions that address the effects of program duration and dog-handler experience on efficacy, as well as the importance of considering implementation fidelity and diversity in handlers and participants.

Dogs have a special place in the hearts of millions of us worldwide but also in human history. In fact, the crucial evolutionary link between dogs and humans underlies the bonds that we currently share with this amazing species. Understanding their behavior and cognition in our homes and neighborhoods not only satisfies our curiosity about this endearing species but directly informs how we interact with them as companions and as providers of support and well-being.

Acknowledgments Organizing the 69th Annual Nebraska Symposium on Motivation was a joy and a privilege. The success of the symposium relied on the support and hard work of many people. I am grateful for the financial support from the University of Nebraska-Lincoln Chancellor Ronnie Green and from the late Professor Cora L. Friedline's bequest to the University of Nebraska Foundation in memory of Professor Harry K. Wolfe. The symposium would not be possible without their generous gifts. I would also like to thank Professor Lisa Crockett, the symposium series editor, for organizing the symposium series. The symposium went off without a hitch, primarily due to the superb organization of Pam Waldvogel and the assistance of London Wolff and Jessica Barela. Thank you for your time and hard work. Finally, I am ever grateful to the symposium speakers, for sharing their wonderful views of the role of dogs in our lives.

References

Algoe, S. B., Kurtz, L. E., & Grewen, K. (2017). Oxytocin and social bonds: The role of oxytocin in perceptions of romantic partners' bonding behavior. *Psychological Science, 28*(12), 1763–1772. https://doi.org/10.1177/0956797617716922

American Veterinary Medical Association. (2022). *Pet ownership and demographics sourcebook.* American Veterinary Medical Association.

Aria, M., Alterisio, A., Scandurra, A., Pinelli, C., & D'Aniello, B. (2021). The scholar's best friend: Research trends in dog cognitive and behavioral studies. *Animal Cognition, 24*(3), 541–553. https://doi.org/10.1007/s10071-020-01448-2

Bensky, M. K., Gosling, S. D., & Sinn, D. L. (2013). The world from a dog's point of view: A review and synthesis of dog cognition research. In H. J. Brockmann, T. J. Roper, M. Naguib, J. C. Mitani, L. W. Simmons, & L. Barrett (Eds.), *Advances in the study of behavior* (Vol. 45, pp. 209–406). Academic Press. https://doi.org/10.1016/B978-0-12-407186-5.00005-7

Blouin, D. D. (2013). Are dogs children, companions, or just animals? Understanding variations in people's orientations toward animals. *Anthrozoös, 26*(2), 279–294. https://doi.org/10.2752/175303713X13636846944402

Bray, E. E., Otto, C. M., Udell, M. A. R., Hall, N. J., Johnston, A. M., & MacLean, E. L. (2021). Enhancing the selection and performance of working dogs. *Frontiers in Veterinary Science, 8.* https://doi.org/10.3389/fvets.2021.644431

Darwin, C. (1859). *The origin of species.* Penguin.

Darwin, C. (1868). *The variation of animals and plants under domestication.* Murray.

Darwin, C. (1871). *The descent of man and selection in relation to sex.* Murray.

Darwin, C. (1872). *The expression of the emotions in man and animals.* Murray.

Darwin, C. (2014). Letter no. 8817. In F. Burkhardt, J. A. Secord, & The Editors of the Darwin Correspondence Project (Eds.), *The correspondence of Charles Darwin: Volume 21: 1873* (Vol. 21). Cambridge University Press. https://doi.org/10.1017/CBO9781107280403

Feldman, R., Weller, A., Zagoory-Sharon, O., & Levine, A. (2007). Evidence for a neuroendocrinological foundation of human affiliation: Plasma oxytocin levels across pregnancy and the postpartum period predict mother-infant bonding. *Psychological Science, 18*(11), 965–970. https://doi.org/10.1111/j.1467-9280.2007.02010.x

Gompper, M. E. (2013). The dog-human-wildlife interface: Assessing the scope of the problem. In *Free-ranging dogs and wildlife conservation* (pp. 9–54). Oxford University Press.

Graziano, J. (2022). *Noodle and the no bones day.* https://www.simonandschuster.com/books/Noodle-and-the-No-Bones-Day/Jonathan-Graziano/9781665927109

Helton, W. S. (2009). *Canine ergonomics: The science of working dogs.* CRC Press.

Herzog, H. (2011). The impact of pets on human health and psychological well-being: Fact, fiction, or hypothesis? *Current Directions in Psychological Science, 20*(4), 236–239. https://doi.org/10.1177/0963721411415220

Ho, J., Hussain, S., & Sparagano, O. (2021). Did the COVID-19 pandemic spark a public interest in pet adoption? *Frontiers in Veterinary Science, 8.* https://www.frontiersin.org/articles/10.3389/fvets.2021.647308

Kaminski, J., Waller, B. M., Diogo, R., Hartstone-Rose, A., & Burrows, A. M. (2019). Evolution of facial muscle anatomy in dogs. *Proceedings of the National Academy of Sciences,* 201820653. https://doi.org/10.1073/pnas.1820653116

Kim, S., Fonagy, P., Koos, O., Dorsett, K., & Strathearn, L. (2014). Maternal oxytocin response predicts mother-to-infant gaze. *Brain Research, 1580,* 133–142. https://doi.org/10.1016/j.brainres.2013.10.050

Lord, K., Feinstein, M., Smith, B., & Coppinger, R. (2013). Variation in reproductive traits of members of the genus Canis with special attention to the domestic dog (*Canis familiaris*). *Behavioural Processes, 92,* 131–142. https://doi.org/10.1016/j.beproc.2012.10.009

Lord, K., Schneider, R. A., & Coppinger, R. (2016). Evolution of working dogs. In J. Serpell (Ed.), *The domestic dog: Its evolution, behavior and interactions with people* (2nd ed., pp. 42–66). Cambridge University Press. https://doi.org/10.1017/9781139161800.004

ManyDogs Project, Alberghina, D., Bray, E., Buchsbaum, D., Byosiere, S.-E., Espinosa, J., Gnanadesikan, G., Guran, C.-N. A., Hare, E., Horschler, D., Huber, L., Kuhlmeier, V. A., MacLean, E., Pelgrim, M. H., Perez, B., Ravid-Schurr, D., Rothkoff, L., Sexton, C., Silver, Z., & Stevens, J. R. (2023). ManyDogs Project: A big team science approach to investigating canine behavior and cognition. *Comparative Cognition and Behavior Reviews, 18*, 59–77. https://doi.org/10.3819/CCBR.2023.180004

McMichael, M. A., & Singletary, M. (2021). Assistance, service, emotional support, and therapy togs. *Veterinary Clinics of North America: Small Animal Practice, 51*(4), 961–973. https://doi.org/10.1016/j.cvsm.2021.04.012

Miklósi, Á. (2015). *Dog behaviour, evolution, and cognition* (2nd ed.). Oxford University Press.

Nagasawa, M., Mitsui, S., En, S., Ohtani, N., Ohta, M., Sakuma, Y., Onaka, T., Mogi, K., & Kikusui, T. (2015). Oxytocin-gaze positive loop and the coevolution of human-dog bonds. *Science, 348*(6232), 333–336. https://doi.org/10.1126/science.1261022

Volsche, S. (2021). Pet parenting in the United States: Investigating an evolutionary puzzle. *Evolutionary Psychology, 19*(3), 14747049211038296. https://doi.org/10.1177/14747049211038297

Chapter 2
Biological and Hormonal Approaches to the Evolution of Human-Canine Relationships

Gwendolyn Wirobski, Martina Lazzaroni, Sarah Marshall-Pescini, and Friederike Range

2.1 Domestication

The domestication of animals and plants is an evolutionary process involving a species' adaptation to life near humans. It is arguably one of the most impactful and significant transitions that occurred during the history of humankind (Larson et al., 2014). A domesticated species may be modified in ways to make it more useful to humans compared to its wild ancestors (Diamond, 2002), entailing changes in morphology, physiology, and behavior. These changes brought about by domestication, i.e., the domestic phenotype, are the result of an intricate interplay of developmental effects and genetic alterations resulting from natural and artificial selection (Price, 1999). Most prominently, domesticated animals typically exhibit a markedly reduced fear response to the presence of humans, altered intraspecific behavioral patterns, and differences in social communication compared to their wild-type ancestors (Driscoll et al., 2009). In addition, many (but not all) domesticates share morphological features such as short snouts, floppy ears, and piebald-colored coats (Sánchez-Villagra et al., 2016). These are commonly referred to as part of the "domestication syndrome," which is thought to be caused by a deficit in neural crest cell development (Wilkins et al., 2014; but see Johnsson et al., 2021 for a recent critique of the neural crest cell hypothesis).

A particularly interesting model species to study domestication effects is the domestic dog (*Canis familiaris*). Dogs represent the first domesticated animal species, living alongside humans for at least 15,000 years (Diamond, 2002; Bergström et al., 2020; Serpell, 2021), sharing a common progenitor with their extant cousins,

G. Wirobski · M. Lazzaroni · S. Marshall-Pescini · F. Range (✉)
Domestication Lab, Konrad Lorenz Institute of Ethology, Department of Interdisciplinary Life Sciences, University of Veterinary Medicine Vienna, Vienna, Austria
e-mail: Friederike.range@vetmeduni.ac.at

gray wolves (*Canis lupus*). Dogs' accessibility, their diverse interactions with humans, and the existence of a closely related wild-living species make them ideal for comparative studies of domestication-related effects.

2.2 The Putative Origin of Dogs

Two main theories exist how wolf domestication may have started. The *commensal scavenger* hypothesis (also referred to as *self-domestication* hypothesis; originally coined by Lorenz, 1950, later elaborated on by Coppinger & Coppinger, 2001) suggests that a founder group of bolder, less fearful wolves approached human encampments to scavenge leftover meat and remains from kills. Gradually, those wolves further lost their fear of humans. With time, animals' whose lower stress response facilitated staying, feeding, and breeding in proximity to humans would have been favored by natural selection. Subsequent generations would eventually have also been subject to artificial selection by humans who might have selected the tamest pups for (hand)raising, culled the aggressive or shy ones, and thus step by step, established some control over the animals' breeding. Those proto-dogs would have been useful as barking sentinels guarding the camps at night, and some may have eventually become valuable hunting companions (Driscoll et al., 2009). However, the existence of sufficient amounts of leftover protein to sustain a scavenging wolf population at the proposed time of initial wolf domestication has been questioned (Jung & Pörtl, 2018; Serpell, 2021).

The second idea which has been suggested is the *cross-species adoption* hypothesis (also referred to as *pet-keeping* hypothesis; recently discussed and supported by Germonpré et al., 2021; Serpell, 2021; Mech & Janssens, 2021). It relies mainly on the observation of pet keeping practices among recent hunter-gatherer societies. It states that wolf domestication started when wolf pups were deliberately adopted and hand-raised by humans, which facilitated the evolution of proto-dogs in an active social process from both sides (Pörtl & Jung, 2017, 2019). This theory places special emphasis on the early development of an emotional bond between humans and "their" proto-dogs. Over the course of time, many of these early pets would have escaped (or been driven away once old enough to fend for themselves) and reverted to the wild, but some might have stayed close to humans and eventually founded the breeding stock for subsequent generations of pet wolves/proto-dogs with increasing propensities to affiliate with humans.

Although it will likely remain elusive what the initial steps in the domestication process exactly looked like, we can study how domestication has altered modern-day dogs compared to wolves and sculpted them into such well-adapted and flexible social partners for humans.

2.3 Behavioral and Endocrine Changes Linked to Domestication

Likely due to selective pressures during the domestication process, dogs have been found to build close relationships with their human caretakers (Miklósi & Topál, 2013). These relationships have been claimed to resemble the attachment bond that characterizes the relationship between human infants and their mothers (Topál et al., 1998; Palmer & Custance, 2008) and to differ fundamentally to those wolves can establish with humans (Topál et al., 2005 but see Wheat et al., 2020). Various domestication hypotheses have been brought forward to explain this extraordinary capacity. Most of these hypotheses emphasize an increase in docility, tameness, and sociability (*selection for tameness* hypothesis, Belyaev, 1979; Trut et al., 2009; *hyper-sociability* hypothesis, vonHoldt et al., 2017) alongside a reduction in the fearful and/or aggressive response toward humans (*emotional reactivity* hypothesis, Hare & Tomasello, 2005) in dogs compared to wolves. Despite these core ideas being likely linked to significant physiological alterations (Buttner, 2016), very few studies to date have in fact investigated these comparatively.

The endocrine system interacts closely with the nervous system, and hormones fulfill a wide array of biological functions, such as regulating cell growth, metabolism, reproduction, and behavior (Garland et al., 2016). Hormones may affect behavioral phenotypes during development and throughout life (i.e., organizational-activational hypothesis; Phoenix et al., 1959; Arnold, 2009). They are important regulators of gene expression (Beato, 1993; Richards, 1994), interacting dynamically with internal and external factors. Hence, the endocrine system represents a crucial mechanism driving behavioral change during natural and artificial selection processes such as domestication.

Evidence regarding which (neuro)endocrine pathways may be particularly relevant for domestication-related behavioral alterations stems from the Russian farm-fox experiment (Belyaev, 1979). In brief, this famous long-term experiment was based on the hypothesis that tamability (i.e., a species' genetic predisposition for docile and friendly behavior toward humans) was the main trait selected for during animal domestication. Thus, to mimic the domestication process and study its correlated physiological changes, Dmitry Belyaev and his colleagues bred silver foxes solely based on their behavioral response to a human experimenter (Trut, 1999). Specifically, they rigorously selected animals that showed reduced levels of fear and aggression in response to a human experimenter standing next to their cage (Trut, 1999). By consistently breeding the least fearful/aggressive individuals with each other, after just six generations, they had created a cohort of tame, "domesticated" foxes, which approached and licked the experimenter "like dogs" (Trut, 1999). For comparative purposes, they kept an unselected control cohort (farm-bred for fur production) and later also created an "aggressive" breeding line by selectively breeding the most fearful/aggressive individuals (see Kukekova et al., 2008 for a description of the behavioral selection criteria). Interestingly, the behavioral changes of the tame and aggressive foxes vs. the control animals were accompanied by a variety of alterations in neurotransmitter systems. Specifically, the serotonergic, glutaminergic, and catecholaminergic signaling pathways were upregulated in several brain regions in tame compared to control and aggressive foxes (Nikulina, 1990; Popova et al., 1991, 1997; Popova, 2006; Wang et al., 2018). In contrast, basal and stress-induced (i.e., capture and handling by humans) concentrations of adrenocorticotropic hormone (ACTH) and glucocorticoids (GC), the main endocrine correlates of the body's stress response, were significantly lower in the tame foxes compared to the aggressive and the unselected groups (Gulevich et al., 2004; Trut et al., 2009).

2.4 The Hypothalamo-Pituitary-Adrenal Axis and Emotional Reactivity

The hypothalamo-pituitary-adrenal (HPA) axis, oftentimes called the stress axis, is the key regulator of the body's physiological and behavioral response to fear-inducing stimuli and physical challenges to homeostasis (Smith & Vale, 2006). Genomic evidence for an alteration of the HPA axis' functional state during the evolution of the domestic phenotype is widely recognized and discussed, in humans as well as in animals (O'Rourke & Boeckx, 2020). Support for attenuated HPA axis (re)activity in association with more docile temperaments comes from selective breeding experiments and comparisons of closely related domestic and wild-type species (rats, Naumenko et al., 1989; Albert et al., 2008; chickens, Løtvedt et al., 2017; Fallahsharoudi et al., 2015; Ericsson et al., 2014; finches, Suzuki et al., 2012; pigs, Weiler et al., 1998; foxes, Harri et al., 2003; Gulevich et al., 2004; Trut et al., 2009; minks, Malmkvist et al., 2003; ducks, Martin, 1978; guinea pigs, Künzl & Sachser, 1999; Künzl et al., 2003; Zipser et al., 2014).

Curiously, relatively few studies have compared behavioral-endocrine profiles and (stress) hormone concentrations of wolves and dogs. An early study by McLeod et al. (1996) reported similar basal concentrations of urinary glucocorticoids in wolves and dogs, yet the attenuation of dogs' HPA axis, compared to wolves', is regularly invoked and discussed as a requisite and hallmark of their domestication process (Hare & Tomasello, 2005; Buttner, 2016; Pörtl & Jung, 2017; Herbeck & Gulevich, 2018; Kikusui et al., 2019).

For example, the *emotional reactivity* hypothesis (Hare & Tomasello, 2005) is built around the notion that dogs' ability to skillfully use human communicative gestures is a by-product of their domestication process, enabled by an initial reduction of fear and stress levels. This idea is mainly supported by the abovementioned Russian fox experiment in which selection for tame behavior alone resulted in correlated changes such as reduced HPA axis activity (as a proxy of reduced fear and stress levels) and enhanced human-directed socio-cognitive skills (i.e., understanding of human pointing gestures) in the experimentally domesticated fox kits compared to the control population (Hare et al., 2005). Hence, regarding the wolf-dog comparison, the *emotional reactivity* hypothesis would predict that dogs show less fear- and stress-related behavior and have lower glucocorticoid concentrations, as an indicator of a dampened HPA axis (re)activity, than wolves, particularly in contexts where humans are present.

2.5 The Oxytocinergic System and Hyper-Sociability

Besides a reduced fear response, domesticated animals also appear to actively seek human proximity more and faster than wild-type species, as shown in comparative studies of selectively bred foxes and controls (Hare et al., 2005), selectively bred rats and controls (Albert et al., 2008), and chickens and their wild ancestors, red junglefowl (Campler et al., 2009). Further studies have described active human-directed contact seeking in other domesticates, such as horses (Malavasi & Huber, 2016), pigs (Pérez Fraga et al., 2020), and goats (Langbein et al., 2018).

It has recently been suggested that the neuropeptide and hormone oxytocin (OT) may be an important driver of the increased sociability typical of domesticated animals, specifically of dogs (Nagasawa et al., 2015; Buttner, 2016; Herbeck et al., 2017; Herbeck & Gulevich, 2018; Kikusui et al., 2019). Oxytocin facilitates contact-seeking behavior with social partners (Lukas et al., 2011; Preckel et al., 2014) by interacting with the dopaminergic reward circuit (Gordon et al., 2011; Love, 2014). Through motivating repeated affiliative interactions with the same partners, oxytocin thereby promotes partner preference and, eventually, social bond formation. Thus far, oxytocin was primarily studied in the context of mother-offspring bonding (Nagasawa et al., 2012) and pair-bonding (Neumann, 2008), but interestingly, oxytocin concentrations were also found to be elevated in response to human-dog interactions (see Powell et al., 2019 for a review of the human-dog literature). Yet this was not the case following human-wolf interactions (Nagasawa et al., 2015). Hence, it appears plausible that dogs' oxytocinergic system has been altered, promoting increased willingness to approach and interact with humans, compared to wolves. Indeed, a genetic study found that the oxytocinergic system has likely been under selection during the dog domestication process and that it contributes to dogs' phenotypic social plasticity (Kis et al., 2014; Oliva et al., 2016; Bence et al., 2017; Cimarelli et al., 2017; Banlaki et al., 2017; Kubinyi et al., 2017; Persson et al., 2017; Sahlén et al., 2021). Compared to the wolf genome, a specific region on the dog genome showed similarity to a human neurodevelopmental disorder, the Williams-Beuren syndrome, which is related to heightened oxytocinergic system activity and behavioral hyper-sociability (vonHoldt et al., 2010, 2017). The identified region also revealed large numbers of polymorphic structural variants in dog but not wolf genomes, which were associated with behavioral measures of hyper-sociability in dogs (vonHoldt et al., 2017). Hyper-sociability, defined as the exaggerated motivation to seek out social contact with (unfamiliar) humans or conspecifics, has been proposed to be a typical behavioral feature of adult dogs but not wolves (Bentosela et al., 2016). Indeed, dogs show high levels of human-directed social motivation and quickly bond with unfamiliar humans (Gácsi et al., 2001), whereas wolves require intense, early-onset socialization and often remain wary of unfamiliar humans as adults (Ujfalussy et al., 2017). For this reason, dogs' behavioral phenotype has been characterized as "hyper-social," supposedly mediated by elevated oxytocinergic activity and a positive feedback loop facilitating the human-dog relationship (Nagasawa et al., 2015). Accordingly, the *hyper-sociability* hypothesis (vonHoldt et al., 2017) describes a genetic mechanism for selection to act upon dogs' hyper-social behavior during domestication and predicts that dogs should show higher social motivation to interact with humans (and conspecifics) than wolves, associated with higher oxytocinergic system (re)activity in response to social contact. However, these predictions remained largely untested until recently.

The few studies that have compared human-directed sociability of pet dogs and human-socialized, enclosure-living wolves (Bentosela et al., 2016), and included measures of oxytocinergic activity (Nagasawa et al., 2015), however, did not account for previous life experiences, social environment, or the quality of the dog-owner bond, thereby potentially confounding phylogenetic and ontogenetic effects. Hence, the conclusions that can be drawn from these data may be limited (Fiset & Plourde, 2015; Kekecs et al., 2016). To move forward, there is a clear need to test dogs living in diverse settings (with different levels of socialization with humans) as well as comparing similarly raised domesticates and wild types, thereby allowing to tease apart the relative influence of life experience and domestication.

2.6 Interactions of the Hypothalamo-Pituitary-Adrenal Axis and the Oxytocinergic System

Throughout the course of domestication, animals gradually lost their fear of humans, presumably facilitated by a reduced stress response (Trut et al., 2009). These less fearful, more docile individuals would have spent more time around humans. An increased motivation to approach and interact with humans, perhaps mediated by increased oxytocinergic activity, would eventually have resulted in the formation of interspecific social bonds (Herbeck et al., 2022). Thus, both the HPA axis and the oxytocinergic system likely have played an important part in this transition from wild to domestic phenotype. Crucially, oxytocin is a major modulator of the neuroendocrine stress response, and accordingly, there is an intricate interplay between both systems (Neumann et al., 2000; Cohen et al., 2010; Winter & Jurek, 2019). The HPA axis and the oxytocinergic system are neuroanatomically connected to the paraventricular nucleus (PVN) of the hypothalamus. During stress exposure, noradrenaline from nerve terminals in the brainstem is released into the paraventricular nucleus, triggering the secretion of corticotropin-releasing hormone (CRH) (Douglas, 2005).

Corticotropin-releasing hormone modulates the release of adrenocorticotropic hormone (ACTH) into the bloodstream, which regulates glucocorticoid secretion from the adrenal glands. In addition, oxytocin is released both into the paraventricular nucleus and into the bloodstream upon stress exposure (Nishioka et al., 1998; Wotjak et al., 1998). This may result in simultaneously high concentrations of oxytocin and glucocorticoids in the body's periphery at certain points following stress exposure (Brown et al., 2016). In the hypothalamus, oxytocin modulates the molecular stress cascade, mainly via inhibition of corticotropin-releasing hormone neurons (Neumann et al., 2000; Windle et al., 2004) and enhancement of the negative feedback loop (Winter & Jurek, 2019), thereby attenuating the behavioral stress response (Smith & Wang, 2014). This mode of oxytocinergic action is thought to underlie the stress-buffering effect of social support (Cavanaugh et al., 2016; McQuaid et al., 2016), gentle touch (Morrison, 2016), and affiliative human-animal interactions (Beetz et al., 2012). However, despite this well-known interplay of the oxytocinergic system and the HPA axis, many studies in the field of animal behavior science have thus far omitted to investigate both endocrine systems simultaneously. This has led to a limited understanding of oxytocin's complex contribution to an animal's inner state. Indeed, elevated oxytocin concentrations have widely been considered solely markers of positive valence and well-being (Mitsui et al., 2011) without consideration of (social) context or implementation of adequate (non-social) control conditions (see Rault et al., 2017 for a critical review on this topic).

Hence, findings of high oxytocinergic (re)activity may be misinterpreted if no physiological or behavioral correlates of negative emotional states to control for valence and general arousal are included. Given the clear support for HPA axis and oxytocin involvement in shaping the domestic phenotype (Trut et al., 2009; von-Holdt et al., 2017), it seems that comparative studies of domesticated and wild-type species as well as domesticated populations living in different environments would benefit especially from including both glucocorticoid and oxytocin measures in behavioral studies to better distinguish between different inner states of the study animals.

2.7 Investigating the Human-Canine Relationship

As both early life experiences and ongoing exposure to different environmental stimuli can affect behavior and physiology (Foyer et al., 2013; Puurunen et al., 2020), to tease apart the relative roles of domestication and life experience on dog-wolf differences, it is crucial to conduct research on populations of wolves and dogs with comparable experiences as well as populations of dogs differing in their social experience with humans. The presented research involving the comparison of wolves and dogs was therefore conducted at the Wolf Science Center (WSC), Ernstbrunn, Austria. At the WSC, wolves and dogs are hand-raised by animal professionals from an early age (i.e., from 10 days old) and later housed in conspecific packs. Both wolves and dogs at the Wolf Science Center experience regular contact with humans throughout their lives (Figs. 2.1 and 2.2). Differences found between their social behavior and hormonal correlates are thus likely attributable to genetic

Fig. 2.1 Wolf at the Wolf Science Center. (Photo credit: Thomas Suchanek/Vetmeduni)

Fig. 2.2 Dogs at the Wolf Science Center. (Photo credit: Thomas Suchanek/Vetmeduni)

factors (i.e., domestication-related effects) rather than differences in ontogeny. To complement the picture, we additionally compared WSC dogs with pet dogs living in Vienna, in a typical "Western" pet-owner relationship/management style. Furthermore, to assess the relative importance of life experience on dogs' behavior, in some studies, we also included tests with a population of free-ranging dogs in Morocco (Fig. 2.3) that, although social toward humans, do not have the same kind

Fig. 2.3 Free-ranging dogs in Morocco. (Photo credit: Martina Lazzaroni)

of close preferential bond with an "owner." Unfortunately, due to the difficulties of collecting hormonal measures from free-ranging animals, these have thus far not been included in our studies of free-ranging dogs.

2.7.1 Study 1

Do dogs and wolves differ in their motivation to interact with humans, and does life experience affect dogs' motivation for social contact? The aim of this study was to investigate the effect of domestication and life experience on the value that dogs attribute to human social contact over food (Lazzaroni et al., 2020). To this end, we compared equally raised Wolf Science Center wolves and dogs and additionally two populations of dogs widely differing in their life experience with humans (i.e., pet dogs and free-ranging dogs). We presented the wolves and dogs with a simple test, divided into two phases: in the pre-test phase, the animals were exposed to two people in succession. First, an experimenter invited the animal to a social/cuddle session by crouching down (social contact provider). If the animal approached, it was gently stroked and cuddled until it decided to leave again. After 30 s, the human left, and a second person appeared in front of the subject. This person fed the animal small pieces of sausage for the same duration as the other person had been present in front of the animal (food provider). The order of appearing in front of the animal was counterbalanced across subjects. After both people had either cuddled or fed the animal, the test phase started. Here, both persons reappeared in front of the subject at the same time and positioned themselves 2 m apart from each other. The animals could then choose which of the two persons to approach, while both stood quietly in a neutral posture. Since the test procedure varied slightly for the different groups, we could only directly compare Wolf Science Center dogs with wolves and pet dogs with free-ranging dogs.

Based on the *hyper-sociability* hypothesis, which predicts dogs to be more interested in social contact with humans than wolves, we expected Wolf Science Center dogs to spend more time with the humans and choose social contact over food more often than Wolf Science Center wolves. Moreover, since the *hyper-sociability* hypothesis suggests that the tendency to seek inter-species social proximity is genetically determined, we expected only a minor influence of life experience and predicted pet dogs and free-ranging dogs to be equally interested in social contact with humans. Indeed, we found that Wolf Science Center dogs spent more time in contact with the experimenter that provided social contact than the wolves in the pre-test phase, and they approached the experimenters more often than the wolves in the test phase. However, they displayed no preference for the cuddler over the food provider. Wolves showed a similar choice behavior – if they made a choice – they showed no clear preference for one person over the other (Fig. 2.4). However, instead of spending time with the person in the pre-test phase and making choices in the test phase, they preferred to move around exploring the test enclosure in line with results showing their higher exploratory tendencies compared to dogs (Moretti et al., 2015; Marshall-Pescini et al., 2017). As predicted, despite their reduced

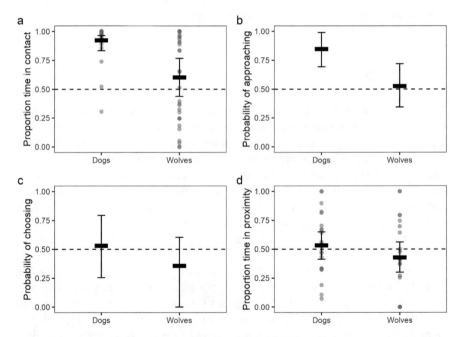

Fig. 2.4 Comparison between Wolf Science Center dogs and wolves: (**a**) proportion of time spent in contact with the experimenter in the pre-test phase, (**b**) probability of approaching the experimenter, (**c**) probability of choosing the experimenter that provided social contact (CP), and (**d**) proportion of time spent in proximity with the experimenter that provided social contact (CP). Thick horizontal lines represent the fitted model estimates, and error bars represent their confidence intervals. Dots in (**a**) and (**d**) depict individual observations with darker dots indicating overlapping observations. (Redrawn from Lazzaroni et al., 2020)

socialization to humans, free-ranging dogs did not differ from pet dogs in the time spent being cuddled by the human in the pre-test phase, and they did not show a preference for the food provider over the cuddler, again behaving similarly to pet dogs. Overall, this study showed a more marked effect of domestication and a relatively minor effect of life experience on the dogs' behavior toward humans. However, the wolves' and dogs' (of the different populations) underlying motivation or "emotional status" when interacting with humans remained an open question from this study, a question which hormonal analyses may help answer.

2.7.2 Study 2

How do active interactions with humans affect behavior and the hormonal correlates of dogs and wolves? In a first investigation combining human-directed behavior and hormonal parameters, we tested if positively reinforced training interactions with humans may differently affect the behavior and glucocorticoid levels (as a proxy for stress) of the wolves and dogs raised and housed at the Wolf Science Center (Vasconcellos et al., 2016). Each animal was tested three times in 5-min training sessions with different animal trainers, who had raised the animals from puppyhood (Fig. 2.5). In each of the training interactions, the animals were asked to respond to familiar cues (sit, lie, etc.) and were rewarded with food when responding correctly to the cue.

Dogs spent longer in proximity and oriented with their face toward the trainer than wolves, whereas (similarly to the study above) wolves spent more time

Fig. 2.5 Wolf-human interaction training session. (Reprinted from Vasconcellos et al., 2016; licensed under CC-BY 4.0)

exploring the room than the dogs. Furthermore, dogs responded to a greater number of cues and did so faster than wolves. This difference is not surprising especially considering that also in other contexts, wolves appear to be less forthcoming than dogs when asked to follow commands (Frank, 2011; Range et al., 2019). Moreover, the animals exhibited no self-directed (putatively stress-related) behaviors (e.g., panting, lip licking, pacing, tucked tail) during the training sessions. Both wolves and dogs showed a significant decrease in glucocorticoid concentrations after the training session, suggesting that individuals from both species viewed this as a positive social interaction. Interestingly, dogs' salivary glucocorticoid concentrations were higher than those of the wolves, both before and after the test sessions (Fig. 2.6), which contradicts predictions deriving from the *emotional reactivity* hypothesis. Overall, the inclusion of hormonal measures as well as behavior added to our understanding of wolf-dog responses to the test, since although from the analyses of behavior alone, there emerged a reduced engagement by wolves (who responded less to the cues) in the task, the hormonal analyses clearly showed a "positive" response to the situation by both species. These results highlight how hormonal analyses may add important nuances to our interpretation of behavioral data.

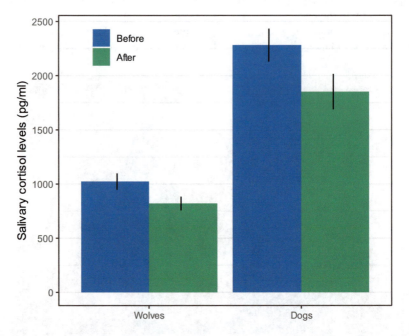

Fig. 2.6 Salivary cortisol concentrations in wolves and dogs at the Wolf Science Center, before and after a training session with a familiar human. Error bars represent standard error of the mean. (Redrawn from Vasconcellos et al., 2016)

2.7.3 Study 3

Do dogs and wolves differ in their behavioral and hormonal response to social contact with humans? How does life experience affect dogs' responses in these contexts? In the final study we present here, we combined the use of hormonal (in this case both glucocorticoid and oxytocin concentrations) and behavioral analyses to further test the *emotional reactivity* and *hyper-sociability* hypotheses of dog domestication by comparing Wolf Science Center wolves and dogs. Additionally, we also investigated the relative weight of life experience by testing pet dogs in the same paradigm (Wirobski et al., 2021). In the study, the animals were presented with a dyadic social interaction test with two different human partners – either a closely bonded (hand-raiser) or a familiar person that the animals knew but had formed no relationship with. In the case of pet dogs, the interaction was either with the owners or a familiar person that the pet dogs knew and saw on a regular basis. In all cases, we measured their urinary oxytocin and glucocorticoid concentrations after the interactions and compared it to a previously obtained baseline.

More specifically, the subjects were exposed to a 5-min "cuddle session," in which animals were invited to approach the fence and be petted by the respective person (Fig. 2.7), and a 5-min training session, in which animals were asked to respond to known cues in exchange for a piece of sausage. In addition to the social conditions, all animals were tested in two control conditions: (1) a food condition, in which a trainer who did not participate in the hand-raising of the focal animal (or the experimenter for the pet dogs) threw pieces of food over the enclosure fence without verbal or physical interaction, and (2) a baseline, in which the animals were observed for an hour resting with their packmates in the enclosure (pet dogs were sampled following 60 min of resting in their familiar environment with the owner present). Forty-five to sixty minutes after each condition, the animals were taken for a short walk, and their urine was collected for later hormonal analyses. Comparing the social interaction conditions with the control conditions allowed us to evaluate whether physical interaction per se was responsible for specific hormonal changes. In the social interaction conditions, we measured human-directed behaviors

Fig. 2.7 Dyadic social interaction test in the animal's home enclosure. Interaction test with a human partner with (**a**) a wolf and (**b**) a pack-living dog. (Reprinted from Wirobski et al., 2021; licensed under CC-BY 4.0)

including proximity and contact seeking as a measure of sociability and self-directed behaviors, e.g., yawning, lip licking, and head and body shaking as behaviors that are thought to indicate fear and distress in dogs (Beerda et al., 1998; Csoltova et al., 2017).

In accordance with the first study presented here, we found that regardless of their relationship, Wolf Science Center dogs showed overall more interest in the human partners (approaching, staying in physical contact, and allowing themselves to be petted) than wolves. However, both the dogs and the wolves spent more time in physical contact with the closely bonded compared to the familiar partner. Wolves' human-directed behavior was more varied than dogs' in both conditions but even more so with the familiar partner, whom some wolves did not approach close enough for physical contact. On the hormonal side, neither Wolf Science Center dogs nor wolves showed an increase in oxytocin concentrations after the social interactions with either human partner compared to the baseline (control) condition. They did however show elevated oxytocin concentrations in the food condition (Fig. 2.8). This finding contradicts the idea that dogs may have evolved higher oxytocinergic system activity in response to social contact with humans (Nagasawa et al., 2015; vonHoldt et al., 2017) and, together with some of the behavioral results, questions the notion of generalized hyper-sociability toward humans in dogs as postulated by the *hyper-sociability* hypothesis.

In contrast, a different picture emerged for the pet dogs: In this population, there was a positive correlation between dogs' oxytocin concentrations and the proportion of interaction time they spent cuddling with their owners (Fig. 2.9). Interestingly, no such correlation was apparent after cuddling with the familiar person, although

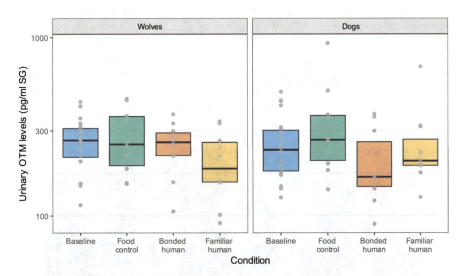

Fig. 2.8 Urinary oxytocin metabolite (OTM) concentrations (pg/ml SG) across all four conditions (baseline, food control, bonded human, and familiar human) in pack-living dogs ($N = 11$) and wolves ($N = 10$). Thick horizontal lines represent medians, boxes represent interquartile ranges, and gray dogs represent individual observations. (Redrawn from Wirobski et al., 2021)

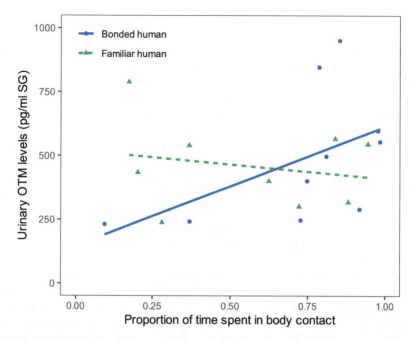

Fig. 2.9 Oxytocin and social contact with humans in pet dogs. Link between urinary oxytocin metabolite (OTM; pg/mL SG) concentrations, proportion of interaction time spent in body contact, and condition (i.e., relationship strength of the interaction partner – owner/bonded = blue dots, solid line; familiar = green triangles; dotted line) in pet dogs ($N = 10$; data points shown of 9 pet dogs in "familiar" condition due to unavailability of one dog for further tests; data points shown of all pet dogs in "bonded/owner" condition). (Redrawn from Wirobski et al., 2021)

behavioral analysis confirmed that they interacted with both partners for similar durations. Finally, in both wolves and Wolf Science Center dogs, physical contact with the familiar partner was positively associated with glucocorticoid concentrations, which was not the case in the pet dogs. However, in both Wolf Science Center and pet dogs, rates of self-directed behaviors during the social interactions were markedly higher than in wolves and – in Wolf Science Center dogs – positively related to contact time in the familiar partner condition.

2.8 The Influence of Life Experience and Domestication on the Human-Canine Relationship

It is often stated that the domestication process has profoundly changed dogs' behavior toward humans compared to wolves, their closest non-domesticated relatives. This notion is widely accepted, and domestication hypotheses such as the *emotional reactivity* and *hyper-sociability* hypotheses derive from it. They predict lower stress levels (behaviorally and physiologically) and a higher intrinsic motivation to approach and interact with humans (potentially driven by the oxytocinergic system) in dogs than wolves. Previous studies appeared to support these claims (Bentosela et al., 2016; Nagasawa et al., 2015) but have been criticized for comparing enclosure-living wolves with pet dogs, thereby confounding domestication-related with ontogenetic effects (Fiset & Plourde, 2015; Kekecs et al., 2015). Hence, as outlined above, studies aiming to test domestication hypotheses must account for previous experience and socialization of the subjects.

Indeed, when these factors are kept comparable, results reported above support a more nuanced picture of dog-wolf behavioral and hormonal differences. Although some consistent differences were evident between the Wolf Science Center wolves and dogs, they were not as profound as predicted, and some were partly in contrast with the *emotional reactivity* and *hyper-sociability* hypotheses. Moreover, although behaviorally there were not many differences between pet dogs, Wolf Science Center dogs, and free-ranging dogs, suggesting that very little previous experience with humans is sufficient to allow close interactions, hormonal measures provided a different picture.

Overall, Wolf Science Center dogs showed more interest than wolves in interacting with humans. In all three studies, the dogs spent more time with the experimenters and appeared more willing to interact with them, while the wolves spent more time exploring the environment and seemed less focused on the humans compared to the dogs. However, Wolf Science Center dogs and wolves both preferentially interacted with their hand-raisers rather than the familiar persons, which does not support the idea that dogs show generalized hyper-sociability toward any human. It also calls into question whether the capacity to develop an attachment bond with human caregivers is indeed a unique feature of dogs' social competence that is absent in wolves (see also Wheat et al., 2020). Moreover, no differences in oxytocinergic reactivity in response to human social contact were evident in the Wolf Science Center animals. In fact, oxytocin concentrations were higher after receiving a food reward in both the dogs and the wolves than after the social interaction with the human partners, suggesting that food may be a stronger reinforcer than social contact (although this was not evident behaviorally in study 1).

Both Wolf Science Center dogs' and wolves' glucocorticoid concentrations correlated positively with the time spent interacting with the lesser-known partner, indicating that an activation of the stress response was associated with the testing situation in both species. This contrasts with findings of a decrease in glucocorticoid concentrations following a training session in study 2. Importantly, the training session in study 2 was carried out with a bonded person and it did not involve physical contact, whereas in the social interaction test (study 3), physical contact preceded the training session, and indeed, it was the "contact time" with the person that was positively correlated with glucocorticoid concentrations and self-directed behaviors for both wolves and dogs. Interestingly, whereas all Wolf Science Center dogs approached and stayed in close contact with the familiar person despite their increase in stress levels (as evidenced by the glucocorticoid response), about a third of wolves rather chose not to engage in physical contact with the human partner at all. This raises the possibility that the dogs' behavior reflects a greater tendency to comply with human needs and wants rather than a higher sociability compared to the wolves', while the latter rather choose to just do things they are comfortable with (*deferential behavior* hypothesis; Range et al., 2019).

In contrast to the Wolf Science Center dogs, in pet dogs, body contact with their owners was linked to higher oxytocin concentrations, whereas contact with the familiar person was not, despite no clear behavioral preference for one person over the other. Behaviorally, Wolf Science Center dogs, pet dogs, and free-ranging dogs did not differ greatly in their human-directed contact-seeking behavior despite their wide difference in life experience and socialization with humans in study 1. Hence, it seems that although no clear behavioral differences emerge between populations in human contact seeking tests, hormonal responses differ widely, suggesting the underlying emotional state of the same behaviors may be very different between individuals of the different populations. In other words, although socialization experiences and the formation of an individual dog-owner bond appear to be crucial for the activation of dogs' oxytocinergic system and modulation of their HPA axis response, behavioral manifestations of human-directed sociability may not differ very much between different dog populations. At face value, i.e., based only on behavior alone, results may appear to lend support to the *hyper-sociability* hypothesis. However, when the hormonal underpinnings are also considered, the motivation to be in contact with humans seems to differ between different dog populations rather than between wolves and dogs at least of those that have the same experiences. Considering such results highlights the need to include hormonal analyses in behavior studies of dog domestication, especially in free-ranging dog populations where detailed behavioral and physiological data are currently largely missing.

2.9 Conclusion

Both the *emotional reactivity* and the *hyper-sociability* hypotheses are based on the core assumption that the domestication process has resulted in less fearful and less aggressive but more tolerant, cooperative, and sociable individuals, in intra- as well as interspecific contexts. Yet empirical evidence regarding the comparison of dogs and wolves upon which some of these initial notions were based appear to be rather inconsistent with, and in part even contradictory, to the predictions of these hypotheses (Range & Marshall-Pescini, 2022). Studies on human-socialized and comparatively raised wolves and dogs at the Wolf Science Center have shown repeatedly and across experimental paradigms that wolves accept humans as social partners and cooperate similarly well with them as dogs (Range & Virányi, 2013; Heberlein et al., 2016; Range et al., 2019). Crucially though, upon closer inspection, their "interaction styles" with humans differ: Dogs appear to wait for and follow humans more readily than wolves and show less inclinations to take over the leading role in a string-pulling task (Range et al., 2019). Wolves, on the other hand, had a higher tendency to steal the rope from the human partner if it was their preferred side and initiate cooperation. This may demonstrate a higher assertiveness in wolves than dogs over human preferences (in line with study 3's contact time during the social interaction test). Together, findings are in line with the idea of the *deferential behavior* hypothesis, which suggests that dogs have been selected for increased compliance and readiness to submit to human needs, making them easier social partners than wolves (Range et al., 2019).

In summary, the wolves and dogs at the Wolf Science Center shared more similarities in their hormonal response to human contact than Wolf Science Center dogs and pet dogs, highlighting the need to carefully control for the animals' previous experiences in comparative studies on domestication-related effects. Yet Wolf Science Center dogs, pet dogs, and free-ranging dogs, despite their profoundly different socialization histories, behaved similarly when interacting with humans. In contrast, differences were relatively clear at the hormonal level between Wolf Science Center dogs and pet dogs. Together, these findings question a general, clear-cut domestication effect as predicted by the *emotional reactivity* and *hypersociability* hypotheses but rather provide hints that epigenetic modulation during development may be a fruitful avenue for future investigation (Udell & Wynne, 2010; Cimarelli et al., 2017; Kovács et al. 2018).

Finally, to move ahead, further comparative research including other domesticated species and their wild-type relatives using paradigms that combine behavior and hormonal markers is needed to close gaps in our understanding of endocrine mechanisms shaping the domestication process. However, it is important to note that these mechanisms may vary from species to species, in relation to its domestication purpose (i.e., food production vs. companion animal, etc.). Conducting research on a greater variety of domesticated species will contribute to the ongoing discussion whether a universal "domestication syndrome" exists (Wilkins et al., 2014).

Acknowledgments The writing of the article was inspired and supported by research funded by the Austrian Science Fund (Project number: P34675-G and I5052-B) and from the Vienna Science and Technology Fund (Project Number: CS15-018).

References

Albert, F. W., Shchepina, O., Winter, C., Römpler, H., Teupser, D., Palme, R., Ceglarek, U., Kratzsch, J., Sohr, R., Trut, L. N., Thiery, J., Morgenstern, R., Plyusnina, I. Z., Schöneberg, T., & Pääbo, S. (2008). Phenotypic differences in behavior, physiology and neurochemistry between rats selected for tameness and for defensive aggression towards humans. *Hormones and Behavior, 53*(3), 413–421. https://doi.org/10.1016/j.yhbeh.2007.11.010

Arnold, A. P. (2009). The organizational-activational hypothesis as the foundation for a unified theory of sexual differentiation of all mammalian tissues. *Hormones and Behavior, 55*(5), 570–578. https://doi.org/10.1016/j.yhbeh.2009.03.011

Banlaki, Z., Cimarelli, G., Viranyi, Z., Kubinyi, E., Sasvari-Szekely, M., & Ronai, Z. (2017). DNA methylation patterns of behavior-related gene promoter regions dissect the gray wolf from domestic dog breeds. *Molecular Genetics and Genomics: MGG, 292*(3), 685–697. https://doi.org/10.1007/s00438-017-1305-5

Beato, M. (1993). Gene regulation by steroid hormones. In *Gene expression* (pp. 43–75). Birkhäuser.
Beerda, B., Schilder, M. B. H., van Hooff, J. A. R. A. M., de Vries, H. W., & Mol, J. A. (1998). Behavioural, saliva cortisol and heart rate responses to different types of stimuli in dogs. *Applied Animal Behaviour Science, 58*(3–4), 365–381. https://doi.org/10.1016/s0168-1591(97)00145-7
Beetz, A., Uvnäs-Moberg, K., Julius, H., & Kotrschal, K. (2012). Psychosocial and psychophysiological effects of human-animal interactions: The possible role of oxytocin. *Frontiers in Psychology, 3*, 234. https://doi.org/10.3389/fpsyg.2012.00234
Belyaev, D. K. (1979). Destabilizing selection as a factor in domestication. *The Journal of Heredity, 70*(5), 301–308. https://doi.org/10.1093/oxfordjournals.jhered.a109263
Bence, M., Marx, P., Szantai, E., Kubinyi, E., Ronai, Z., & Banlaki, Z. (2017). Lessons from the canine Oxtr gene: Populations, variants and functional aspects. *Genes, Brain, and Behavior, 16*(4), 427–438. https://doi.org/10.1111/gbb.12356
Bentosela, M., Wynne, C. D. L., D'Orazio, M., Elgier, A., & Udell, M. A. R. (2016). Sociability and gazing toward humans in dogs and wolves: Simple behaviors with broad implications: Sociability and gazing in dogs and wolves. *Journal of the Experimental Analysis of Behavior, 105*(1), 68–75. https://doi.org/10.1002/jeab.191
Bergström, A., Frantz, L., Schmidt, R., Ersmark, E., Lebrasseur, O., Girdland-Flink, L., Lin, A. T., Storå, J., Sjögren, K.-G., Anthony, D., Antipina, E., Amiri, S., Bar-Oz, G., Bazaliiskii, V. I., Bulatović, J., Brown, D., Carmagnini, A., Davy, T., Fedorov, S., et al. (2020). Origins and genetic legacy of prehistoric dogs. *Science (New York, N.Y.), 370*(6516), 557–564. https://doi.org/10.1126/science.aba9572
Brown, C. A., Cardoso, C., & Ellenbogen, M. A. (2016). A meta-analytic review of the correlation between peripheral oxytocin and cortisol concentrations. *Frontiers in Neuroendocrinology, 43*, 19–27. https://doi.org/10.1016/j.yfrne.2016.11.001
Buttner, A. P. (2016). Neurobiological underpinnings of dogs' human-like social competence: How interactions between stress response systems and oxytocin mediate dogs' social skills. *Neuroscience and Biobehavioral Reviews, 71*, 198–214. https://doi.org/10.1016/j.neubiorev.2016.08.029
Campler, M., Jöngren, M., & Jensen, P. (2009). Fearfulness in red junglefowl and domesticated white leghorn chickens. *Behavioural Processes, 81*(1), 39–43. https://doi.org/10.1016/j.beproc.2008.12.018
Cavanaugh, J., Carp, S. B., Rock, C. M., & French, J. A. (2016). Oxytocin modulates behavioral and physiological responses to a stressor in marmoset monkeys. *Psychoneuroendocrinology, 66*, 22–30. https://doi.org/10.1016/j.psyneuen.2015.12.027
Cimarelli, G., Virányi, Z., Turcsán, B., Rónai, Z., Sasvári-Székely, M., & Bánlaki, Z. (2017). Social behavior of pet dogs is associated with peripheral OXTR methylation. *Frontiers in Psychology, 8*, 549. https://doi.org/10.3389/fpsyg.2017.00549
Cohen, H., Kaplan, Z., Kozlovsky, N., Gidron, Y., Matar, M. A., & Zohar, J. (2010). Hippocampal microinfusion of oxytocin attenuates the behavioural response to stress by means of dynamic interplay with the glucocorticoid-catecholamine responses. *Journal of Neuroendocrinology, 22*(8), 889–904. https://doi.org/10.1111/j.1365-2826.2010.02003.x
Coppinger, R., & Coppinger, L. (2001). *Dogs: A startling new understanding of canine origin, behavior & evolution*. Simon and Schuster.
Csoltova, E., Martineau, M., Boissy, A., & Gilbert, C. (2017). Behavioral and physiological reactions in dogs to a veterinary examination: Owner-dog interactions improve canine well-being. *Physiology & Behavior, 177*, 270–281. https://doi.org/10.1016/j.physbeh.2017.05.013
Diamond, J. (2002). Evolution, consequences and future of plant and animal domestication. *Nature, 418*(6898), 700–707. https://doi.org/10.1038/nature01019
Douglas, A. J. (2005). Central noradrenergic mechanisms underlying acute stress responses of the hypothalamo-pituitary-adrenal axis: Adaptations through pregnancy and lactation. *Stress (Amsterdam, Netherlands), 8*(1), 5–18. https://doi.org/10.1080/10253890500044380
Driscoll, C. A., Macdonald, D. W., & O'Brien, S. J. (2009). From wild animals to domestic pets, an evolutionary view of domestication. *Proceedings of the National Academy of Sciences*

of The United States of America, 106(supplement_1), 9971–9978. https://doi.org/10.1073/pnas.0901586106

Ericsson, M., Fallahsharoudi, A., Bergquist, J., Kushnir, M. M., & Jensen, P. (2014). Domestication effects on behavioural and hormonal responses to acute stress in chickens. *Physiology & Behavior, 133*, 161–169. https://doi.org/10.1016/j.physbeh.2014.05.024

Fallahsharoudi, A., de Kock, N., Johnsson, M., Ubhayasekera, S. J. K. A., Bergquist, J., Wright, D., & Jensen, P. (2015). Domestication effects on stress induced steroid secretion and adrenal gene expression in chickens. *Scientific Reports, 5*(1), 15345. https://doi.org/10.1038/srep15345

Fiset, S., & Plourde, V. (2015). Commentary: Oxytocin-gaze positive loop and the coevolution of human-dog bonds. *Frontiers in Psychology, 6*, 1845. https://doi.org/10.3389/fpsyg.2015.01845

Foyer, P., Wilsson, E., Wright, D., & Jensen, P. (2013). Early experiences modulate stress coping in a population of German shepherd dogs. *Applied Animal Behaviour Science, 146*(1–4), 79–87. https://doi.org/10.1016/j.applanim.2013.03.013

Frank, H. (2011). Wolves, dogs, rearing and reinforcement: Complex interactions underlying species differences in training and problem-solving performance. *Behavior Genetics, 41*(6), 830–839. https://doi.org/10.1007/s10519-011-9454-5

Gácsi, M., Topál, J., Miklósi, Á., Dóka, A., & Csányi, V. (2001). Attachment behavior of adult dogs (Canis familiaris) living at rescue centers: Forming new bonds. *Journal of Comparative Psychology (Washington, D.C.: 1983), 115*(4), 423–431. https://doi.org/10.1037/0735-7036.115.4.423

Garland, T., Jr., Zhao, M., & Saltzman, W. (2016). Hormones and the evolution of complex traits: Insights from artificial selection on behavior. *Integrative and Comparative Biology, 56*(2), 207–224. https://doi.org/10.1093/icb/icw040

Germonpré, M., Van den Broeck, M., Lázničková-Galetová, M., Sablin, M. V., & Bocherens, H. (2021). Mothering the orphaned pup: The beginning of a domestication process in the upper Palaeolithic. *Human Ecology: An Interdisciplinary Journal, 49*(6), 677–689. https://doi.org/10.1007/s10745-021-00234-z

Gordon, I., Martin, C., Feldman, R., & Leckman, J. F. (2011). Oxytocin and social motivation. *Developmental Cognitive Neuroscience, 1*(4), 471–493. https://doi.org/10.1016/j.dcn.2011.07.007

Gulevich, R. G., Oskina, I. N., Shikhevich, S. G., Fedorova, E. V., & Trut, L. N. (2004). Effect of selection for behavior on pituitary-adrenal axis and proopiomelanocortin gene expression in silver foxes (Vulpes vulpes). *Physiology & Behavior, 82*(2–3), 513–518. https://doi.org/10.1016/j.physbeh.2004.04.062

Hare, B., & Tomasello, M. (2005). Human-like social skills in dogs? *Trends in Cognitive Sciences, 9*, 439–444.

Hare, B., Plyusnina, I., Ignacio, N., Schepina, O., Stepika, A., Wrangham, R., & Trut, L. (2005). Social cognitive evolution in captive foxes is a correlated by-product of experimental domestication. *Current Biology: CB, 15*(3), 226–230. https://doi.org/10.1016/j.cub.2005.01.040

Harri, M., Mononen, J., Ahola, L., Plyusnina, I., & Rekilä, T. (2003). Behavioural and physiological differences between silver foxes selected and not selected for domestic behaviour. *Animal Welfare, 12*, 305–314.

Heberlein, M. T. E., Turner, D. C., Range, F., & Virányi, Z. (2016). A comparison between wolves, Canis lupus, and dogs, Canis familiaris, in showing behaviour towards humans. *Animal Behaviour, 122*, 59–66. https://doi.org/10.1016/j.anbehav.2016.09.023

Herbeck, Y. E., & Gulevich, R. G. (2018). Neuropeptides as facilitators of domestication. *Cell and Tissue Research, 375*(1), 295–307. https://doi.org/10.1007/s00441-018-2939-2

Herbeck, Y. E., Gulevich, R. G., Shepeleva, D. V., & Grinevich, V. V. (2017). Oxytocin: Co-evolution of human and domesticated animals. *Russian Journal of Genetics, 7*, 235–242.

Herbeck, Y. E., Eliava, M., Grinevich, V., & MacLean, E. L. (2022). Fear, love, and the origins of canid domestication: An oxytocin hypothesis. *Comprehensive Psychoneuroendocrinology, 9*, 100100. https://doi.org/10.1016/j.cpnec.2021.100100

Johnsson, M., Henriksen, R., & Wright, D. (2021). The neural crest cell hypothesis: No unified explanation for domestication. *Genetics, 219*(1). https://doi.org/10.1093/genetics/iyab097

Jung, C., & Pörtl, D. (2018). Scavenging hypothesis: Lack of evidence for dog domestication on the waste dump. *Dog Behavior, 4*, 41–56.

Kekecs, Z., Szollosi, A., Palfi, B., Szaszi, B., Kovacs, K. J., Dienes, Z., & Aczel, B. (2016). Commentary: Oxytocin-gaze positive loop and the coevolution of human-dog bonds. *Frontiers in Neuroscience, 10*, 155. https://doi.org/10.3389/fnins.2016.00155

Kikusui, T., Nagasawa, M., Nomoto, K., Kuse-Arata, S., & Mogi, K. (2019). Endocrine regulations in human – Dog coexistence through domestication. *Trends in Endocrinology and Metabolism, 30*, 793–806.

Kis, A., Bence, M., Lakatos, G., Pergel, E., Turcsán, B., Pluijmakers, J., Vas, J., Elek, Z., Brúder, I., Földi, L., Sasvári-Székely, M., Miklósi, Á., Rónai, Z., & Kubinyi, E. (2014). Oxytocin receptor gene polymorphisms are associated with human directed social behavior in dogs (Canis familiaris). *PLoS One, 9*(1), e83993. https://doi.org/10.1371/journal.pone.0083993

Kubinyi, E., Bence, M., Koller, D., Wan, M., Pergel, E., Ronai, Z., Sasvari-Szekely, M., & Miklósi, Á. (2017). Oxytocin and opioid receptor gene polymorphisms associated with greeting behavior in dogs. *Frontiers in Psychology, 8*, 1520. https://doi.org/10.3389/fpsyg.2017.01520

Kukekova, A. V., Trut, L. N., Chase, K., Shepeleva, D. V., Vladimirova, A. V., Kharlamova, A. V., Oskina, I. N., Stepika, A., Klebanov, S., Erb, H. N., & Acland, G. M. (2008). Measurement of segregating behaviors in experimental silver fox pedigrees. *Behavior Genetics, 38*(2), 185–194. https://doi.org/10.1007/s10519-007-9180-1

Künzl, C., & Sachser, N. (1999). The behavioral endocrinology of domestication: A comparison between the domestic guinea pig (Cavia aperea f. porcellus) and its wild ancestor, the cavy (Cavia aperea). *Hormones and Behavior, 35*, 28–37.

Künzl, C., Kaiser, S., Meier, E., & Sachser, N. (2003). Is a wild mammal kept and reared in captivity still a wild animal? *Hormones and Behavior, 43*(1), 187–196. https://doi.org/10.1016/s0018-506x(02)00017-x

Langbein, J., Krause, A., & Nawroth, C. (2018). Human-directed behaviour in goats is not affected by short-term positive handling. *Animal Cognition, 21*(6), 795–803. https://doi.org/10.1007/s10071-018-1211-1

Larson, G., Piperno, D. R., Allaby, R. G., Purugganan, M. D., Andersson, L., Arroyo-Kalin, M., Barton, L., Climer Vigueira, C., Denham, T., Dobney, K., Doust, A. N., Gepts, P., Gilbert, M. T. P., Gremillion, K. J., Lucas, L., Lukens, L., Marshall, F. B., Olsen, K. M., Pires, J. C., et al. (2014). Current perspectives and the future of domestication studies. *Proceedings of the National Academy of Sciences of the United States of America, 111*(17), 6139–6146. https://doi.org/10.1073/pnas.1323964111

Lazzaroni, M., Range, F., Backes, J., Portele, K., Scheck, K., & Marshall-Pescini, S. (2020). The effect of domestication and experience on the social interaction of dogs and wolves with a human companion. *Frontiers in Psychology, 11*. https://doi.org/10.3389/fpsyg.2020.00785

Lorenz, K. Z. (1950). *Man meets dog*. Dr. G. Borotha-Schoeler.

Løtvedt, P., Fallahshahroudi, A., Bektic, L., Altimiras, J., & Jensen, P. (2017). Chicken domestication changes expression of stress-related genes in brain, pituitary and adrenals. *Neurobiology of Stress, 7*, 113–121. https://doi.org/10.1016/j.ynstr.2017.08.002

Love, T. M. (2014). Oxytocin, motivation and the role of dopamine. *Pharmacology, Biochemistry, and Behavior, 119*, 49–60. https://doi.org/10.1016/j.pbb.2013.06.011

Lukas, M., Toth, I., Reber, S. O., Slattery, D. A., Veenema, A. H., & Neumann, I. D. (2011). The neuropeptide oxytocin facilitates pro-social behavior and prevents social avoidance in rats and mice. *Neuropsychopharmacology: Official Publication of the American College of Neuropsychopharmacology, 36*(11), 2159–2168. https://doi.org/10.1038/npp.2011.95

Malavasi, R., & Huber, L. (2016). Evidence of heterospecific referential communication from domestic horses (Equus caballus) to humans. *Animal Cognition, 19*(5), 899–909. https://doi.org/10.1007/s10071-016-0987-0

Malmkvist, J., Hansen, S. W., & Damgaard, B. M. (2003). Effect of the serotonin agonist buspirone on behaviour and hypothalamic-pituitary-adrenal axis in confident and fearful mink. *Physiology & Behavior, 78*(2), 229–240. https://doi.org/10.1016/s0031-9384(02)00964-2

Marshall-Pescini, S., Virányi, Z., Kubinyi, E., & Range, F. (2017). Motivational factors underlying problem solving: Comparing wolf and dog puppies' explorative and neophobic behaviors at 5, 6, and 8 weeks of age. *Frontiers in Psychology, 8*, 180. https://doi.org/10.3389/fpsyg.2017.00180

Martin, J. T. (1978). Embryonic pituitary adrenal axis, behavior development and domestication in birds. *American Zoologist, 18*(3), 489–499. https://doi.org/10.1093/icb/18.3.489

McLeod, P. J., Moger, W. H., Ryon, J., Gadbois, S., & Fentress, J. C. (1996). The relation between urinary cortisol levels and social behaviour in captive timber wolves. *Canadian Journal of Zoology, 74*(2), 209–216. https://doi.org/10.1139/z96-026

McQuaid, R. J., McInnis, O. A., Paric, A., Al-Yawer, F., Matheson, K., & Anisman, H. (2016). Relations between plasma oxytocin and cortisol: The stress buffering role of social support. *Neurobiology of Stress, 3*, 52–60. https://doi.org/10.1016/j.ynstr.2016.01.001

Mech, L. D., & Janssens, L. A. A. (2021). An assessment of current wolf Canis lupus domestication hypotheses based on wolf ecology and behaviour. *Mammal Review*. https://doi.org/10.1111/mam.12273

Mitsui, S., Yamamoto, M., Nagasawa, M., Mogi, K., Kikusui, T., Ohtani, N., & Ohta, M. (2011). Urinary oxytocin as a noninvasive biomarker of positive emotion in dogs. *Hormones and Behavior, 60*(3), 239–243. https://doi.org/10.1016/j.yhbeh.2011.05.012

Moretti, L., Hentrup, M., Kotrschal, K., & Range, F. (2015). The influence of relationships on neophobia and exploration in wolves and dogs. *Animal Behaviour, 107*, 159–173. https://doi.org/10.1016/j.anbehav.2015.06.008

Morrison, I. (2016). Keep calm and cuddle on: Social touch as a stress buffer. *Adaptive Human Behavior and Physiology, 2*(4), 344–362. https://doi.org/10.1007/s40750-016-0052-x

Nagasawa, M., Okabe, S., Mogi, K., & Kikusui, T. (2012). Oxytocin and mutual communication in mother-infant bonding. *Frontiers in Human Neuroscience, 6*, 31. https://doi.org/10.3389/fnhum.2012.00031

Nagasawa, M., Mitsui, S., En, S., Ohtani, N., Ohta, M., Sakuma, Y., Onaka, T., Mogi, K., & Kikusui, T. (2015). Oxytocin-gaze positive loop and the coevolution of human-dog bonds. *Science, 348*(6232), 333–336. https://doi.org/10.1126/science.1261022

Naumenko, E. V., Popova, N. K., Nikulina, E. M., Dygalo, N. N., Shishkina, G. T., Borodin, P. M., & Markel, A. L. (1989). Behavior, adrenocortical activity, and brain monoamines in Norway rats selected for reduced aggressiveness towards man. *Pharmacology, Biochemistry, and Behavior, 33*(1), 85–91. https://doi.org/10.1016/0091-3057(89)90434-6

Neumann, I. D. (2008). Brain oxytocin: A key regulator of emotional and social behaviours in both females and males. *Journal of Neuroendocrinology, 20*(6), 858–865. https://doi.org/10.1111/j.1365-2826.2008.01726.x

Neumann, I. D., Krömer, S. A., Toschi, N., & Ebner, K. (2000). Brain oxytocin inhibits the (re)activity of the hypothalamo-pituitary-adrenal axis in male rats: Involvement of hypothalamic and limbic brain regions. *Regulatory Peptides, 96*(1–2), 31–38. https://doi.org/10.1016/s0167-0115(00)00197-x

Nikulina, E. M. (1990). The brain catecholamines during domestication of the silver fox Vulpes fulvus. *Zhurnal Evoliutsionnoĭ Biokhimii i Fiziologii, 26*(2), 156–160.

Nishioka, T., Anselmo-Franci, J. A., Li, P., Callahan, M. F., & Morris, M. (1998). Stress increases oxytocin release within the hypothalamic paraventricular nucleus. *Brain Research, 781*(1–2), 57–61. https://doi.org/10.1016/s0006-8993(97)01159-1

O'Rourke, T., & Boeckx, C. (2020). Glutamate receptors in domestication and modern human evolution. *Neuroscience and Biobehavioral Reviews, 108*, 341–357. https://doi.org/10.1016/j.neubiorev.2019.10.004

Oliva, J. L., Wong, Y. T., Rault, J.-L., Appleton, B., & Lill, A. (2016). The oxytocin receptor gene, an integral piece of the evolution of Canis familiaris from Canis lupus. *Pet Behaviour Science, 2*, 1. https://doi.org/10.21071/pbs.v0i2.4000

Palmer, R., & Custance, D. (2008). A counterbalanced version of Ainsworth's strange situation procedure reveals secure-base effects in dog–human relationships. *Applied Animal Behaviour Science, 109*(2–4), 306–319. https://doi.org/10.1016/j.applanim.2007.04.002

Pérez Fraga, P., Gerencsér, L., & Andics, A. (2020). Human proximity seeking in family pigs and dogs. *Scientific Reports, 10*(1), 20883. https://doi.org/10.1038/s41598-020-77643-5

Persson, M. E., Trottier, A. J., Bélteky, J., Roth, L. S. V., & Jensen, P. (2017). Intranasal oxytocin and a polymorphism in the oxytocin receptor gene are associated with human-directed social behavior in golden retriever dogs. *Hormones and Behavior, 95*, 85–93. https://doi.org/10.1016/j.yhbeh.2017.07.016

Phoenix, C. H., Goy, R. W., Gerall, A. A., & Young, W. C. (1959). Organizing action of prenatally administered testosterone propionate on the tissues mediating mating behavior in the female guinea pig. *Endocrinology, 65*, 369–382.

Popova, N. K. (2006). From genes to aggressive behavior: The role of serotonergic system. *BioEssays: News and Reviews in Molecular, Cellular and Developmental Biology, 28*(5), 495–503. https://doi.org/10.1002/bies.20412

Popova, N. K., Voitenko, N. N., Kulikov, A. V., & Avgustinovich, D. F. (1991). Evidence for the involvement of central serotonin in mechanism of domestication of silver foxes. *Pharmacology, Biochemistry, and Behavior, 40*(4), 751–756. https://doi.org/10.1016/0091-3057(91)90080-1

Popova, N. K., Kulikov, A. V., Avgustinovich, D. F., Voĭtenko, N. N., & Trut, L. N. (1997). Effect of domestication of the silver fox on the main enzymes of serotonin metabolism and serotonin receptors. *Genetika, 33*(3), 370–374.

Pörtl, D., & Jung, C. (2017). Is dog domestication due to epigenetic modulation in brain? *Dog Behavior, 3*, 21–32.

Pörtl, D., & Jung, C. (2019). Physiological pathways to rapid prosocial evolution. *Biologia Futura, 70*(2), 93–102. https://doi.org/10.1556/019.70.2019.12

Powell, L., Guastella, A. J., McGreevy, P., Bauman, A., Edwards, K. M., & Stamatakis, E. (2019). The physiological function of oxytocin in humans and its acute response to human-dog interactions: A review of the literature. *Journal of Veterinary Behavior: Clinical Applications and Research: Official Journal of: Australian Veterinary Behaviour Interest Group, International Working Dog Breeding Association, 30*, 25–32. https://doi.org/10.1016/j.jveb.2018.10.008

Preckel, K., Scheele, D., Kendrick, K. M., Maier, W., & Hurlemann, R. (2014). Oxytocin facilitates social approach behavior in women. *Frontiers in Behavioral Neuroscience, 8*, 191. https://doi.org/10.3389/fnbeh.2014.00191

Price, E. O. (1999). Behavioral development in animals undergoing domestication. *Applied Animal Behaviour Science, 65*(3), 245–271. https://doi.org/10.1016/s0168-1591(99)00087-8

Puurunen, J., Hakanen, E., Salonen, M. K., Mikkola, S., Sulkama, S., Araujo, C., & Lohi, H. (2020). Inadequate socialisation, inactivity, and urban living environment are associated with social fearfulness in pet dogs. *Scientific Reports, 10*(1), 3527. https://doi.org/10.1038/s41598-020-60546-w

Range, F., & Marshall-Pescini, S. (2022). Comparing wolves and dogs: current status and implications for human 'self-domestication'. *Trends in Cognitive Sciences, 26*, 1–13.

Range, F., & Virányi, Z. (2013). Social learning from humans or conspecifics: Differences and similarities between wolves and dogs. *Frontiers in Psychology, 4*, 868. https://doi.org/10.3389/fpsyg.2013.00868

Range, F., Marshall-Pescini, S., Kratz, C., & Virányi, Z. (2019). Wolves lead and dogs follow, but they both cooperate with humans. *Scientific Reports, 9*(1), 3796. https://doi.org/10.1038/s41598-019-40468-y

Rault, J., Munkhof, M., & Buisman-Pijlman, F. T. A. (2017). Oxytocin as an indicator of psychological and social well-being in domesticated animals: A critical review. *Frontiers in Psychology, 8*, 1521.

Richards, J. S. (1994). Hormonal control of gene expression in the ovary. *Endocrine Reviews, 15*(6), 725–751. https://doi.org/10.1210/er.15.6.725

Sahlén, P., Yanhu, L., Xu, J., Kubinyi, E., Wang, G.-D., & Savolainen, P. (2021). Variants that differentiate wolf and dog populations are enriched in regulatory elements. *Genome Biology and Evolution, 13*(4). https://doi.org/10.1093/gbe/evab076

Sánchez-Villagra, M. R., Geiger, M., & Schneider, R. A. (2016). The taming of the neural crest: A developmental perspective on the origins of morphological covariation in domesticated mammals. *Royal Society Open Science, 3*(6), 160107. https://doi.org/10.1098/rsos.160107

Serpell, J. A. (2021). Commensalism or cross-species adoption? A critical review of theories of wolf domestication. *Frontiers in Veterinary Science, 8*, 662370. https://doi.org/10.3389/fvets.2021.662370

Smith, S. M., & Vale, W. W. (2006). The role of the hypothalamic-pituitary-adrenal axis in neuroendocrine responses to stress. *Dialogues in Clinical Neuroscience, 8*(4), 383–395. https://doi.org/10.31887/dcns.2006.8.4/ssmith

Smith, A. S., & Wang, Z. (2014). Hypothalamic oxytocin mediates social buffering of the stress response. *Biological Psychiatry, 76*(4), 281–288. https://doi.org/10.1016/j.biopsych.2013.09.017

Suzuki, K., Yamada, H., Kobayashi, T., & Okanoya, K. (2012). Decreased fecal corticosterone levels due to domestication: A comparison between the white-backed Munia (Lonchura striata) and its domesticated strain, the Bengalese finch (Lonchura striata var. domestica) with a suggestion for complex song evolution: Domestication effects on fecal corticosterone. *Journal of Experimental Zoology. Part A, Ecological Genetics and Physiology, 317*(9), 561–570. https://doi.org/10.1002/jez.1748

Topál, J., Miklósi, Á., Csányi, V., & Dóka, A. (1998). Attachment behavior in dogs (Canis familiaris): A new application of Ainsworth's (1969) Strange Situation Test. *Journal of Comparative Psychology (Washington, D.C.: 1983), 112*(3), 219–229. https://doi.org/10.1037/0735-7036.112.3.219

Topál, J., Gácsi, M., Miklósi, Á., Virányi, Z., Kubinyi, E., & Csányi, V. (2005). Attachment to humans: A comparative study on hand-reared wolves and differently socialized dog puppies. *Animal Behaviour, 70*(6), 1367–1375. https://doi.org/10.1016/j.anbehav.2005.03.025

Trut, L. N. (1999). Early canid domestication: The farm-fox experiment: Foxes bred for tamability in a 40-year experiment exhibit remarkable transformations that suggest an interplay between behavioral genetics and development. *American Scientist, 87*, 160–169.

Trut, L., Oskina, I., & Kharlamova, A. (2009). Animal evolution during domestication: The domesticated fox as a model. *BioEssays: News and Reviews in Molecular, Cellular and Developmental Biology, 31*(3), 349–360. https://doi.org/10.1002/bies.200800070

Udell, M. A. R., & Wynne, C. D. L. (2010). Ontogeny and phylogeny: Both are essential to human-sensitive behaviour in the genus Canis. *Animal Behaviour, 79*, e9–e14.

Ujfalussy, D. J., Kurys, A., Kubinyi, E., Gácsi, M., & Virányi, Z. (2017). Differences in greeting behaviour towards humans with varying levels of familiarity in hand-reared wolves (Canis lupus). *Royal Society Open Science, 4*(6), 160956. https://doi.org/10.1098/rsos.160956

Vasconcellos, S., Virányi, Z., Range, F., & Ades, C. (2016). Training reduces stress in human-socialised wolves to the same degree as in dogs. *PLoS One*, 1–19. https://doi.org/10.1371/journal.pone.0162389

vonHoldt, B. M., Pollinger, J. P., Lohmueller, K. E., Han, E., Parker, H. G., Quignon, P., Degenhardt, J. D., Boyko, A. R., Earl, D. A., Auton, A., Reynolds, A., Bryc, K., Brisbin, A., Knowles, J. C., Mosher, D. S., Spady, T. C., Elkahloun, A., Geffen, E., Pilot, M., et al. (2010). Genome-wide SNP and haplotype analyses reveal a rich history underlying dog domestication. *Nature, 464*(7290), 898–902. https://doi.org/10.1038/nature08837

vonHoldt, B. M., Shuldiner, E., Koch, I. J., Kartzinel, R. Y., Hogan, A., Brubaker, L., Wanser, S., Stahler, D., Wynne, C. D. L., Ostrander, E. A., Sinsheimer, J. S., & Udell, M. A. R. (2017). Structural variants in genes associated with human Williams-Beuren syndrome underlie stereotypical hypersociability in domestic dogs. *Science Advances, 3*(7), e1700398. https://doi.org/10.1126/sciadv.1700398

Wang, X., Pipes, L., Trut, L. N., Herbeck, Y., Vladimirova, A. V., Gulevich, R. G., Kharlamova, A. V., Johnson, J. L., Acland, G. M., Kukekova, A. V., & Clark, A. G. (2018). Genomic responses to selection for tame/aggressive behaviors in the silver fox (Vulpes vulpes). *Proceedings of the National Academy of Sciences of the United States of America, 115*(41), 10398–10403. https://doi.org/10.1073/pnas.1800889115

Weiler, U., Claus, R., Schnoebelen-Combes, S., & Louveau, I. (1998). Influence of age and genotype on endocrine parameters and growth performance: A comparative study in wild boars, Meishan and large white boars. *Livestock Production Science, 54*(1), 21–31. https://doi.org/10.1016/s0301-6226(97)00165-6

Wheat, C. H., Larsson, L., Berner, P., & Temrin, H. (2020). Hand-reared wolves show attachment comparable to dogs and use human caregiver as a social buffer in the Strange Situation Test. *bioRxiv.* https://doi.org/10.1101/2020.02.17.952663

Wilkins, A. S., Wrangham, R. W., & Fitch, W. T. (2014). The "domestication syndrome" in mammals: A unified explanation based on neural crest cell behavior and genetics. *Genetics, 197*(3), 795–808. https://doi.org/10.1534/genetics.114.165423

Windle, R. J., Kershaw, Y. M., Shanks, N., Wood, S. A., Lightman, S. L., & Ingram, C. D. (2004). Oxytocin attenuates stress-induced c-fos mRNA expression in specific forebrain regions associated with modulation of hypothalamo-pituitary-adrenal activity. *The Journal of Neuroscience: The Official Journal of the Society for Neuroscience, 24*(12), 2974–2982. https://doi.org/10.1523/JNEUROSCI.3432-03.2004

Winter, J., & Jurek, B. (2019). The interplay between oxytocin and the CRF system: Regulation of the stress response. *Cell and Tissue Research, 375*(1), 85–91. https://doi.org/10.1007/s00441-018-2866-2

Wirobski, G., Range, F., Schaebs, F. S., Palme, R., Deschner, T., & Marshall-Pescini, S. (2021). Life experience explains dogs' hormonal responses to human contact better than domestication. *Scientific Reports, 11*(1), 1–12.

Zipser, B., Schleking, A., Kaiser, S., & Sachser, N. (2014). Effects of domestication on biobehavioural profiles: A comparison of domestic guinea pigs and wild cavies from early to late adolescence. *Frontiers in Zoology, 11*(1), 30. https://doi.org/10.1186/1742-9994-11-30

Chapter 3
Measuring the Dog Side of the Dog-Human Bond

Jordan G. Smith and Jeffrey S. Katz

3.1 Introduction

"Man's best friend" is a sentiment that is echoed by dog owners worldwide. For many years now, dogs (*Canis familiaris*) have been invited into human social circles and even function as a source of social support (McConnell et al., 2011). Dogs also fulfill many roles within human society, including serving on the police force, assisting individuals with disabilities, and helping with search and rescue efforts. However, despite the commonality of the relationship between dogs and humans, only recently have researchers begun to understand the foundational aspects of dog-human attachment.

Attachment is defined as a bond between two specific individuals (Bowlby, 1982). Although human attachment theory extends to many different types of relationships, researchers have found significant similarities between the dog-human relationship and the infant-mother relationship (Palmer & Custance, 2008). For example, in this form of attachment, attached individuals (i.e., infant or dog) display proximity-seeking behaviors toward the attachment figure (i.e., mother/primary caregiver or owner), and the attachment figure acts as a secure base from which the attached individual can move off to interact with their environment confidently (Ainsworth, 1989; Bowlby, 1958). As researchers continue to learn more about the dog-human relationship, it is important to consider previous methods that have been used to measure interactions between dogs and humans to establish a foundation for the theory of dog-human attachment. Additionally, integrating various methods will allow researchers to create a more comprehensive model of attachment in dogs that can be compared to previously established models of human attachment. In this

J. G. Smith (✉) · J. S. Katz
Department of Psychological Sciences, Auburn University, Auburn, AL, USA
e-mail: jag0125@auburn.edu

chapter, we will discuss the evolution of canine research as it relates to dog-human interactions and how this research provides support for dog-human attachment. We will also cover various methods that should be considered moving forward to provide additional support for this theory.

Of note, this chapter is not intended to function as a comprehensive review of any of the discussed measures (see Bensky et al. (2013) for a review of canine socio-cognitive measures, Payne et al. (2015) and Payne et al. (2016) for reviews of dog-human attachment measures, and Thompkins et al. (2016) and Bunford et al. (2017) for reviews of dog fMRI research). Rather, the goal of this chapter is to explore methodological considerations in regard to dog-human attachment. Specific tasks will be highlighted that not only inform conclusions regarding attachment in dogs but also provide useful tools to measure attachment in future research efforts.

3.2 Socio-Cognitive Measures

Researchers have been evaluating the socio-cognitive abilities of dogs for decades, sparking the current rise in research evaluating the behavioral and cognitive capacities of the domestic dog (Aria et al., 2021). Because of the domestication process, dogs are thought to have evolved functionally similar social skills to humans, essentially creating a model in which to study human social skills (Miklósi et al., 2007). However, socio-cognitive measures also provide insight into dogs' perceptions of humans in a variety of contexts. While these measures may not provide a direct assessment of the dog-human bond, they do allow researchers to evaluate factors affecting how dogs use humans as a social reference point (Payne et al., 2015). The bond between dogs and humans can also explain why dogs have a greater propensity to understand and engage with human communicative interactions relative to other species (Miklósi & Topál, 2013). In this section, specific tasks that measure dogs' abilities to understand human communicative cues and also use human-directed behaviors will be discussed.

3.2.1 Object-Choice Task

The *object-choice task* measures the ability of dogs to follow a variety of different communicative gestures given by humans. Typically, this task involves a two-choice paradigm in which an experimenter hides a reward in one of two opaque containers (Fig. 3.1, bottom panel). The experimenter then gestures toward the container with the reward while the dog observes. If the dog is able to choose the location of the reward significantly above chance, it is considered to understand the communicative nature of the human gesture used in that testing scenario. In 1998, two studies using the object-choice task first demonstrated that dogs were able to use a variety of cues given by the experimenters, ranging in saliency from pointing to glancing (Hare

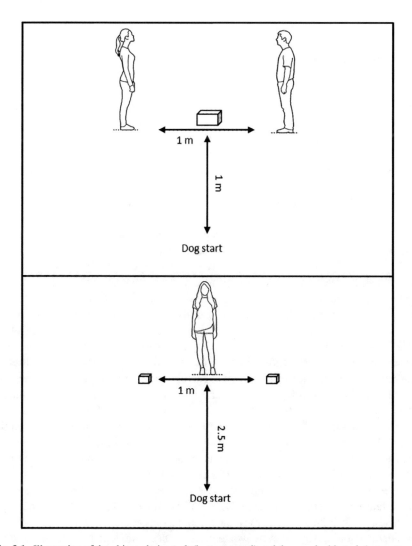

Fig. 3.1 Illustration of the object-choice task (bottom panel) and the unsolvable task (upper panel) from Lazarowski et al. (2020). In the object-choice task, an experimenter holds the dog at a starting location, while another experimenter stands between two containers, gesturing toward one. A dog's choice is recorded by noting which container the dog approached first. In the unsolvable task, the dog is released from a starting position and permitted to interact with the apparatus for a given amount of time. Gazing directed toward individuals positioned around the apparatus is also recorded

et al., 1998; Miklösi et al., 1998). Interestingly, dogs in Miklösi et al. (1998) not only appeared to learn some of the cues over the testing period, but some even demonstrated prior understanding of specific gestures.

Researchers continued to use the object-choice task to further understand the nuances and limitations of dog's abilities to understand human gestures. Agnetta et al. (2000) showed that dogs have the ability to use a novel cue by placing a physical marker near the location of the hidden reward. However, dogs appear to rely on visual observation of the marker placement by the human experimenter and were not able to use the marker itself as a cue (Agnetta et al., 2000). Udell et al. (2008b) further expanded these findings, demonstrating that dogs have greater accuracy for human cues than nonhuman cues. Dogs are also sensitive to attentional cues paired with communicative gestures, with dogs achieving higher accuracy when the experimenters made eye contact while gesturing toward the hidden food reward (Udell et al., 2008b). Kaminski et al. (2012) demonstrated similar findings and additionally illustrated that dogs will rely on other attentional cues, such as name calling, when eye contact is not available. Concerning the familiarity of the person providing the cues, researchers have found that companion dogs are more likely to follow cues from their owner (Cunningham & Ramos, 2014; Lazarowski et al., 2020). However, another study observed no differences in performance in cues given by familiar and unfamiliar individuals (Marshall-Pescini et al., 2011).

Researchers have also compared wolves (*Canis lupus*) and dogs on the object-choice task to determine if the ability to understand human cues is a product of domestication. Several studies found that dogs generally outperformed human-reared wolves on the object-choice task, illustrating a difference between species even when wolves had experienced extensive interactions with humans (Hare et al., 2002; Miklósi et al., 2003). Even with training, wolves only met the performance of naïve dogs on the object-choice task (Virányi et al., 2008). However, Udell et al. (2008a) found that when environmental factors and rearing conditions were controlled for during testing, wolves can outperform dogs in specific contexts. Specifically, the authors found that hand-reared wolves tested in an outdoor environment with a familiar experimenter performed significantly above chance on the object-choice task, whereas companion dogs tested in a similar environment performed at chance levels. Additionally, shelter dogs tested in an indoor environment with an unfamiliar experimenter performed significantly worse than companion dogs tested in a similar environment and wolves tested in an outdoor environment with a familiar experimenter. Lazarowski and Dorman (2015) also found that rearing history can influence accuracy on the object-choice task, with kennel-reared dogs demonstrating significantly worse performance compared to companion dogs. Therefore, while the domestication process may have provided the dog a particular advantage over closely related species, environmental experiences also appear to heavily influence the ability to understand human gestures.

3.2.2 Unsolvable Task

Another task used to measure the socio-cognitive abilities of dogs is the *unsolvable task*. In this task, a food reward is hidden in an apparatus, and the dog receives the reward through manipulation of the apparatus (Fig. 3.1, upper panel). However, after several reinforced trials, the apparatus is secured to prevent the dog from obtaining the reward (i.e., unsolvable trial). The dog's behavior during the unsolvable trial is usually evaluated in several ways, including human-directed gazing, gaze alteration behaviors, and persistence in attempting to open the apparatus. Specifically, human-directed gazing and gaze alteration behaviors are considered to be communicative behaviors indicative of the dog seeking human assistance with the apparatus (Marshall-Pescini et al., 2013, 2017; however, see Lazzaroni et al., 2020, for alternative explanations).

Using this task, researchers have been able to evaluate the different factors that can influence human-directed gazing in dogs. Genetic variability accounts for some variation in human-directed behavior (Persson et al., 2015), and breed differences also support the idea that human-directed behavior can be influenced by selection (Konno et al., 2016; Passalacqua et al., 2011). However, environmental experiences also produce extensive variation in these behaviors. Human-directed gazing has been shown to increase with age, likely due to extended experience interacting with humans (Passalacqua et al., 2011). Rearing history (D'Aniello & Scandurra, 2016) and training experience (Marshall-Pescini et al., 2009) also impact human-directed gazing. Dogs are also sensitive to the attentional state of humans during the unsolvable task, exhibiting increased gaze alteration toward attentive individuals (Marshall-Pescini et al., 2013).

When comparing dogs to wolves on the unsolvable task, Miklósi et al. (2003) found that dogs look at humans sooner and longer on the unsolvable task than wolves. However, when persistence during the unsolvable trial was included as a variable, Marshall-Pescini et al. (2017) observed no differences in human-directed gazing between dogs and wolves. Instead, the main factor driving differences in human-directed gazing was persistence, with more persistent dogs gazing at humans less regardless of species. Interestingly, wolves were more persistent than dogs overall, suggesting that differences between species in explorative behaviors and reward motivation may influence the use of human-directed behaviors.

3.2.3 Summary of Socio-cognitive Measures

These tasks provide valuable assessments of the socio-cognitive abilities of dogs and allow researchers to evaluate how the dog-human bond may influence these abilities. The object-choice task specifically measures dog's ability to understand human cues and gestures, and researchers have shown that dogs not only demonstrate high levels of performance with a variety of gestures on this task but are also able to learn new cues. In addition, many factors, including environmental experiences and rearing history, seem to influence this ability. Alternatively, the unsolvable task predominantly measures dog's use of human-directed behavior. Researchers have shown that selection for specific traits across breeds influences performance on this task, as well as other factors such as rearing history and training experiences. Persistence at manipulating the apparatus has also been shown to account for much of the variation observed in human-directed behavior on the unsolvable task. Overall, these tasks show that dogs use humans as a social reference point in many different contexts, allowing them to interpret communicative cues and exhibit human-directed behavior. While dogs seem uniquely primed to interact with humans in this way, these abilities are heavily influenced by social experiences and also potentially by bonds formed with specific individuals. More research is needed to determine how socio-cognitive abilities may interact with the dog-human bond by evaluating how different factors, such as the quality of the bond between dogs and their attachment figure, can influence performance on these tasks.

3.3 Dog-Human Attachment Measures

In an attempt to quantify the dog-human bond, researchers have modified behavioral measures previously used to measure attachment in humans as a method of measuring attachment in dogs. While some tests compare a dog's interactions with an attachment figure (usually the owner or primary caretaker) and an unfamiliar person, others focus primarily on behaviors directed toward the attachment figure. However, despite slight differences in methodology, the central goal of these measures is to demonstrate that dog-human bonds exhibit the four features that typify human caregiver-infant relationships (Payne et al., 2015):

1. Proximity-seeking behaviors directed toward the attachment figure.
2. Separation-related distress in the absence of the attachment figure.
3. The safe-haven effect illustrated by the presence of the attachment figure diminishing the impact of a stressful event.
4. The secure base effect characterized by an increase in social and explorative behaviors in the presence of the attachment figure.

The predominant measures of dog-human attachment are discussed below, along with a summary addressing the current perspectives on dog-human attachment based on this literature.

3.3.1 Strange Situation Test

One test that has been frequently used to measure dog-human attachment is Ainsworth's *strange situation test* (Fig. 3.2), which was initially developed to measure mother-infant attachment (Ainsworth & Bell, 1970). Topál et al. (1998) first adapted this task to be used in dogs and used various episodes to measure the dog's reaction to being separated and reunited with the owner on multiple occasions. Typically, the strange situation test episodes occur in the following order:

1. The owner and the dog are present in an unfamiliar room together.
2. An unfamiliar person (i.e., stranger) enters and joins the owner and the dog.

3 Measuring the Dog Side of the Dog-Human Bond

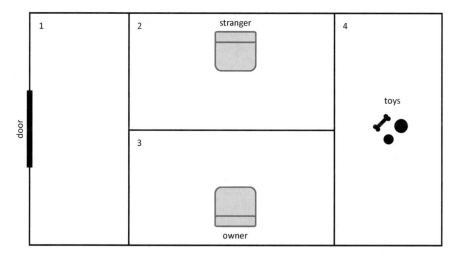

Fig. 3.2 An example of the testing environment for the strange situation test. Two chairs are present in the room, one for the attachment figure (i.e., owner) and one for the stranger. Other objects, such as toys, can also be included to measure other behaviors of interest (i.e., play behaviors). The testing room is typically divided into separate areas to facilitate behavioral interpretation during this test. For example, time spent in Area 1 could be characterized as door-directed behavior triggered by the exit of the owner, whereas time spent in Area 2 could be classified as interaction with the stranger

3. The owner exits the room, leaving the dog in the room with the stranger.
4. The owner re-enters the room, and the stranger leaves.
5. The dog is left alone in the room.
6. The stranger re-enters the room with the dog.
7. The owner enters the room, and the stranger exits.

The purpose of this test is to activate attachment behaviors by separating and reuniting the dog with the owner on multiple different occasions and also show how the dog's interactions with the stranger are mediated by the presence of the owner.

While Topál et al. (1998) provided evidence indicative of a dog's preference for its owner over the stranger, they failed to report on any behaviors that are typically used to measure attachment, including security-, proximity-, and comfort-seeking behaviors (Palmer & Custance, 2008). However, Prato-Previde et al. (2003) illustrated that dogs tested on the strange situation test do display evidence of these attachment behaviors with their owners, but habituation to the testing environment due to order effects inherent within the test ultimately limited their conclusions. When conditions within the test were counterbalanced, evidence of attachment behaviors remained and clearly demonstrated the secure base effect in dogs (Palmer & Custance, 2008). Rehn et al. (2013) confirmed these findings, indicating that counterbalancing the episodes in the strange situation test is necessary to avoid order effects when measuring attachment behaviors in dogs.

These initial studies illustrated that the strange situation test could be used to measure dog-human attachment, but this test was also developed to classify individuals according to attachment styles (Ainsworth et al., 1978). Schöberl et al. (2016) and Solomon et al. (2019) both demonstrated that the classification systems previously developed for humans could be applied to dogs based on behavioral responses exhibited during the strange situation test. These classification systems confirmed that dogs possessed either a secure attachment style (i.e., exhibits distress when separated but seeks proximity when reunited with the attachment figure) or some form of an insecure attachment style, typically characterized by a lack of distress upon being separated and/or an inability to return to a normal behavioral status after being reunited with the attachment figure. Solomon et al. (2019) actually found that the proportions of dogs classified with secure and insecure attachment styles were similar to those previously observed in human toddlers. Furthermore, evaluating differences in specific behavioral patterns during the strange situation test can help improve the classification of dogs by attachment styles in future studies (Riggio et al., 2021).

Dogs appear to develop attachments to humans at an early age. Although no evidence of attachment was observed in 2-month-old puppies (Mariti et al., 2020), Topál et al. (2005) found that 4-month old puppies tested on the strange situation test exhibited attachment behaviors toward their owner. Topál et al. (2005) also compared dog and wolf puppies on the strange situation test to determine if attachment behaviors differed between species. Overall, the authors found that unlike the dog puppies, hand-reared wolf puppies did not demonstrate clear evidence of attachment for their primary caretaker, despite high levels of socialization.

Dog characteristics and life experiences also influence the dog-human bond as measured by the strange situation test. Specifically, the level of attachment between dogs and owners is more influenced by a dog's current experiences and less so by experiences during critical socialization periods (Marinelli et al., 2007). Deprivation of human contact also seems to facilitate the rapid formation of new bonds, with shelter dogs demonstrating evidence of attachment after 30 minutes of interaction with a handler (Gácsi et al., 2001). In addition, while breed does not appear to influence dog-human attachment (Lenkei et al., 2021), differences in temperament influence dog attachment styles (Parthasarathy & Crowell-Davis, 2006). Sex has also been shown to impact behavioral responses during the strange situation test, with females exhibiting greater distress when separated from the owner compared to males (D'Aniello et al., 2022).

Several researchers have used the strange situation test to measure the effects of training experiences on the dog-human bond. In guide dogs, behavioral responses exhibited during the strange situation test were more controlled than companion dogs (Fallani et al., 2006) despite significant increases in heart rate during separation periods (Fallani et al., 2007). In addition, the breaking of previous bond attachments during the training process does not appear to influence guide dogs' abilities to form secure attachments later in life (Fallani et al., 2006; Valsecchi et al., 2010). However, the effect of training experiences on attachment appears to be influenced by the type of training, with other studies demonstrating only minor differences between companion dogs and dogs with extensive training experiences, specifically search and rescue (Mariti et al., 2013) and water rescue (Scandurra et al., 2016).

3.3.2 Secure Base Test

Another measure of attachment more recently developed for use in dogs is the *secure base test* (Fig. 3.3). This test was modified from a previous experiment measuring attachment in primates (Harlow, 1958) and was first used with dogs by Thielke et al. (2017). Essentially, the secure base test is a shortened version of the strange situation test that only measures interactions with the attachment figure across three episodes: (1) dog is with the attachment figure in an unfamiliar room, (2) dog is alone, and (3) dog is reunited with the attachment figure. Several studies have now demonstrated that the secure base test can be used as a measure of attachment in dogs and that the behaviors exhibited during this test can be used to categorize dogs by attachment style (Thielke et al., 2017; Thielke & Udell, 2019, 2020; Wanser & Udell, 2019).

Researchers have used this measure to evaluate how attachment in dogs may be influenced by participation in animal-assisted interventions. Wanser and Udell (2019) found that dogs with insecure attachment styles gazed longer at their owner during animal-assisted interventions, indicating that these dogs could be using gaze to maintain contact with the owner when physical contact is unavailable. In addition, Wanser et al. (2020) found that dogs with a secure attachment to their primary caregiver were more likely to have a secure attachment with a child in the same family. Dog-parent attachment style not only predicted whether a secure attachment style would exist between the dog and the child, but it was also related to the probability of a secure attachment developing with that child during an animal-assisted intervention. Overall, these studies demonstrate how the secure base test can be used to measure attachment styles in dogs and also how differences in attachment styles can influence dogs' experience in animal-assisted interventions.

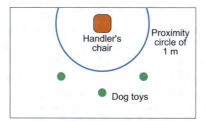

Fig. 3.3 An example of the testing environment for the secure base test by Wanser and Udell (2019). Because this test only evaluates a dog's interactions with its attachment figure, only one chair is present in the testing room. An area marked around the chair facilitates classification of behavioral interactions with the attachment figure. (Redrawn from Wanser & Udell, 2019)

The secure base test was also used by Thielke and Udell (2020) to evaluate how environmental and social experiences may affect dog-human attachment by comparing attachment styles observed in shelter and foster dogs to companion dogs. The authors supplemented the secure base test findings with two other measures: a paired attachment test comparing general preferences for the attachment figure to an unfamiliar person and the Lexington Attachment to Pets Scale, which is considered to be a measure of the strength of attachment bonds as reported by humans (Ramírez et al., 2014). Overall, the authors found that the proportion of shelter dogs with secure attachment was significantly lower than the proportions previously reported in companion dogs (Schöberl et al., 2016; Thielke et al., 2017; Wanser & Udell, 2019). In addition, another study by Thielke and Udell (2019) found that attachment style in foster dogs also influenced performance on the object-choice task, with securely attached dogs demonstrating better performance on the task overall. Scores from the Canine Behavioral Assessment and Research Questionnaire (C-BARQ), a validated survey used to measure various aspects of a dog's personality (Serpell & Hsu, 2001), also illustrated that foster dogs exhibit more attachment and attention-seeking behaviors than shelter dogs. These studies demonstrate how populations of companion dogs with different environmental and social experiences may display varying styles of attachment and how attachment style can affect performance on a socio-cognitive task.

3.3.3 Summary of Attachment Measures

Researchers using the strange situation test and the secure base test have demonstrated that both of these tests provide a valuable measure of the dog-human bond, despite being developed to measure attachment in humans. After initial research illustrated that dogs display behaviors characteristic of attachment using the strange situation test, other researchers showed that dogs exhibit different attachment styles similar to humans. The strange situation test has also been used to show that dog-human attachment is affected by age, sex, life experiences, temperament, and training. More recently, researchers have begun to use the secure base test as a more rapid measure of dog-human attachment. Although shorter than the strange situation test, this test is still an effective measure of attachment behaviors in dogs and has been used to measure how differences in attachment styles influence dogs' experiences during animal-assisted interventions and how the attachment styles of companion dogs differ from shelter dogs. The secure base test has also been used to illustrate how attachment style may influence socio-cognitive abilities, specifically the ability to use human gestures during the object-choice task. Overall, these measures not only provide a method of demonstrating how dog-human relationships exhibit characteristics associated with infant-caregiver relationships but also allow researchers to observe the effects of various factors on dog-human attachment.

3.4 Functional Magnetic Resonance Imaging

Although researchers had established many measures of evaluating dog-human interactions and attachment, the neural basis for these behaviors was still unknown. However, Berns et al. (2012) presented evidence that dogs could be trained to undergo functional magnetic resonance imaging (fMRI) scans while awake and unrestrained, providing realistic fMRI data that was not affected by the dog being immobilized or restrained during the scan (Fig. 3.4). FMRI allows researchers to evaluate brain activity noninvasively by measuring the flow of oxygenated blood that is tied to activity in specific areas of the brain. Subjects must remain still for the duration of a scan, which often lasts for an extended period of time; however, methods have been developed that show dogs can be trained to hold their head still in the scanner, resulting in usable fMRI data that is not influenced by the dog being restrained for the scan. Specifically, Berns et al. (2012) demonstrated that caudate activation was related to reward expectancy by training dogs to differentiate between two different hand signals: a reward signal and a no reward signal. Since caudate activation has been linked to rewarding stimuli and situations across species (Daw et al., 2011; Knutson et al., 2001; Schultz et al., 1997), the results presented by Berns et al. (2012) aligned with previous research and provided the first canine contribution to the functional neuroimaging literature in relation to stimulus presentation.

Researchers built off the methodology established by Berns et al. (2012) to evaluate how differences in familiarity with humans may influence neural responses to various stimuli in dogs. Using the same reward and no reward hand signals, Cook

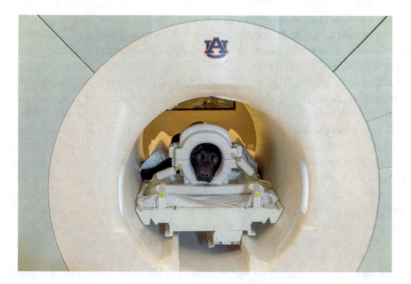

Fig. 3.4 A dog laying in an MRI scanner with its head positioned in a human knee coil for scanning from Thompkins et al. (2021)

et al. (2014) found that the temperament of the dog and the familiarity of the person giving the hand signals influenced the caudate response to the two hand signals. Specifically, dogs with lower levels of aggression demonstrated a significant difference in caudate activation when a familiar person was providing the signals, whereas more aggressive dogs showed a significant difference when an unfamiliar person was giving the signals. These results are likely driven by more aggressive dogs experiencing higher levels of arousal when an unfamiliar person presented the signals, resulting in greater activation due to the increased salience of the signals. In addition, when presented with olfactory stimuli, dogs demonstrate greater caudate activation to the odor of a familiar human relative to an unfamiliar human (Berns et al., 2015). Overall, the results from these studies suggest that dogs associate humans with positive expectations and rewards and that dogs can differentiate between familiar and unfamiliar humans through multiple sensory modalities.

While other researchers were evaluating neural responses in dogs to visual and olfactory stimuli, Andics et al. (2014) were the first to explore activation patterns in the auditory regions of the dog brain when presented with both dog and human vocalizations. While the authors found that dogs showed greater activation for dog vocalizations relative to human vocalizations, dogs also demonstrated sensitivity to the emotional valence of both dog and human vocalizations in a region near the primary auditory cortex. These results suggest that although conspecific vocalizations may carry greater ecological relevance for dogs, they have also developed the ability to detect differences in the emotional valence of human vocalizations. Andics et al. (2016) expanded these findings by testing lexical-intonation effects in dogs using human vocalizations. In this study, dogs were given praising and neutral words in similarly praising and neutral intonations while in the MRI scanner. Overall, dogs demonstrate lexical-intonation effects (i.e., greater activation for praising words delivered in a praising tone) in reward regions of the brain, specifically the caudate, ventral tegmental area, and the substantia nigra. Therefore, dogs appear to rely on both the meaning and the intonation of a word when determining the reward value of a verbal cue.

Another area of dog fMRI research has focused on finding an area of the brain that processes facial stimuli, building off behavioral evidence indicating dogs have the ability to discriminate between human faces (Huber et al., 2013). Dilks et al. (2015) provided the first evidence of a face processing area in the dog brain by evaluating differences in activation levels when dogs viewed human and dog faces compared to everyday objects. The authors found a region in the temporal lobe that demonstrated a greater response to faces than everyday objects, but they did not observe any difference in activation between human and dog faces. Another study found similar results when having dogs view pictures of human faces and everyday objects, illustrating greater activation for faces in a region of the temporal lobe similar to Dilks et al. (2015) and also some differences in the caudate, thalamus, and frontal cortex (Cuaya et al., 2016).

Although initial research suggested dogs process conspecific and heterospecific faces in the same area of the brain (Dilks et al., 2015), Thompkins et al. (2018) found different areas of the dog brain that show preferential activation for human and dog faces separately. In this study, the authors presented dogs with pictures of familiar and unfamiliar dog and human faces. The results revealed two different areas of interest, with one area showing greater activation for dog faces (i.e., dog face area [DFA]) and the other showing greater activation for human faces (i.e., human face area [HFA]). The authors then mapped both the DFA and the HFA onto functionally analogous regions of the human brain by matching connectivity networks to determine if the face areas in the dog brain corresponded to similar areas used to process faces in the human brain. Through this analysis, Thompkins et al. (2018) found that the HFA maps onto the human fusiform face area, while the DFA maps onto the human superior temporal sulcus, both of which are associated with face processing in humans (Bernstein & Yovel, 2015). Overall, the results of this study provide additional evidence for face-sensitive areas in the dog brain. However, recent research indicates these areas may not be face selective and provides additional controls and explanations to consider in future studies (Bunford et al., 2020; Szabó et al., 2020).

While studies using fMRI in dogs have provided valuable information about the neural processes underlying dog behavior and cognition, the experimental nature of this new field of research often leads to tentative interpretations of the data. Therefore, researchers have begun to use multimodal approaches that relate behavioral and cognitive measures with fMRI results. One recent study used eye-tracking, a behavioral preference test, and fMRI to evaluate how dogs react to images of their caregiver compared to images of a stranger (Karl et al., 2020). The fMRI results demonstrated that dogs display greater activation in areas of the brain related to emotion and attachment processing in humans when viewing their caregiver, specifically the bilateral insula, the rostral dorsal cingulate gyrus, and the amygdala. The caudate was also activated when viewing the caregiver, corroborating previous research indicating dogs may associate familiar individuals with positive expectations (Berns et al., 2015; Cook et al., 2014). The multimodal approach used by the authors provided further support for these results, with both the behavioral preference test (i.e., dogs tended to approach the image of their caregiver instead of a stranger) and the eye-tracking data (i.e., dogs looked longer at their caregiver compared to a familiar person) aligning with the fMRI findings. A follow-up study evaluating dogs' ability to differentiate between their caregiver and a stranger in more complex social interactions observed differential activation in the hypothalamus, suggesting that dogs may be emotionally affected by watching their caregiver interact with another dog in a positive way (Karl et al., 2021). An additional study using a multimodal approach evaluated how different levels of attachment in dogs would influence the neural response to their owner's voice (Gábor et al., 2021). The authors found that dogs with greater attachment as measured by the strange situation test also exhibited greater activation in the caudate when their owners were praising them. Both of these studies not only support the theory of dog-human attachment using a multimodal approach, but they also provide evidence for a neural attachment network in dogs.

Another recent study employed a multimodal approach to evaluate an additional aspect of the dog-human relationship, specifically how dogs react to differences in human face familiarity and emotions (Thompkins et al., 2021). Dogs were presented with images of human faces varying in familiarity and emotional valence during MRI scans. Both the amygdala and the caudate were influenced by the familiarity and emotional valence of the human faces. The hippocampus was also affected by the emotional content of the faces, which has previously been associated with emotion processing in humans (Iidaka et al., 2003). The dogs were also tested on the unsolvable task to see if human-directed behavior would differ between the familiar and unfamiliar person. Relating the dogs' unsolvable task scores with their fMRI data revealed several significant correlations between the two measures. Specifically, dogs with a bias for the familiar person in the unsolvable task showed greater activation for familiar faces in the amygdala, caudate, and hippocampus and also showed greater activation for positive faces in the hippocampus. This study provides additional support for dog-human attachment and demonstrates that dogs can use facial stimuli to make discriminations based on emotional valence and familiarity.

In sum, although canine fMRI research is still in its early stages of development, this area of research has already expanded researchers' knowledge of dog behavior and cognition. Over the past decade, studies have shown that dogs associate humans with positive expectations, can discriminate between humans across several sensory modalities, and are sensitive to words and faces. In addition, multimodal approaches using behavioral, cognitive, and neural measures have contributed significantly to the development of a neural model of attachment in dogs by relating neural activation patterns directly to behavioral and cognitive responses outside of the scanner. Overall, fMRI research continues to support previous studies of dog social cognition and dog-human attachment, illustrating that dogs are sensitive to a variety of human cues and develop bonds with specific individuals.

3.5 Neural Model of Human Attachment as a Model for Dogs

The study of attachment in dogs has often relied on the use of methods that measured aspects of human attachment, like the strange situation test. However, researchers were able to use these measures to guide hypotheses and ultimately demonstrate evidence of attachment behaviors in dogs. As the use of fMRI develops as a method for measuring the neural correlates of attachment in dogs, researchers can also rely on human models to guide hypotheses regarding various dog brain areas that might be involved in dog-human attachment.

Because of the extensive research on the neural basis of human attachment, researchers have been able to develop comprehensive neuro-anatomical models of human attachment (Fig. 3.5). For example, Long et al. (2020) proposed a functional neuro-anatomical model of human attachment that was divided into two systems: emotional mentalization and cognitive mentalization. The emotional mentalization system refers to a collection of bottom-up processing mechanisms that describe the

3 Measuring the Dog Side of the Dog-Human Bond

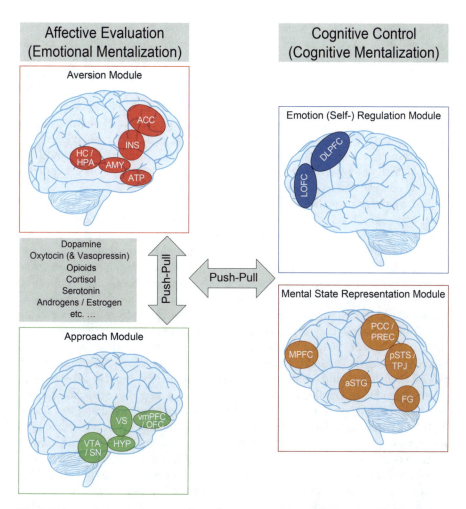

Fig. 3.5 An example of a neural model of human attachment that researchers could reference when evaluating the neural model of attachment in dogs from Long et al. (2020). This model illustrates the various parts of the brain that are likely involved in the emotional and cognitive mentalization of attachment in humans. (Reprinted from Long et al., 2020; licensed under CC-BY 4.0)

reactive, and potentially even unconscious, processing related to human attachment. Long et al. (2020) further divided the emotional mentalization system into an aversion module and an approach module. The aversion module is responsible for encoding negative social states, usually associated with threat detection, fear responses, and the subsequent fight-or-flight response. Brain regions in the aversion module include the anterior cingulate cortex (Eisenberger et al., 2003; Koban et al., 2010); the insula (Lamm et al., 2011); the hippocampus, which is also involved in regulating the hypothalamus-pituitary-adrenal axis (Foley & Kirschbaum, 2010; Kim et al., 2015); the amygdala (Engell et al., 2007); and the anterior temporal pole

(Lévesque et al., 2003). In contrast, the approach module processes positive social states and involves primarily reward-related, dopaminergic areas of the brain including the ventral striatum (Haber & Knutson, 2010; Strathearn et al., 2009), the ventral tegmental area (Aron et al., 2005; Fletcher et al., 2015), the substantia nigra (Swain et al., 2007), and the ventromedial prefrontal/orbitofrontal cortex (Kim et al., 2017; Minagawa-Kawai et al., 2009; Nitschke et al., 2004; Xu et al., 2012). The hypothalamus, which is responsible for the release of oxytocin, is also included in the approach module due to its close connection to the dopaminergic circuits (Strathearn et al., 2009; Swain et al., 2007). Although these modules are independent, the authors suggest that these systems are in a "push-pull" balance, highlighting their complementary nature.

The cognitive mentalization system proposed by Long et al. (2020) includes brain areas associated with top-down, intentional processing mechanisms and is responsible for behavioral regulation and cognitive representations of others. This system is further divided into two modules: the emotional regulation module and the mental state representation module. The emotional regulation module controls behavioral and emotional regulation during social experiences, such as directing attention toward certain stimuli or cognitive reappraisal of a situation. Brain areas in the emotional regulation module include the dorsolateral prefrontal cortex and the lateral orbitofrontal cortex (Callaghan & Tottenham, 2016; Lieberman, 2007; Martin & Ochsner, 2016; Ochsner et al., 2012). The mental state representation module encodes and maintains internal representations of others, associating it with processes such as theory of mind. This module is ultimately responsible for remembering previous interactions with individuals and generating expectation about future interactions, and it contains a series of brain regions including the medial prefrontal cortex, anterior superior temporal gyrus, fusiform gyrus, posterior cingulate cortex, precuneus, posterior superior temporal sulcus, and temporo-parietal junction (Kanske, 2018; Spreng & Grady, 2010; Uddin et al., 2005). Overall, while the emotional and cognitive mentalization systems proposed by Long et al. (2020) cover separate components of attachment, a "push-pull" balance between these two systems illustrates their interdependent nature, providing a comprehensive model of the neuro-anatomical correlates of human attachment.

Although using functional neuro-anatomical models of human attachment as a reference can provide a starting point for an attachment model in dogs, there are several limitations to this method that should be considered. Primarily, attachment between conspecifics (i.e., human-human attachment) is likely to recruit different neural pathways than attachment between heterospecifics (i.e., dog-human attachment). This effect is illustrated in a fMRI study in which mothers were shown images of their own child and their dog (Stoeckel et al., 2014). Of the sample tested, 93% of the women considered their dog a member of their family, indicating high levels of attachment. This finding was additionally supported by significant overlap in activation areas when viewing their own child and dog, including the amygdala, hippocampus, medial orbitofrontal cortex, dorsal putamen, thalamus, and fusiform gyrus. Despite many similarities, several key differences were observed that indicate the women had formed different types of attachment with their infants and their dogs. Specifically, increased activation in reward-related areas of the brain (ventral tegmental area and substantia nigra) was observed when the mothers were viewing images of their child but not their dogs. In addition, the women exhibited greater activation in the fusiform gyrus when viewing images of their dogs compared to their child. Given that the fusiform gyrus is associated with face perception and social cognition (Kanwisher et al., 1997; Long et al., 2020), this finding highlights a key perceptual difference that may influence human attachment with dogs, namely, the reliance on facial cues due to the inability to communicate using verbal language (Stoeckel et al., 2014). In sum, while similarities exist between human attachment to both dogs and other humans, attachment between heterospecifics demonstrates distinct differences relative to conspecific attachment.

Another limitation of applying a neuro-anatomical model of human attachment to dogs is the difficulty associated with procuring evidence for processes related to cognitive mentalization. Research with nonhuman animals relies primarily on behavioral and physiological responses to stimuli, and self-reporting on internal thought processes is not possible due to the lack of verbal communication. Consequently, researchers attempting to demonstrate evidence for cognitive mentalization, such as theory of mind, in nonhuman animals must have carefully constructed and controlled methods (Krupenye & Call, 2019). While some methods relying on perspective-taking abilities have suggested that dogs may possess theory of mind mechanisms (Maginnity & Grace, 2014; Virányi et al., 2004), these testing methods would be difficult to use during an fMRI study, limiting the ability to test the neural correlates of theory of mind in dogs. While initial studies have provided some evidence for emotional mentalization of attachment in dogs (Gábor et al., 2021; Karl et al., 2020; Thompkins et al., 2021), continued development of current methods is needed to determine if dogs demonstrate cognitive mentalization of attachment.

3.6 Future Methodological Considerations

As researchers continue to evaluate dog-human attachment, it is important to consider what kinds of studies may provide more explicit evidence for a neural attachment model in dogs. Specifically, studies combining previously established methods (i.e., socio-cognitive and dog-human attachment measures) with developing methods (i.e., fMRI) can provide a comprehensive measure of attachment in dogs. While studies utilizing fMRI will inevitably require significant time and resources to properly train dogs (Karl et al., 2020; Strassberg et al., 2019), evaluations of how individual differences influence training success can improve the selection of dogs for fMRI studies (Karl et al., 2020). The neural model of human attachment can also be used as a reference as more complicated models of the dog attachment network are developed.

Considering some of the limitations associated with measuring dog-human attachment, study designs specifically evaluating bond formation may provide beneficial information regarding the dog attachment network. Using this design, dogs could be scanned both before and after bonding occurred with a specific person, and differences in activation patterns when observing the attachment figure and unfamiliar individuals could reveal neural networks related to attachment in dogs. This same design could also be applied to humans to observe how activation patterns may change over the course of a bonding period with a specific dog. To employ a multimodal approach, attachment measures like the secure base test can be used to evaluate how behavioral evidence of attachment develops over the course of the bonding period. Surveys that provide a measure of attachment behaviors and bonds, such as the Canine Behavioral Assessment and Research Questionnaire (Serpell & Hsu, 2001) and Lexington Attachment to Pets Scale (Ramírez et al., 2014), could also be filled out by the attachment figure to measure changes across the bonding period. Using fMRI to measure differences in activation over the course of a bonding period, and supporting these findings with behavioral evidence of attachment, provides a relatively controlled method of evaluating the various regions of the brain that may support attachment in dogs. In addition, comparing these findings to the activation patterns observed in the bonded humans provides a unique opportunity to evaluate similarities and differences in dog and human attachment.

Although this type of study would provide a more controlled evaluation of the attachment network in dogs, several key issues make this study design particularly difficult to execute. Primarily, this type of study requires a cohort of dogs that are already trained for fMRI. Most studies using fMRI in dogs have relied on companion dog populations for participants (e.g., Andics et al., 2014; Berns et al., 2015; Karl et al., 2020), evaluating interactions between these dogs and their owners. However, using companion dogs in a study measuring bond formation presents several issues, namely, these dogs are typically bonded to their owner when recruited for fMRI studies. While it may be possible to conduct a longitudinal study to see how activation patterns for companion dogs change over the course of time when viewing their owners, researchers are unlikely to obtain a baseline measure prior to the formation of the dog-human bond. However, other populations of dogs, such as shelter dogs and working dogs, provide potential alternatives for a study evaluating bond formation. Shelter dogs, which have previously been used in studies of attachment (Gácsi et al., 2001; Thielke & Udell, 2019), could feasibly be trained for fMRI scans prior to adoption. Researchers could then observe changes in activation patterns when dogs view their new owner after a specified bonding period. Alternatively, working dogs could also be used in studies of bond formation, specifically those housed in a kennel environment. With this population, it would be possible to evaluate bond formation with a trainer or with an unfamiliar individual over a given period of time by scanning dogs both before and after a bonding period. Therefore, while companion dogs have typically represented most of the fMRI data to date (although see Thompkins et al. (2018, 2021), Jia et al. (2014, 2016), and Berns et al. (2017) for fMRI studies using working dogs), other populations of dogs that have not formed strong bonds with caretakers may provide a unique opportunity to measure the attachment network in dogs. In addition, these populations also offer researchers the opportunity to characterize attachment to dogs in humans, allowing for potential comparisons between the neural models of human and dog attachment.

3.7 Conclusion

Although researchers have been using behavioral measures of dog-human attachment for years, recent development in the field of fMRI research has allowed for evaluation of the neural correlates underlying these behaviors. Studies employing a multimodal approach provide the best opportunity for future research to evaluate how neural activation patterns associated with dog-human attachment are additionally supported by behavioral and cognitive evidence. Specifically, studies measuring bond formation between dogs and humans allow for a more controlled method of evaluating the attachment network in dogs to observe how activation patterns change both before and after bonding has occurred. Using this method, comparisons can be made between both the human and dog attachment networks to observe quantitative and qualitative similarities and differences between how dogs and humans attach to each other.

References

Agnetta, B., Hare, B., & Tomasello, M. (2000). Cues to food location that domestic dogs (*Canis familiaris*) of different ages do and do not use. *Animal Cognition, 3*(2), 107–112. https://doi.org/10.1007/s100710000070

Ainsworth, M. D. S. (1989). Attachments beyond infancy. *The American Psychologist, 44*(4), 709–716. https://doi.org/10.1037//0003-066x.44.4.709

Ainsworth, M. D. S., & Bell, S. M. (1970). Attachment, exploration, and separation: Illustrated by the behavior of one-year-olds in a strange situation. *Child Development, 41*(1), 49–67. https://doi.org/10.2307/1127388

Ainsworth, M. D. S., Blehar, M. C., Waters, E., & Wall, S. (1978). *Patterns of attachment: A psychological study of the strange situation*. Lawrence Erlbaum.

Andics, A., Gácsi, M., Faragó, T., Kis, A., & Miklósi, Á. (2014). Voice-sensitive regions in the dog and human brain are revealed by comparative fMRI. *Current Biology, 24*(5), 574–578. https://doi.org/10.1016/j.cub.2014.01.058

Andics, A., Gábor, A., Gácsi, M., Faragó, T., Szabó, D., & Miklósi, Á. (2016). Neural mechanisms for lexical processing in dogs. *Science, 353*(6303), 1030–1032. https://doi.org/10.1126/science.aaf3777

Aria, M., Alterisio, A., Scandurra, A., Pinelli, C., & D'Aniello, B. (2021). The scholar's best friend: Research trends in dog cognitive and behavioral studies. *Animal Cognition, 24*(3), 541–553. https://doi.org/10.1007/s10071-020-01448-2

Aron, A., Fisher, H., Mashek, D. J., Strong, G., Li, H., & Brown, L. L. (2005). Reward, motivation, and emotion systems associated with early-stage intense romantic love. *Journal of Neurophysiology, 94*(1), 327–337. https://doi.org/10.1152/jn.00838.2004

Bensky, M. K., Gosling, S. D., & Sinn, D. L. (2013). The world from a dog's point of view: A review and synthesis of dog cognition research. In H. J. Brockmann, T. J. Roper, M. Naguib,

J. C. Mitani, L. W. Simmons, & L. Barrett (Eds.), *Advances in the study of behavior* (pp. 209–406). Academic Press. https://doi.org/10.1016/B978-0-12-407186-5.00005-7

Berns, G. S., Brooks, A. M., & Spivak, M. (2012). Functional MRI in awake unrestrained dogs. *PLoS One, 7*(5), e38027. https://doi.org/10.1371/journal.pone.0038027

Berns, G. S., Brooks, A. M., & Spivak, M. (2015). Scent of the familiar: An fMRI study of canine brain responses to familiar and unfamiliar human and dog odors. *Behavioural Processes, 110*, 37–46. https://doi.org/10.1016/j.beproc.2014.02.011

Berns, G. S., Brooks, A. M., Spivak, M., & Levy, K. (2017). Functional MRI in awake dogs predicts suitability for assistance work. *Scientific Reports, 7*(1), 43704. https://doi.org/10.1038/srep43704

Bernstein, M., & Yovel, G. (2015). Two neural pathways of face processing: A critical evaluation of current models. *Neuroscience and Biobehavioral Reviews, 55*, 536–546. https://doi.org/10.1016/j.neubiorev.2015.06.010

Bowlby, J. (1958). The nature of the child's tie to his mother. *International Journal of Psycho-Analysis, 39*, 350–373.

Bowlby, J. (1982). *Attachment and loss* (2nd ed.). Basic Books.

Bunford, N., Andics, A., Kis, A., Miklósi, Á., & Gácsi, M. (2017). Canis familiaris as a model for non-invasive comparative neuroscience. *Trends in Neurosciences, 40*(7), 438–452. https://doi.org/10.1016/j.tins.2017.05.003

Bunford, N., Hernández-Pérez, R., Farkas, E. B., Cuaya, L. V., Szabó, D., Szabó, Á. G., Gácsi, M., Miklósi, Á., & Andics, A. (2020). Comparative brain imaging reveals analogous and divergent patterns of species and face sensitivity in humans and dogs. *Journal of Neuroscience, 40*(43), 8396–8408. https://doi.org/10.1523/JNEUROSCI.2800-19.2020

Callaghan, B. L., & Tottenham, N. (2016). The neuro-environmental loop of plasticity: A cross-species analysis of parental effects on emotion circuitry development following typical and adverse caregiving. *Neuropsychopharmacology, 41*(1), 163–176. https://doi.org/10.1038/npp.2015.204

Cook, P. F., Spivak, M., & Berns, G. S. (2014). One pair of hands is not like another: Caudate BOLD response in dogs depends on signal source and canine temperament. *PeerJ, 2*, e596. https://doi.org/10.7717/peerj.596

Cuaya, L. V., Hernández-Pérez, R., & Concha, L. (2016). Our faces in the dog's brain: Functional imaging reveals temporal cortex activation during perception of human faces. *PLoS One, 11*(3), e0149431. https://doi.org/10.1371/journal.pone.0149431

Cunningham, C. L., & Ramos, M. F. (2014). Effect of training and familiarity on responsiveness to human cues in domestic dogs (Canis familiaris). *Animal Cognition, 17*(3), 805–814. https://doi.org/10.1007/s10071-013-0714-z

D'Aniello, B., & Scandurra, A. (2016). Ontogenetic effects on gazing behaviour: A case study of kennel dogs (Labrador retrievers) in the impossible task paradigm. *Animal Cognition, 19*(3), 565–570. https://doi.org/10.1007/s10071-016-0958-5

D'Aniello, B., Scandurra, A., Pinelli, C., Marinelli, L., & Mongillo, P. (2022). Is this love? Sex differences in dog-owner attachment behavior suggest similarities with adult human bonds. *Animal Cognition, 25*(1), 137–148. https://doi.org/10.1007/s10071-021-01545-w

Daw, N. D., Gershman, S. J., Seymour, B., Dayan, P., & Dolan, R. J. (2011). Model-based influences on humans' choices and striatal prediction errors. *Neuron, 69*(6), 1204–1215. https://doi.org/10.1016/j.neuron.2011.02.027

Dilks, D. D., Cook, P., Weiller, S. K., Berns, H. P., Spivak, M., & Berns, G. S. (2015). Awake fMRI reveals a specialized region in dog temporal cortex for face processing. *PeerJ, 3*, e1115. https://doi.org/10.7717/peerj.1115

Eisenberger, N. I., Lieberman, M. D., & Williams, K. D. (2003). Does rejection hurt? An fMRI study of social exclusion. *Science, 302*(5643), 290–292. https://doi.org/10.1126/science.1089134

Engell, A. D., Haxby, J. V., & Todorov, A. (2007). Implicit trustworthiness decisions: Automatic coding of face properties in the human amygdala. *Journal of Cognitive Neuroscience, 19*(9), 1508–1519. https://doi.org/10.1162/jocn.2007.19.9.1508

Fallani, G., Previde, E. P., & Valsecchi, P. (2006). Do disrupted early attachments affect the relationship between guide dogs and blind owners? *Applied Animal Behaviour Science, 100*(3–4), 241–257. https://doi.org/10.1016/j.applanim.2005.12.005

Fallani, G., Prato Previde, E., & Valsecchi, P. (2007). Behavioral and physiological responses of guide dogs to a situation of emotional distress. *Physiology & Behavior, 90*(4), 648–655. https://doi.org/10.1016/j.physbeh.2006.12.001

Fletcher, G. J. O., Simpson, J. A., Campbell, L., & Overall, N. C. (2015). Pair-bonding, romantic love, and evolution: The curious case of homo sapiens. *Perspectives on Psychological Science, 10*(1), 20–36. https://doi.org/10.1177/1745691614561683

Foley, P., & Kirschbaum, C. (2010). Human hypothalamus–pituitary–adrenal axis responses to acute psychosocial stress in laboratory settings. *Neuroscience & Biobehavioral Reviews, 35*(1), 91–96. https://doi.org/10.1016/j.neubiorev.2010.01.010

Gábor, A., Andics, A., Miklósi, Á., Czeibert, K., Carreiro, C., & Gácsi, M. (2021). Social relationship-dependent neural response to speech in dogs. *NeuroImage, 243*, 118480. https://doi.org/10.1016/j.neuroimage.2021.118480

Gácsi, M., Topál, J., Miklósi, Á., Dóka, A., & Csányi, V. (2001). Attachment behavior of adult dogs (*Canis familiaris*) living at rescue centers: Forming new bonds. *Journal of Comparative Psychology, 115*(4), 423–431. https://doi.org/10.1037/0735-7036.115.4.423

Haber, S. N., & Knutson, B. (2010). The reward circuit: Linking primate anatomy and human imaging. *Neuropsychopharmacology, 35*(1), 4–26. https://doi.org/10.1038/npp.2009.129

Hare, B., Call, J., & Tomasello, M. (1998). Communication of food location between human and dog (*Canis familiaris*). *Evolution of Communication, 2*(1), 137–159. https://doi.org/10.1075/eoc.2.1.06har

Hare, B., Brown, M., Williamson, C., & Tomasello, M. (2002). The domestication of social cognition in dogs. *Science, 298*(5598), 1634–1636. https://doi.org/10.1126/science.1072702

Harlow, H. F. (1958). The nature of love. *American Psychologist, 13*(12), 673–685. https://doi.org/10.1037/h0047884

Huber, L., Racca, A., Scaf, B., Virányi, Z., & Range, F. (2013). Discrimination of familiar human faces in dogs (*Canis familiaris*). *Learning and Motivation, 44*(4), 258–269. https://doi.org/10.1016/j.lmot.2013.04.005

Iidaka, T., Terashima, S., Yamashita, K., Okada, T., Sadato, N., & Yonekura, Y. (2003). Dissociable neural responses in the hippocampus to the retrieval of facial identity and emotion: An event-related fMRI study. *Hippocampus, 13*(4), 429–436. https://doi.org/10.1002/hipo.10059

Jia, H., Pustovyy, O. M., Waggoner, P., Beyers, R. J., Schumacher, J., Wildey, C., Barrett, J., Morrison, E., Salibi, N., Denney, T. S., Vodyanoy, V. J., & Deshpande, G. (2014). Functional MRI of the olfactory system in conscious dogs. *PLoS One, 9*(1), e86362. https://doi.org/10.1371/journal.pone.0086362

Jia, H., Pustovyy, O. M., Wang, Y., Waggoner, P., Beyers, R. J., Schumacher, J., Wildey, C., Morrison, E., Salibi, N., Denney, T. S., Vodyanoy, V. J., & Deshpande, G. (2016). Enhancement of odor-induced activity in the canine brain by zinc nanoparticles: A functional MRI study in fully unrestrained conscious dogs. *Chemical Senses, 41*(1), 53–67. https://doi.org/10.1093/chemse/bjv054

Kaminski, J., Schulz, L., & Tomasello, M. (2012). How dogs know when communication is intended for them. *Developmental Science, 15*(2), 222–232. https://doi.org/10.1111/j.1467-7687.2011.01120.x

Kanske, P. (2018). The social mind: Disentangling affective and cognitive routes to understanding others. *Interdisciplinary Science Reviews, 43*(2), 115–124. https://doi.org/10.1080/03080188.2018.1453243

Kanwisher, N., McDermott, J., & Chun, M. M. (1997). The fusiform face area: A module in human extrastriate cortex specialized for face perception. *Journal of Neuroscience, 17*(11), 4302–4311. https://doi.org/10.1523/JNEUROSCI.17-11-04302.1997

Karl, S., Boch, M., Virányi, Z., Lamm, C., & Huber, L. (2020). Training pet dogs for eye-tracking and awake fMRI. *Behavior Research Methods, 52*(2), 838–856. https://doi.org/10.3758/s13428-019-01281-7

Karl, S., Sladky, R., Lamm, C., & Huber, L. (2021). Neural responses of pet dogs witnessing their caregiver's positive interactions with a conspecific: An fMRI study. *Cerebral Cortex Communications, 2*(3), tgab047. https://doi.org/10.1093/texcom/tgab047

Kim, E. J., Pellman, B., & Kim, J. J. (2015). Stress effects on the hippocampus: A critical review. *Learning & Memory, 22*(9), 411–416. https://doi.org/10.1101/lm.037291.114

Kim, S., Iyengar, U., Mayes, L. C., Potenza, M. N., Rutherford, H. J. V., & Strathearn, L. (2017). Mothers with substance addictions show reduced reward responses when viewing their own infant's face. *Human Brain Mapping, 38*(11), 5421–5439. https://doi.org/10.1002/hbm.23731

Knutson, B., Adams, C. M., Fong, G. W., & Hommer, D. (2001). Anticipation of increasing monetary reward selectively recruits nucleus accumbens. *Journal of Neuroscience, 21*(16), RC159. https://doi.org/10.1523/JNEUROSCI.21-16-j0002.2001

Koban, L., Pourtois, G., Vocat, R., & Vuilleumier, P. (2010). When your errors make me lose or win: Event-related potentials to observed errors of cooperators and competitors. *Social Neuroscience, 5*(4), 360–374. https://doi.org/10.1080/17470911003651547

Konno, A., Romero, T., Inoue-Murayama, M., Saito, A., & Hasegawa, T. (2016). Dog breed differences in visual communication with humans. *PLoS One, 11*(10), e0164760. https://doi.org/10.1371/journal.pone.0164760

Krupenye, C., & Call, J. (2019). Theory of mind in animals: Current and future directions. *WIREs Cognitive Science, 10*(6), e1503. https://doi.org/10.1002/wcs.1503

Lamm, C., Decety, J., & Singer, T. (2011). Meta-analytic evidence for common and distinct neural networks associated with directly experienced pain and empathy for pain. *NeuroImage, 54*(3), 2492–2502. https://doi.org/10.1016/j.neuroimage.2010.10.014

Lazarowski, L., & Dorman, D. C. (2015). A comparison of pet and purpose-bred research dog (*Canis familiaris*) performance on human-guided object-choice tasks. *Behavioural Processes, 110*, 60–67. https://doi.org/10.1016/j.beproc.2014.09.021

Lazarowski, L., Thompkins, A., Krichbaum, S., Waggoner, L. P., Deshpande, G., & Katz, J. S. (2020). Comparing pet and detection dogs (*Canis familiaris*) on two aspects of social cognition. *Learning & Behavior, 48*(4), 432–443. https://doi.org/10.3758/s13420-020-00431-8

Lazzaroni, M., Marshall-Pescini, S., Manzenreiter, H., Gosch, S., Přibilová, L., Darc, L., McGetrick, J., & Range, F. (2020). Why do dogs look back at the human in an impossible task? Looking back behaviour may be over-interpreted. *Animal Cognition, 23*(3), 427–441. https://doi.org/10.1007/s10071-020-01345-8

Lenkei, R., Carreiro, C., Gácsi, M., & Pongrácz, P. (2021). The relationship between functional breed selection and attachment pattern in family dogs (*Canis familiaris*). *Applied Animal Behaviour Science, 235*, 105231. https://doi.org/10.1016/j.applanim.2021.105231

Lévesque, J., Eugène, F., Joanette, Y., Paquette, V., Mensour, B., Beaudoin, G., Leroux, J.-M., Bourgouin, P., & Beauregard, M. (2003). Neural circuitry underlying voluntary suppression of sadness. *Biological Psychiatry, 53*(6), 502–510. https://doi.org/10.1016/S0006-3223(02)01817-6

Lieberman, M. D. (2007). Social cognitive neuroscience: A review of core processes. *Annual Review of Psychology, 58*(1), 259–289. https://doi.org/10.1146/annurev.psych.58.110405.085654

Long, M., Verbeke, W., Ein-Dor, T., & Vrtička, P. (2020). A functional neuro-anatomical model of human attachment (NAMA): Insights from first- and second-person social neuroscience. *Cortex, 126*, 281–321. https://doi.org/10.1016/j.cortex.2020.01.010

Maginnity, M. E., & Grace, R. C. (2014). Visual perspective taking by dogs (*Canis familiaris*) in a Guesser–Knower task: Evidence for a canine theory of mind? Animal Cognition, 17(6), 1375–1392. doi:https://doi.org/10.1007/s10071-014-0773-9.

Marinelli, L., Adamelli, S., Normando, S., & Bono, G. (2007). Quality of life of the pet dog: Influence of owner and dog's characteristics. *Applied Animal Behaviour Science, 108*(1–2), 143–156. https://doi.org/10.1016/j.applanim.2006.11.018

Mariti, C., Ricci, E., Carlone, B., Moore, J. L., Sighieri, C., & Gazzano, A. (2013). Dog attachment to man: A comparison between pet and working dogs. *Journal of Veterinary Behavior, 8*(3), 135–145. https://doi.org/10.1016/j.jveb.2012.05.006

Mariti, C., Lenzini, L., Carlone, B., Zilocchi, M., Ogi, A., & Gazzano, A. (2020). Does attachment to man already exist in 2 months old normally raised dog puppies? A pilot study. *Dog Behavior, 6*(1), 1–11. https://doi.org/10.4454/db.v6i1.96

Marshall-Pescini, S., Passalacqua, C., Barnard, S., Valsecchi, P., & Prato-Previde, E. (2009). Agility and search and rescue training differently affects pet dogs' behaviour in socio-cognitive tasks. *Behavioural Processes, 81*(3), 416–422. https://doi.org/10.1016/j.beproc.2009.03.015

Marshall-Pescini, S., Prato-Previde, E., & Valsecchi, P. (2011). Are dogs (*Canis familiaris*) misled more by their owners than by strangers in a food choice task? *Animal Cognition, 14*(1), 137–142. https://doi.org/10.1007/s10071-010-0340-y

Marshall-Pescini, S., Colombo, E., Passalacqua, C., Merola, I., & Prato-Previde, E. (2013). Gaze alternation in dogs and toddlers in an unsolvable task: Evidence of an audience effect. *Animal Cognition, 16*(6), 933–943. https://doi.org/10.1007/s10071-013-0627-x

Marshall-Pescini, S., Virányi, Z., Kubinyi, E., & Range, F. (2017). Motivational factors underlying problem solving: Comparing wolf and dog puppies' explorative and neophobic behaviors at 5, 6, and 8 weeks of age. *Frontiers in Psychology, 8*, 180. https://doi.org/10.3389/fpsyg.2017.00180

Martin, R. E., & Ochsner, K. N. (2016). The neuroscience of emotion regulation development: Implications for education. *Current Opinion in Behavioral Sciences, 10*, 142–148. https://doi.org/10.1016/j.cobeha.2016.06.006

McConnell, A. R., Brown, C. M., Shoda, T. M., Stayton, L. E., & Martin, C. E. (2011). Friends with benefits: On the positive consequences of pet ownership. *Journal of Personality & Social Psychology, 101*(6), 1239–1252. https://doi.org/10.1037/a0024506

Miklósi, Á., & Topál, J. (2013). What does it take to become 'best friends'? Evolutionary changes in canine social competence. *Trends in Cognitive Sciences, 17*(6), 287–294. https://doi.org/10.1016/j.tics.2013.04.005

Miklósi, Á., Polgárdi, R., Topál, J., & Csányi, V. (1998). Use of experimenter-given cues in dogs. *Animal Cognition, 1*(2), 113–121. https://doi.org/10.1007/s100710050016

Miklósi, Á., Kubinyi, E., Topál, J., Gácsi, M., Virányi, Z., & Csányi, V. (2003). A simple reason for a big difference: Wolves do not look back at humans, but dogs do. *Current Biology, 13*(9), 763–766. https://doi.org/10.1016/S0960-9822(03)00263-X

Miklósi, Á., Topál, J., & Csányi, V. (2007). Big thoughts in small brains? Dogs as a model for understanding human social cognition. *Neuroreport, 18*(5), 467–471. https://doi.org/10.1097/WNR.0b013e3280287aae

Minagawa-Kawai, Y., Matsuoka, S., Dan, I., Naoi, N., Nakamura, K., & Kojima, S. (2009). Prefrontal activation associated with social attachment: Facial-emotion recognition in mothers and infants. *Cerebral Cortex, 19*(2), 284–292. https://doi.org/10.1093/cercor/bhn081

Nitschke, J. B., Nelson, E. E., Rusch, B. D., Fox, A. S., Oakes, T. R., & Davidson, R. J. (2004). Orbitofrontal cortex tracks positive mood in mothers viewing pictures of their newborn infants. *NeuroImage, 21*(2), 583–592. https://doi.org/10.1016/j.neuroimage.2003.10.005

Ochsner, K. N., Silvers, J. A., & Buhle, J. T. (2012). Functional imaging studies of emotion regulation: A synthetic review and evolving model of the cognitive control of emotion. *Annals of the New York Academy of Sciences, 1251*(1), E1–E24. https://doi.org/10.1111/j.1749-6632.2012.06751.x

Palmer, R., & Custance, D. (2008). A counterbalanced version of Ainsworth's Strange Situation Procedure reveals secure-base effects in dog–human relationships. *Applied Animal Behaviour Science, 109*(2–4), 306–319. https://doi.org/10.1016/j.applanim.2007.04.002

Parthasarathy, V., & Crowell-Davis, S. L. (2006). Relationship between attachment to owners and separation anxiety in pet dogs (*Canis lupus familiaris*). *Journal of Veterinary Behavior, 1*(3), 109–120. https://doi.org/10.1016/j.jveb.2006.09.005

Passalacqua, C., Marshall-Pescini, S., Barnard, S., Lakatos, G., Valsecchi, P., & Prato Previde, E. (2011). Human-directed gazing behaviour in puppies and adult dogs, *Canis lupus familiaris*. *Animal Behaviour, 82*(5), 1043–1050. https://doi.org/10.1016/j.anbehav.2011.07.039

Payne, E., Bennett, P. C., & McGreevy, P. D. (2015). Current perspectives on attachment and bonding in the dog–human dyad. *Psychology Research and Behavior Management, 8*, 71–79. https://doi.org/10.2147/PRBM.S74972

Payne, E., DeAraugo, J., Bennett, P., & McGreevy, P. (2016). Exploring the existence and potential underpinnings of dog–human and horse–human attachment bonds. *Behavioural Processes, 125*, 114–121. https://doi.org/10.1016/j.beproc.2015.10.004

Persson, M. E., Roth, L. S. V., Johnsson, M., Wright, D., & Jensen, P. (2015). Human-directed social behaviour in dogs shows significant heritability. *Genes, Brain and Behavior, 14*(4), 337–344. https://doi.org/10.1111/gbb.12194

Prato-Previde, E., Spiezio, C., Sabatini, F., & Custance, D. M. (2003). Is the dog-human relationship an attachment bond? An observational study using Ainsworth's Strange Situation. *Behaviour, 140*(2), 225–254. https://doi.org/10.1163/156853903321671514

Ramírez, M. T. G., del Berumen, L. C. Q., & Hernández, R. L. (2014). Psychometric properties of the Lexington Attachment to Pets Scale: Mexican version (LAPS-M). *Anthrozoös, 27*(3), 351–359. https://doi.org/10.2752/175303714X13903827487926

Rehn, T., McGowan, R. T. S., & Keeling, L. J. (2013). Evaluating the strange situation procedure (SSP) to assess the bond between dogs and humans. *PLoS One, 8*(2), e56938. https://doi.org/10.1371/journal.pone.0056938

Riggio, G., Gazzano, A., Zsilák, B., Carlone, B., & Mariti, C. (2021). Quantitative behavioral analysis and qualitative classification of attachment styles in domestic dogs: Are dogs with a secure and an insecure-avoidant attachment different? *Animals, 11*(1), 14. https://doi.org/10.3390/ani11010014

Scandurra, A., Alterisio, A., & D'Aniello, B. (2016). Behavioural effects of training on water rescue dogs in the Strange Situation Test. *Applied Animal Behaviour Science, 174*, 121–127. https://doi.org/10.1016/j.applanim.2015.10.007

Schöberl, I., Beetz, A., Solomon, J., Wedl, M., Gee, N., & Kotrschal, K. (2016). Social factors influencing cortisol modulation in dogs during a strange situation procedure. *Journal of Veterinary Behavior, 11*, 77–85. https://doi.org/10.1016/j.jveb.2015.09.007

Schultz, W., Dayan, P., & Montague, P. R. (1997). A neural substrate of prediction and reward. *Science, 275*(5306), 1593–1599. https://doi.org/10.1126/science.275.5306.1593

Serpell, J. A., & Hsu, Y. (2001). Development and validation of a novel method for evaluating behavior and temperament in guide dogs. *Applied Animal Behaviour Science, 72*(4), 347–364. https://doi.org/10.1016/S0168-1591(00)00210-0

Solomon, J., Beetz, A., Schöberl, I., Gee, N., & Kotrschal, K. (2019). Attachment security in companion dogs: Adaptation of Ainsworth's strange situation and classification procedures to dogs and their human caregivers. *Attachment & Human Development, 21*(4), 389–417. https://doi.org/10.1080/14616734.2018.1517812

Spreng, R. N., & Grady, C. L. (2010). Patterns of brain activity supporting autobiographical memory, prospection, and theory of mind, and their relationship to the default mode network. *Journal of Cognitive Neuroscience, 22*(6), 1112–1123. https://doi.org/10.1162/jocn.2009.21282

Stoeckel, L. E., Palley, L. S., Gollub, R. L., Niemi, S. M., & Evins, A. E. (2014). Patterns of brain activation when mothers view their own child and dog: An fMRI study. *PLoS One, 9*(10), e107205. https://doi.org/10.1371/journal.pone.0107205

Strassberg, L. R., Waggoner, L. P., Deshpande, G., & Katz, J. S. (2019). Training dogs for awake, unrestrained functional magnetic resonance imaging. *Journal of Visualized Experiments: JoVE, 152*. https://doi.org/10.3791/60192

Strathearn, L., Fonagy, P., Amico, J., & Montague, P. R. (2009). Adult attachment predicts maternal brain and oxytocin response to infant cues. *Neuropsychopharmacology, 34*(13), 2655–2666. https://doi.org/10.1038/npp.2009.103

Swain, J. E., Lorberbaum, J. P., Kose, S., & Strathearn, L. (2007). Brain basis of early parent-infant interactions: Psychology, physiology, and *in vivo* functional neuroimaging studies. *Journal of Child Psychology and Psychiatry, 48*(3–4), 262–287. https://doi.org/10.1111/j.1469-7610.2007.01731.x

Szabó, D., Gábor, A., Gácsi, M., Faragó, T., Kubinyi, E., Miklósi, Á., & Andics, A. (2020). On the face of it: No differential sensitivity to internal facial features in the dog brain. *Frontiers in Behavioral Neuroscience, 14*. https://www.frontiersin.org/article/10.3389/fnbeh.2020.00025

Thielke, L. E., & Udell, M. A. R. (2019). Evaluating cognitive and behavioral outcomes in conjunction with the secure base effect for dogs in shelter and foster environments. *Animals, 9*(11), 932. https://doi.org/10.3390/ani9110932

Thielke, L. E., & Udell, M. A. R. (2020). Characterizing human–dog attachment relationships in foster and shelter environments as a potential mechanism for achieving mutual wellbeing and success. *Animals, 10*(1), 67. https://doi.org/10.3390/ani10010067

Thielke, L. E., Rosenlicht, G., Saturn, S. R., & Udell, M. A. R. (2017). Nasally-administered oxytocin has limited effects on owner-directed attachment behavior in pet dogs (*Canis lupus familiaris*). *Frontiers in Psychology, 8*. https://www.frontiersin.org/articles/10.3389/fpsyg.2017.01699

Thompkins, A. M., Deshpande, G., Waggoner, P., & Katz, J. S. (2016). Functional magnetic resonance imaging of the domestic dog: Research, methodology, and conceptual issues. *Comparative Cognition & Behavior Reviews, 11*, 63–82. https://doi.org/10.3819/ccbr.2016.110004

Thompkins, A. M., Ramaiahgari, B., Zhao, S., Gotoor, S. S. R., Waggoner, P., Denney, T. S., Deshpande, G., & Katz, J. S. (2018). Separate brain areas for processing human and dog faces as revealed by awake fMRI in dogs (*Canis familiaris*). *Learning & Behavior, 46*(4), 561–573. https://doi.org/10.3758/s13420-018-0352-z

Thompkins, A. M., Lazarowski, L., Ramaiahgari, B., Gotoor, S. S. R., Waggoner, P., Denney, T. S., Deshpande, G., & Katz, J. S. (2021). Dog–human social relationship: Representation of human face familiarity and emotions in the dog brain. *Animal Cognition, 24*(2), 251–266. https://doi.org/10.1007/s10071-021-01475-7

Topál, J., Miklósi, A., Csányi, V., & Dóka, A. (1998). Attachment behavior in dogs (*Canis familiaris*): A new application of Ainsworth's (1969) Strange Situation Test. *Journal of Comparative Psychology, 112*(3), 219–229. https://doi.org/10.1037/0735-7036.112.3.219

Topál, J., Gácsi, M., Miklósi, Á., Virányi, Z., Kubinyi, E., & Csányi, V. (2005). Attachment to humans: A comparative study on hand-reared wolves and differently socialized dog puppies. *Animal Behaviour, 70*(6), 1367–1375. https://doi.org/10.1016/j.anbehav.2005.03.025

Uddin, L. Q., Kaplan, J. T., Molnar-Szakacs, I., Zaidel, E., & Iacoboni, M. (2005). Self-face recognition activates a frontoparietal "mirror" network in the right hemisphere: An event-related fMRI study. *NeuroImage, 25*(3), 926–935. https://doi.org/10.1016/j.neuroimage.2004.12.018

Udell, M. A. R., Dorey, N. R., & Wynne, C. D. L. (2008a). Wolves outperform dogs in following human social cues. *Animal Behaviour, 76*(6), 1767–1773. https://doi.org/10.1016/j.anbehav.2008.07.028

Udell, M. A. R., Giglio, R. F., & Wynne, C. D. L. (2008b). Domestic dogs (*Canis familiaris*) use human gestures but not nonhuman tokens to find hidden food. *Journal of Comparative Psychology, 122*(1), 84–93. https://doi.org/10.1037/0735-7036.122.1.84

Valsecchi, P., Previde, E. P., Accorsi, P. A., & Fallani, G. (2010). Development of the attachment bond in guide dogs. *Applied Animal Behaviour Science, 123*, 43–50.

Virányi, Z., Topál, J., Gácsi, M., Miklósi, Á., & Csányi, V. (2004). Dogs respond appropriately to cues of humans' attentional focus. *Behavioural Processes, 66*(2), 161–172. https://doi.org/10.1016/j.beproc.2004.01.012

Virányi, Z., Gácsi, M., Kubinyi, E., Topál, J., Belényi, B., Ujfalussy, D., & Miklósi, Á. (2008). Comprehension of human pointing gestures in young human-reared wolves (*Canis lupus*) and dogs (*Canis familiaris*). *Animal Cognition, 11*(3), 373. https://doi.org/10.1007/s10071-007-0127-y

Wanser, S. H., & Udell, M. A. R. (2019). Does attachment security to a human handler influence the behavior of dogs who engage in animal assisted activities? *Applied Animal Behaviour Science, 210*, 88–94. https://doi.org/10.1016/j.applanim.2018.09.005

Wanser, S. H., Simpson, A. C., MacDonald, M., & Udell, M. A. R. (2020). Considering family dog attachment bonds: Do dog-parent attachments predict dog-child attachment outcomes in animal-assisted interventions? *Frontiers in Psychology, 11.* https://www.frontiersin.org/articles/10.3389/fpsyg.2020.566910

Xu, X., Brown, L., Aron, A., Cao, G., Feng, T., Acevedo, B., & Weng, X. (2012). Regional brain activity during early-stage intense romantic love predicted relationship outcomes after 40 months: An fMRI assessment. *Neuroscience Letters, 526*(1), 33–38. https://doi.org/10.1016/j.neulet.2012.08.004

Chapter 4
A Dog's Life in the Human Jungle

Anindita Bhadra and Rohan Sarkar

The dog is known as man's best friend and the first ever animal to be domesticated by humans (Morey, 2010). Even before our ancestors started practicing agriculture, they had adopted dogs, or perhaps, the dogs had adopted them (Thalmann & Perri, 2019). Though scientists generally agree that dogs have evolved from gray wolf-like ancestors and have changed through centuries of domestication, the exact process of this change is not known. For example, it is understood that ancestral dogs, but not wolves, acquired mutations in their genes that helped them produce enzymes to digest carbohydrates, which in turn helped dogs to adapt to scavenging on human leftovers (Axelsson et al., 2013; Ollivier et al., 2016). Genetic studies have revealed that the earliest dogs were domesticated somewhere in East Asia, and there were probably two waves of domestication (Pang et al., 2009; Savolainen et al., 2002). All breed dogs are much more similar to each other than wolves are to free-ranging or village dogs. This is because the breed dogs are a result of artificial selection by humans, probably starting from a very small population of dogs (Driscoll et al., 2009). While humans were busy breeding dogs for traits of choice, free-ranging dogs faced their own challenges of adapting to a life around human settlements as scavengers, and thus, even today, they represent greater genetic diversity than the breed dogs and share more genes with wolves than with the breed dogs. Yet most research targeted to understand the process of dog domestication focuses on pet dogs.

Free-ranging dogs are ubiquitously present around humans in varied habitats, from the coasts to the mountain tops, in many countries across the Global South. In India, dogs have lived in free-ranging populations for centuries. The earliest

---

A. Bhadra (✉) · R. Sarkar
Department of Biological Sciences, Indian Institute of Science Education and Research Kolkata, Mohanpur, West Bengal, India
e-mail: abhadra@iiserkol.ac.in

© The Author(s), under exclusive license to Springer Nature Switzerland AG 2023
J. R. Stevens (ed.), *Canine Cognition and the Human Bond*, Nebraska Symposium on Motivation 69, https://doi.org/10.1007/978-3-031-29789-2_4

mention of free-ranging dogs in Indian literature dates back to the Rig Veda, the oldest text from the subcontinent, which dates back to at least 1000 BCE (Parpola, 2015). Perhaps the most well-known story of a free-ranging dog from this region is that of a dog following a favorite human far beyond its home range, up into the Himalayas as mentioned in the epic Mahabharata (Debroy, 2008; Sharma & Gaur, 2000). This behavior can still be seen in free-ranging dogs in the region ("This story of a dog who walked 600 km", 2016) as most dog lovers would know. These dogs live in groups, are fiercely territorial, and are primarily scavengers, depending on human generated waste for their sustenance (Sen Majumder et al., 2014b). Unlike pet dogs, they are not cared and provided for by people, but they do interact with humans regularly. They, thus, provide an excellent model system for studying the eco-ethology of dogs and their innate tendencies, especially their ability to communicate with humans.

Since its inception in June 2009, the Dog Lab at the Indian Institution of Science Education and Research (IISER)-Kolkata is engaged in peeping into the private lives of free-ranging dogs in India. We address various proximate questions that can be broadly classified into (a) how dogs interact with each other, (b) how they interact with humans, and (c) how they process information and take decisions. The ultimate question that we aim to answer, using the information we gather from the proximate answers is how the dog became "man's best friend," the evolution of the special relationship between our two species.

4.1 A Dog's Day

Free-ranging dogs are often disliked by people because they bark and bite, they chase vehicles and people, they defecate and urinate on the streets, and they squabble over food and scatter garbage. While there is much qualitative assessment of the activity of dogs, especially pertaining to aggressiveness (Reece, 2007; Sudarshan, 2004), not much objective information exists on the activity patterns of free-ranging dogs. When I (Anindita Bhadra) started considering working on free-ranging dogs, I began to walk around the campus of the Indian Institute of Science, Bangalore, to take scans of free-ranging dogs. I used to note down their coat color, any other morphological features, gender, age class, and behavior at the time of sighting, with the location of the sighting. Using this method, I compiled a list of approximately 60 behaviors of the dogs. When I established the Dog Lab, I continued this exercise on the campus of IISER-Kolkata. Soon, the first student in the lab, Sreejani Sen Majumder, joined this exercise, and the dog ethogram started to grow. Within a year, we had an ethogram with over a 100 behaviors and had started to accumulate data on activity patterns. This data was mostly collected between 0700 and 1900 h, which is when the dogs share the space with humans in most areas.

Using 1941 sightings from the IISER-Kolkata campus at Mohanpur (22° 94′ N, 88° 53′ E) and the township of Kalyani (22° 58′ N, 88° 28′ E) in West Bengal and the Indian Institute of Science campus at Bangalore (12°98′ N, 77°58′ E), Karnataka, we analyzed the activity patterns of the dogs in urban habitats. We found that contrary to the general perception of dogs being aggressive animals, these animals are generally lazy and friendly. We recorded very few interactions with humans during our observations, and most of these were submissive (Sen Majumder et al., 2014a). While this gave us the understanding of the behavior of dogs within human-dominated habitats during the part of the day when they share spaces with humans, we were still interested in delving deeper. Dogs have evolved from wolf-like ancestors, which are primarily nocturnal (Popova & Zlatanova, 2018). Free-ranging dogs are perceived to be active at night, as they can be heard barking, often aggressively, and sometimes engaging in inter-group aggression during the late hours of the night. Hence, we were interested in understanding the activity patterns of dogs throughout the day. Arunita Banerjee carried out an extensive study spanning a whole year to record dog behaviors in different locations at random times of the day. She analyzed 5669 sightings of dogs to understand the time-activity budget of the dogs. Her results confirmed that the dogs are generalists in their habit, being neither completely nocturnal nor diurnal. They remain active when humans are active, with activity levels rising above 50% during the window of 0900 to 2230 h (Banerjee & Bhadra, 2022). This study led to the addition of several new behaviors, which along with other behaviors observed by different students over the years brought the size of the ethogram to 177 behaviors.

4.2 Early Life History

4.2.1 Birth and Death

One of the earliest studies documented births and deaths of pups in the population. This study was spearheaded by Sreejani and Manabi Paul, who had joined the lab a few months after Sreejani. With Sreejani interested in mating behavior and Manabi keen to study maternal care, they made a fine team. Over a span of nearly 5 years (2010–2015), we documented 108 litters and followed 95 until the pups were 7 months old or they died. We recorded their date of birth, the size of the litter, the sex of the pups, and, if possible, the characteristics of the dens including their location. Whenever a pup died, the date and cause of death was recorded. Sometimes we had direct observations, and other times we relied on people in the locality for this information. We observed that pups begin to appear in the population in October, with the number of pups and juveniles reaching a peak during the months of December and January. The death/disappearance rate overtakes the birth rate from January, and the net number of pups and juveniles begins to decrease significantly in the population (linear regression: $R^2 = 0.848$, $\beta = -0.921$, $P = 0.003$), with the number of newborn pups reaching zero by the end of February. This clearly determined the pup emergence season for the dogs (Fig. 4.1) and helped us determine the mating season (Paul et al., 2016).

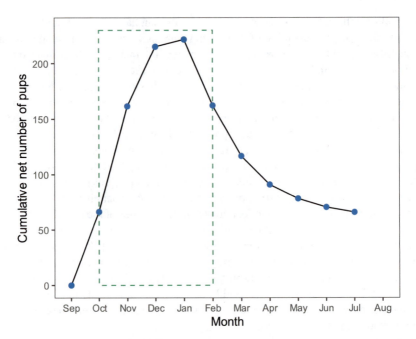

Fig. 4.1 Cumulative net number of pups (births-deaths) observed in each calendar month, for sampling conducted over five denning seasons between 2010 and 2015 (*N* = 108 mother-litter units, 30 pups). The green rectangle represents the pup-rearing season. (Redrawn from Paul et al., 2016)

It was quite evident that the pups were dying in large numbers. In fact, of the 364 pups that we tracked, only 69 survived until the age of 7 months, an 81% mortality rate. In many cases, the entire litter perished. Survival analysis yielded a plot of survival probabilities of the pups corresponding to each ordered time at which the event of removal occurred (Fig. 4.2). The median of the curve corresponded to 82 days (*N* = 364, 95% CL: 72–92 days). The highest mortality was observed at the fourth month of pup age (Paul et al., 2016). Pup mortality was caused by a varied range of factors: natural causes (disease, malnutrition, climatic factors, predation, and injury from fights), human influence (poisoning, beating, accidents, taken away from the population), and disappearances for unknown reasons. Humans accounted for 63% of pup mortality, either directly or indirectly (removal from the natal group). This was quite staggering and showed that humans are not necessarily the best friends of dogs on streets. However, this data also suggested that though there is concern over the growing population of free-ranging dogs, often leading to killing of pups and neutering of the adults, only about one-fifth of the pups born in a year survive to reach adulthood.

Parental care is a composite behavioral repertoire by which parents invest their time, energy, and resources to increase the chances of their offsprings' survival (Clutton-Brock, 1991; Woodroffe & Vincent, 1994). Caring for the young is observed in diverse species, from insects to humans, in myriad forms

4 A Dog's Life in the Human Jungle

Fig. 4.2 Number of pups and juveniles (data from 2010 to 2015) that survived at each month of age decreased significantly (on a $\log_{10}$ scale) with the increase in age. (Redrawn from Paul et al., 2016)

(Clutton-Brock, 1991). Parental care can be as simple as the act of finding a safe and habitable den for laying eggs or giving birth or as elaborate as providing extensive care in the form of nourishment, shelter, protection, and cultural transmission of knowledge (Moehlman, 1979; Tomonaga et al., 2004). The nature and extent of parental care is an important factor that influences the life history strategies of species; this is a very energy-intensive behavior, and parents need to optimize their investment in a batch of offspring to maximize their lifetime reproductive fitness (LRS) (Evans, 1990; Roff, 1992; Stearns, 1992).

Mammals are the only animals in which parental care is mandatory, at least in the form of nursing by the mother (Clutton-Brock, 1991; Woodroffe & Vincent, 1994). While all mammals nurse their offspring, they do not show similar nursing effort, and there is a large variation in the duration over which offspring are nursed, the quality and quantity of milk that is produced by the mother, and the rate at which the offspring grow while being nursed. Maternal care can be defined as the amount of resources invested by the mother to rear her current offspring at the cost of her own survival and future reproduction. Lactation is considered to be the most energetically demanding component of maternal care that can affect the mother's survival and reproduction (Oftedal, 1985; Stearns, 1992). According to Trivers' parental investment theory (Trivers, 1974), a mother should adopt a conservative strategy that ensures her own future reproduction and survival by decreasing the allocation of resources to her current offspring (Festa-Bianchet & Jorgenson, 1998).

Pet dogs are cared and provided for by their owners and breeders from birth. For free-ranging dogs, all the care, in terms of nursing, guarding, grooming, and sheltering, is provided by the mother. Manabi was interested in understanding maternal care in free-ranging dogs. Dog mothers are widely known to be very protective of their pups, often behaving aggressively toward intruding humans. Maternal investment can be measured in terms of the time spent in caregiving to the pups during various stages of their life. We broadly divided maternal care into care pre-birth, through den selection, and care post-birth, through various caregiving behaviors.

4.2.2 What Makes a Good Nursery for Pup Rearing?

Many animals are known to build nests and dens before laying eggs or giving birth. While we tend to easily associate bird nests with their breeding, denning in mammals is a relatively lesser-known behavior. However, there are reports from pet dog owners about their dogs seeking out cozy spaces, digging holes in the soil, or shredding up cloth to prepare "dens" for whelping. We had observed that female free-ranging dogs tend to give birth in dens around human homes. Since den selection can be a crucial factor in determining survival of pups in the early period of development, we carried out a study to understand the denning habits of free-ranging dogs, during 2010–2015 (Sen Majumder et al., 2016). A total of 148 den sites were located during this study.

Dens were found in all kinds of locations, from open fields and roadsides to inside buildings and human artifacts (Fig. 4.3). Likewise, they came in a varying degree of shapes and sizes. We photographed the dens and took measurements of

Fig. 4.3 Images showing different types of dens found in all kinds of locations, from open fields, roadsides, to inside buildings and human artifacts. (Photo credit: Manabi Paul)

their dimensions, lighting conditions (dark or lit), and their distance from resources like food and water and from sources of human disturbance. Combining these parameters, we quantified the "quality" of dens and gave each den a score, with the lowest score being 8 and the highest 24. Our analysis revealed something surprising – the mothers preferred den sites that gave them access to human-provided food over direct scavenging at dustbins and garbage dumping sites, which also translated to higher human disturbance around the den site. Den scores were not correlated with the size of the litter in the respective dens, which suggested that the mothers did not choose the dens based on the expected litter size. There was an overall abundance of medium to larger dens over smaller ones, irrespective of litter sizes, which ranged from 1 to 13. This would lead to the obvious conclusion that the pregnant females were not aware of the size of the litter they would give birth to at the time of den selection. Further analysis revealed that the distance of the den from resources like food and water played an important role in den selection. Mothers with large litters (5 or more pups) appeared to be less choosy, while mothers with small litters (1–4 pups) preferred dens of intermediate distance from resources and had smaller dens (Fig. 4.4). This observation raised two interesting questions – did the pregnant females actually "choose" den sites, and if so, did they have some idea of whether they were expecting small or large litters?

To answer these questions, we carried out a study focused on pregnant females. We identified pregnant females and tracked them twice every alternate day, until they gave birth. For each female, every time she appeared to select a den and rest in

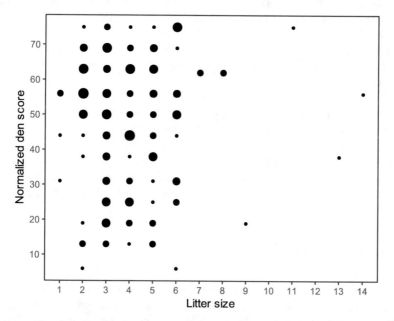

Fig. 4.4 A scatterplot showing the distribution of normalized den scores for various observed litter sizes ($N = 148$ dens). Dot sizes represent number of observations. (Redrawn from Sen Majumder et al., 2016)

it, all characteristics of the den were recorded. We tracked 20 females over three breeding seasons, of which 15 yielded data for a month, while the rest whelped earlier than a month. The identified dens were categorized as first den (D_1), intermediate dens (ID), and final den (D_F), for each female. The route taken by each female while moving during the observations was traced on a map on each day, and the time spent in each den was noted. The pregnant females occupied two to six intermediate dens, spending 4 to 21 days in a den site. The dens were given scores based on their characteristics (as above), and significant variation was observed between the scores of D_1, ID, and D_F; the scores increased from first to final dens: $D_1 <$ ID $< D_F$. The number of intermediate dens that a pregnant female occupied was independent of the time available to her before whelping. The pregnant females covered considerable distances in search of dens every day (mean ± s.d. = 312.5 ± 182.0 m). The difference between the scores of D_F and D_1 increased with the linear distance between the dens but was not correlated with the total distance covered over the total time of observations, considering the actual paths taken by the females. The distance between first and final dens increased with the number of days spent in intermediate dens. The increased time spent in intermediate dens was representative of the increased searching time. This, in turn, led to the dogs covering larger linear distance from the initial dens in search of the final den. The final den score, D_F (as compared to the initial den score, D_1), and the linear distance covered in search of it were found to have a positive relation. In short, female dogs who spent increased searching effort and time and moved a larger linear distance from their initial dens were more likely to find more suitable dens. Most of the final dens had a score of 17 or 18, for both the pregnant females' data set and the population level data, suggesting 17–18 to be the optimal den score (see above for score criteria). This study confirmed that pregnant females actively search for and select dens, settling in one that they preferred, irrespective of the number of den sites they sampled (Sen Majumder et al., 2016).

Maternal care in dogs clearly begins even before pups are born, as the would-be mothers invest time and energy in the process of den selection. This also revealed an interesting fact about the free-ranging dog-human dynamics. Unlike most urban animals (Herr et al., 2010; Thiel et al., 1998), free-ranging dogs don't avoid human proximity during breeding. They don't hide their pups away from humans but prefer to give birth close to humans, sometimes within human homes. Thus, humans are an important resource for free-ranging dogs, both as a source of food and shelter.

4.2.3 Maternal Care

Manabi carried out extensive behavioral observations on 15 groups of free-ranging dogs, which had 22 mother-litter units between them, with several of the groups having more than one lactating female and her offspring. The groups were observed from the third week to 17th week of pup age. Because of the highly defensive nature of the mothers soon after giving birth, it was impossible to collect data during the first 2 weeks, when the pups were always inside the dens and the mother guarded them constantly. Each group was observed for two morning (0900–1200) and two evening (1400–1700) sessions spread over 2-week blocks, using randomly distributed instantaneous scan (1 min each) and all occurrences sessions (5 min each) (Altmann, 1974). This amounted to a total of 8712 scans and 8712 all occurrence sessions of sampling for each mother-litter unit. This study yielded several interesting insights into the dynamics between pups, their mothers, and other members of the group.

The proportion of time, out of the total duration of observations that an animal invests in a certain behavior, is used to calculate its time investment in that behavior. We estimated the time spent by the mothers in parental care out of the total duration of observations every week. Maternal care levels were dependent on pup age and current litter size of the mother. At the third week of pup age, mothers devoted $72 \pm 25\%$ (mean ± standard deviation) of their total time in caring for their pups, and this time investment decreased as the pups grew older. A reduction of the maternal care levels was also seen from lower to higher litter sizes, irrespective of the pup age. For the same age of pups, care decreased with an increase in litter size, suggesting that the mothers regulate their investment in active care according to the litter sizes they have to nurture (Fig. 4.5a). This is indicative of competition between the siblings during the early stages of development for maternal care, which is likely to influence the dynamics within the group at later stages of development. This was further confirmed by estimating active care received per pup in each litter (Fig. 4.5b). Pups having fewer siblings tend to receive higher amount of active maternal care at their early stages of life. The care behaviors include a wide range of active as well

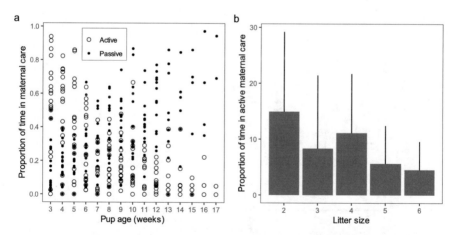

Fig. 4.5 (**a**) Scatterplot showing the relationship between the proportion of time spent in maternal care with the age of the pups. Each dot represents a mother of a mother-litter unit. Black dots represent passive care, open circles represent active care received by each litter at different ages of pups (Redrawn from Paul et al., 2017). (**b**) Mean and standard deviation of the proportion of time spent by the mother in active care toward her pups as a function of litter size (Redrawn from Paul et al., 2017)

passive behaviors, and they were observed to occur at various levels at various ages of the pups. The most important and inevitable maternal care behavior is nursing, which is essential for the survival of the offspring. Hence, we specifically analyzed the mother's investment in nursing (Paul et al., 2017).

4.2.4 Nursing

Mothers invested 18 ± 9% of their total time in nursing in the third week of pup age. This time decreased with increasing pup age (Fig. 4.6) and stopped completely by the 13th week. At their third week of age, pups spent 15 ± 9.25% of their total time in suckling from their mothers. The mismatch in the mother and offspring's time investment in nursing/suckling is due to competition between siblings during suckling. There was no significant variation in nursing rates between mothers for pups of the same age, and there was no evidence of any preferential treatment by the mothers toward any individual pups during nursing initiation. However, the rate (frequency per hour) of care received in terms of suckling by individual pups was regulated by a combination of their age and their current litter size. Thus, though the mothers were impartial in providing care through nursing, sibling rivalry could lead to skewed benefits for individual pups. The duration of nursing bouts decreased with increasing pup age, suggesting the reduced interest of mothers to offer milk to her pups, which is predicted by parent-offspring conflict theory (Trivers, 1974).

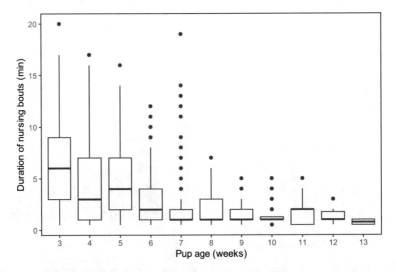

Fig. 4.6 Box plots of duration of nursing/suckling bouts (in minutes) as a function of pup age (in weeks). Nursing/suckling durations decrease as the pups grow older. Thick horizontal lines represent medians, boxes represent interquartile ranges, whiskers represent 1.5 times the interquartile range, and filled dots represent data points beyond 1.5 times the interquartile range. (Redrawn from Paul & Bhadra, 2017)

4 A Dog's Life in the Human Jungle

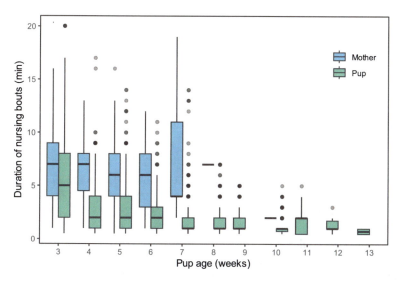

Fig. 4.7 Box plots showing the duration of mother-initiated nursing (blue) and pup-initiated (green) suckling bouts as a function of pup age ($N = 11$ litters). Thick horizontal lines represent medians, boxes represent interquartile ranges, whiskers represent 1.5 times the interquartile range, and filled dots represent data points beyond 1.5 times the interquartile range. (Redrawn from Paul & Bhadra, 2017)

The reduced frequency and duration of nursing could also be an outcome of the pups' increasing efficiency in suckling. Hence, we considered the identity of the initiator for every bout of suckling to understand whether mothers consistently offered to nurse their pups throughout the duration of observations or whether some of the nursing bouts resulted from solicitations by pups. We calculated the proportion of bouts initiated by the mother and pups at every week of pup age. The proportion of mother-initiated nursing and pup-initiated suckling bouts were inversely related to each other in the context of increasing pup age. Thus, as pups grew older, instances of nursing bouts initiated by the mother decreased, whereas instances of pup initiated suckling bouts increased. (Fig. 4.7). Thus, both the mother's reduced interest in nursing and the pups' efforts at suckling from the mother contributed to the observed pattern of nursing behavior. We concluded that mothers actively balanced their investment in parental care, reducing investment in care as the pups grew older, and not overinvesting with increasing litter sizes (Paul & Bhadra, 2017).

4.3 The Great Indian Joint Families

Since our observations were carried out on mother-litter units that belonged to larger groups of dogs, they included interactions between all group members. This revealed an interesting set of dynamics between the pups and the other members of the group, both other pups and adults. The most important interactions between the focal pups and adults were alloparental care, i.e., care behavior shown toward the pups by an adult other than their mother. Such behavior is also found in other animals like elephants (matrifocal), spotted hyenas, birds, and canids such as wolves (both sexes) (Riedman, 1982).

4.3.1 Helping Relatives

We observed allocare in 19 of the 23 litters, of which 10 litters received all three types of care, i.e., maternal care, male care, and female allocare (Paul & Bhadra, 2018) (Fig. 4.8). Male care and female allocare were observed in 14 litters each. Allomaternal care was mostly (93%) shown by female relatives of the pups; for a single litter, there could be multiple allomothers, who could be their grandmothers, aunts, or siblings from earlier litters. All the males that showed care had been observed to have mated with the mothers of the pups receiving care. However, since the dogs have a promiscuous mating system, this was not enough to conclude the paternity of the pups. Hence, we designated the caregiving males as "putative fathers." There was a special case of one litter of pups receiving only allocare from their grandmother and putative father, as their mother died in an accident a day after their birth.

Female allocare, especially when it includes allonursing, imposes high metabolic costs (in terms of lactation) on the caregiver, though it is likely to be less intensive than maternal care. Often, pups received female allocare as early as their third week of age, but the level of female allocare is significantly lower than maternal care. The level of allomaternal care increased from the third week of pup age and reached its peak between ninth and tenth weeks of pup age, decreasing again as the pups grew older. Like maternal care, active care shown by both males and females was

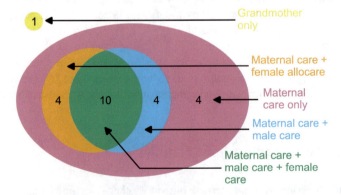

Fig. 4.8 Infographic showing the distribution of alloparenting observed in the 23 litters. The ellipses represent the groups, the numbers represent the number of litters in each category, and the colors differentiate between the types of care received. (Redrawn from Paul & Bhadra, 2018)

dependent on pup age, but unlike maternal care, allocare was independent of litter size. Interestingly, though the allomaternal care received by the pups was significantly lower than the maternal care levels, active care shown by the putative fathers was comparable with that of the mothers.

Mothers and putative fathers seemed to show similar levels of investment in caregiving behaviors but budgeted their time invested differently. For the first 3 weeks of observations (third to fifth weeks of pup age), 76–86% of the active maternal care comprised of nursing and pile sleeping. Play and protection replaced these behaviors as the pups grew older (Fig. 4.9). In case of male care, play and protection consistently contributed to 69 ± 12% of active male allocare, throughout the entire period of observations. Thus, it appears that mothers mostly nursed and groomed the pups, while fathers engaged in play and protection, suggesting some degree of division of labor in care, which would not be possible in litters from small groups or solitary females. Fathers were also seen to regurgitate food for the pups, which is a behavior commonly observed in the mothers as the pups attain the fifth week of age.

While allomaternal care could impose a cost on the allomothers, philopatry could reduce the cost by providing inclusive fitness benefits to females that provided care to the related pups. In a population that faces high early life mortality (Paul et al., 2016), any additional care received by pups could help increase their survival probability, thus making allocaring a stable strategy in such a species. Alloparental

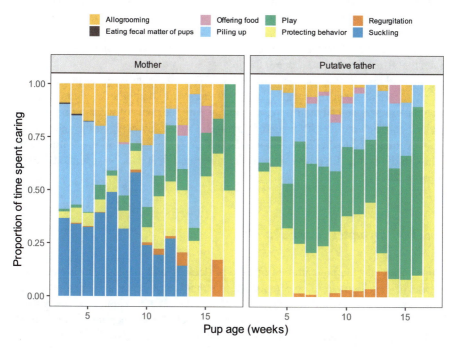

Fig. 4.9 Stacked bar diagram showing the proportion of time spent by the mothers and putative fathers in various caregiving activities as a function of pup age. (Redrawn from Paul & Bhadra, 2018)

care is likely to increase the chances of survival of pups, thus providing an advantage for group living to the dogs.

4.3.2 Selfish Pups

Pups received allocare when they began to emerge from their natal dens, facilitating the increased contact with adult dogs other than their mothers. While allocare in the form of grooming, protection, or even play was not surprising, it was indeed surprising to note that allomaternal care often included allonursing. Since allonursing is likely to be costly to the allomother, leading to sharing of her resources (milk) with pups other than her own, this observation came as a surprise to us, leading to a more detailed analysis of this behavior. For each bout of allonursing, the identity of the initiator and terminator of the nursing bout and the duration of the bout were recorded in 11 mother-litter units. A similar analysis had been carried out for nursing bouts by the mothers, and the two data sets could be now compared.

In 9 of the 11 mother-litter units, we observed high incidence of allonursing (594 bouts), and in eight of these nine units, the allonursing female was related to the pups. 100% of the allonursing bouts were initiated by pups, irrespective of their age, and the allomothers never volunteered to allonurse (Fig. 4.10). Most of the allonursing bouts were terminated by refusals from the allomothers, irrespective of the age of the pups. The average nursing duration was 3.2 ± 2.3 min for the mothers, whereas it was 1.5 ± 0.8 min for the allomothers. The duration of suckling from mothers over the entire period of observations was significantly longer 3.2 ± 2.3 min than that from allomothers 1.5 ± 0.8 min.

Interestingly, during the weaning period (7th to the 13th week of pup age), the durations were equal for suckling from mothers and allomothers, which suggests that the mothers nursed their pups voluntarily until the onset of weaning but tried to reduce care beyond the 7th week of pup age. The allomothers, on the other hand, never volunteered to nurse non-filial pups, and thus, they were victims of milk theft. This study is the first ever report of milk theft behavior in canids (Paul & Bhadra, 2017).

4.3.3 Playmates in the Family

Pups spend considerable amount of time in sleeping and playing. During the early weeks of development, they often sleep together, wrapped around each other in a pile. Sometimes, the mother too sleeps with her pups in this manner, and we call this behavior pile sleeping, which is considered distinctly from sleeping (by oneself). It is likely that pile sleeping helps the pups stay warm and also helps build social bonds among the siblings. Non-sibling pups from the same group are not observed to engage in pile sleeping.

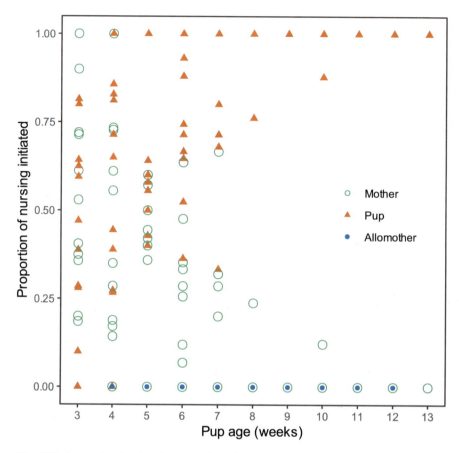

Fig. 4.10 Scatterplot showing the proportion of nursing/suckling initiated by mothers (empty green circle), pups (orange triangles), and allomothers (solid blue circles). The allomothers were never observed to volunteer to allonurse. (Redrawn from Paul & Bhadra, 2017)

The behavior that is most noted in pups, even by the lay observer, is perhaps play. Young mammals are known to engage in play quite extensively, and play has been shown to be of extreme importance during the developmental phase in many species (Burghardt, 2005; Nunes, 2014; Shimada & Sueur, 2014). On one hand, play helps develop social bonds between individuals, especially littermates, and on the other, it is used to establish hierarchies within the group (Bekoff, 1974). Social play is useful in training for hunting, fighting, and even mating (Pellegrini et al., 2007; Smith, 1982). Dogs often play as adults too, and this is considered to be a neotenic trait that is strongly associated with domestication (Bradshaw et al., 2015).

Post analysis of play behavior in all the groups of dogs discussed above, we noted that pups spent 36.6 ± 27.2% of their active time in play. Their most preferred play partners were their littermates, followed by other pups in the group. They solicited play from their mothers at a much lower rate than from other pups, and adults were observed as playmates much less than pups. Social network analysis for play behavior could be carried out for 18 of the litters, in which there were more than six nodes in the network. This revealed "rich clubs" within the networks, comprised primarily of the littermates. A rich club within a social network is a structural property of complex networks in which highly connected nodes are more connected to each other than to other nodes in the network (Wasserman & Fausk, 1994; Zhou & Mondragón, 2004). The fact that the littermates play preferentially with each other, followed by other pups in the group, suggests that play could be a very important social behavior that helps establish social relationships in early life and may influence the dynamics of the group in adulthood. Future studies need to be carried out to understand the role of play in social dynamics in more detail.

These studies showed that the pups grow up in complex social groups, receiving extensive maternal care, which is often supplemented by allomaternal and paternal care. In spite of this, the survival probability of pups remains one in five within the population.

4.4 Survival in the Human Jungle

How have free-ranging dogs adapted to living among humans in the human-dominated habitat? We carried out a series of experiments to test both the physical and socio-cognitive abilities of free-ranging dogs. Here, we review some of the studies that we have carried out to test the cognitive abilities of free-ranging dogs in India, with particular attention to their survival in the human jungle.

4.4.1 Scavenging Skills

One of the very first experiments addressed a simple question – do free-ranging dogs have a preference for meat/animal proteins? This question might sound naïve but has important implications for the dog. In 2013, a study reported that dogs acquired a set of genes that enabled them to digest carbohydrates, which in turn gave them an edge over their relatives, the wolves, as they could feed on the carbohydrate-rich leftovers of humans (Axelsson et al., 2013). The diet of Indians is carbohydrate rich, and dogs typically receive biscuits or bread from humans as a response to begging, and leftovers also consist primarily of rice, breads, vegetable and fruit peels, and bones of fish chicken, lamb, etc. Free-ranging dogs rarely ever hunt in the urban areas, though they are reported to sometimes hunt in large packs in forest fringes and in the outskirts of remote villages. So they primarily depend on carbohydrate-rich food for their sustenance. Anandarup Bhadra wanted to understand if many generations of such a diet have led free-ranging dogs to lose or bypass the preference for meat, which is expected in canids. He carried out a set of choice tests with very small food pellets, which clearly revealed a preference for meat over carbohydrates in the adults. However, the pups (8–10 weeks old) did not display any such preference and ate everything with equal gusto (Bhadra & Bhadra, 2014). Another set of experiments revealed that the adults actually sniffed out meat, even when it was present in trace quantities, and preferentially fed on the option that smelled of meat, rather than the one that was rich in proteins. We concluded that free-ranging dogs use a rule of thumb, "if it smells like meat, eat it," to increase their foraging efficiency (Bhadra et al., 2016). This strategy would be helpful in sniffing out protein-rich food items from a lot of noise in the form of garbage, thereby making them efficient scavengers.

Scientists must always question themselves and never become complacent. After the initial thrill of discovering the rule of thumb, we were suspicious – efficient though they are at sniffing out the meat when provided with choices on a platter (literally!); do they really use the rule of thumb in a more realistic situation, we wondered. The only way to answer this question was to test it with an experiment. So the next student, Rohan Sarkar, designed and executed the "dustbin experiments," which, as one might guess, were quite a handful, given that the experimenters had to carry around baskets and set them up as dustbins, on street sides. The dustbin experiment was simple – we provided choices to individual dogs but in the form of "dustbins" – there were three identical baskets, each half-filled with garbage (paper, plastic, dry leaves, flowers, vegetable peels, etc.) collected from the vicinity. One of the baskets had ten pieces of raw chicken (protein box), another had ten bread (carbohydrate box), and the third had five pieces of chicken and five bread (mixed box). The food was hidden among the garbage, such that the dog would need to search for it. The dogs were provided these baskets together, placed in random order, and they were allowed to explore for 1 min. Records were maintained of the order of sniffing and eating and the choice made. So several months and hundreds of trials later, we were convinced that the dogs did use the rule of thumb even while scavenging. They had eaten more from the protein box and eaten more of the chicken pieces in total than the bread (Fig. 4.11).

Whenever they sniffed the protein box first, they typically ate from the box before moving on to the next box, suggesting the use of a "sniff-and-snatch" strategy. They did eat more chicken, but did not ignore the biscuits, which again suggests their skill as scavengers (Sarkar et al., 2019).

Rohan has carried out more complicated dustbin experiments to understand how competition might influence the choices that dogs make during scavenging and how the reactions of the dogs tested in groups might differ from dogs tested individually. He has also been carrying out a series of experiments to see if the behavior of dogs in groups remain consistent over repeated trials. We hope to soon have answers to these questions.

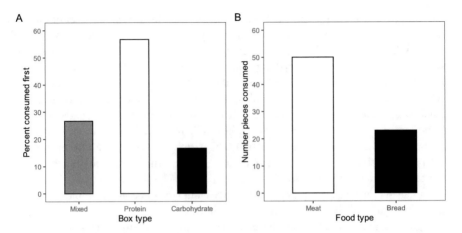

Fig. 4.11 (a) Bar graph showing the percentage of times dog consumed from each box type (mixed, protein, and carbohydrate) first. The protein box was approached first in a significantly higher percentage of cases (goodness-of-fit: $\chi^2 = 7.8$, df = 2, $p = 0.020$). (b) Considering all pieces of food eaten, meat was eaten more than bread (Goodness of Fit: $\chi^2 = 9.986$, df = 1, $p = 0.002$). (Redrawn from Sarkar et al., 2019)

4.4.2 Understanding Human Gestures

Pet dogs have remarkable skills of responding to various human social cues (Hare & Tomasello, 1999, 2005; Miklósi & Soproni, 2006; Soproni et al., 2002). A range of studies have demonstrated their abilities to communicate with humans using pointing gestures, from the simplest to the most complex types (Elgier et al., 2012; Lakatos et al., 2009; Miklósi & Soproni, 2006). Our observations of free-ranging dogs had revealed that their preferred mode of scavenging is begging from humans (Bhadra et al., 2016). The dogs make eye contact and gaze for prolonged duration at a human, especially when the person is eating something (personal observations). Sometimes, individual dogs are fed by specific humans on a regular basis. Since humans are both a source of food and shelter and a threat to the dogs, we were interested in their ability to comprehend human gestures like pointing or threatening postures. Debottam Bhattacharjee was interested in investigating the ability of free-ranging dogs to understand and utilize human gestures. He led a set of experiments with pups (4–8 weeks old), juveniles (3–7 months), and adults to test their ability to understand a simple pointing cue from an unfamiliar human.

The experiment involved an experimenter randomly pointing at one of two covered bowls, one of which had a piece of chicken and the other was sham-baited by rubbing it with chicken. The proximal pointing cue (Bhattacharjee et al., 2017b) was used as referential gesture. Most of the pups followed the pointing and went to the bowl being pointed at, while juveniles and adults tended not to follow the pointing cue. The adults showed an interesting difference from the juveniles and pups – they showed both positive and negative reinforcement. Thus, when they followed pointing and found a reward in a trial, they had a higher probability of following pointing in the text trial (positive reinforcement). However, if they followed pointing and were deceived, they had a lower probability of following pointing in the next trial (negative reinforcement). Each individual was tested in three trials. This suggested that the dogs have an innate tendency to follow human pointing gestures (pups follow the point) but perhaps learn not to rely on unfamiliar humans as they grow, due to the negative experiences with humans. Our data on mortality had revealed that the juvenile stage is the most vulnerable to death caused by human factors. This is also the stage when they begin to become independent of their mothers and are more likely to face threats from humans. However, as they mature, they also learn to take decisions based on immediate experiences, which is reflected in the behavior of the adults (Bhattacharjee et al., 2017b).

Pet dogs are known to follow various kinds of pointing gestures, which is likely to be a result of their experience of living with humans. We tested the ability of free-ranging dogs to follow two kinds of complex gestures – a momentary distal pointing and a dynamic distal pointing. The dogs showed a high degree of point following behavior for both the cues. In both cases, about 80% of the adult dogs followed the point, which was significantly higher than the point following observed in case of the simple pointing cue (Bhattacharjee et al., 2019). This was perhaps because the dogs are more used to people throwing food to them at a distance, rather than pointing out the food from close proximity. Also, the gesture of bending down to point to a bowl might be perceived as a threat by the dogs, as compared to the distal pointing gesture.

Free-ranging dogs experience varied interactions with humans, ranging from highly positive like petting, feeding, etc. to highly negative, like beating, chasing, and even killing by humans. We performed a set of experiments with adult free-ranging dogs to test their responses to human social gestures – neutral, friendly, low threat, and high threat. The neutral cue condition consisted of the experimenter standing in front of a dog, looking straight ahead. In the friendly cue condition, the experimenter called out to the dog while bending slightly and stretching out both arms. The low threat comprised of the experimenter standing before the dog, carrying a stick, while in the high threat condition, the experimenter raised the stick above his head, in a threatening pose. In each condition, a piece of chicken was provided to the dog by the experimenter after providing the social cue. Free-ranging dogs showed varied responses to the cues. They approached more in the friendly cue condition, and in the high impact threatening condition, they failed to approach even on being provided food, preferring to keep a distance from the experimenter (Fig. 4.12).

While the demeanor of the dogs was mostly affiliative in the friendly cue condition, it was mostly anxious in the high impact threatening condition. These experiments highlighted the behavioral plasticity of free-ranging dogs in their interactions with unfamiliar humans. They not only understand different behavioral states of humans but also respond to the same human differently in different situations (Bhattacharjee et al., 2018).

The differential and situation-specific responses of the dogs might be explained by early social interactions with humans (Fox & Stelzner, 1966). Domestication has

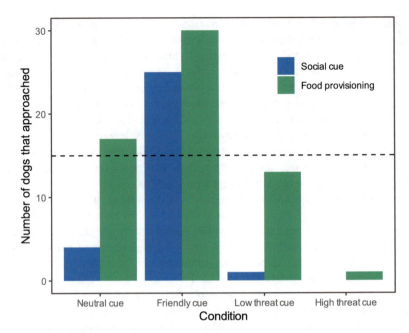

Fig. 4.12 Bar graph showing the number of approaches in the Social Cue Phase and Food Provisioning Phase of the four experimental conditions: neutral cue, friendly cue, low threat cue, and high threat cue. Number of dogs that approached varied between the phases across the conditions (Contingency χ^2: $\chi^2 = 10.44$, df = 3, $p = 0.015$). The dotted line indicated the chance level (50%). (Redrawn from Bhattacharjee et al., 2018)

played a crucial role in shaping the dogs' understanding and sensitivity toward human social cues. It has been shown that even hand-reared wolves fail to adjust behaviors while interacting with humans in ambiguous situations (Bradshaw, 1995). Thus, it can be surmised that an interplay of domestication, the immediate environment, and life experiences with humans influence the responses of the dogs to humans and might shape their personalities.

4.4.3 Love Is the Buzz Word

We often observe free-ranging dogs establishing social bonds with specific humans, interacting with them through friendly gestures like tail-wagging, play bows, licking, and greeting. While conducting experiments with unfamiliar random dogs on streets, we typically find some dogs who are extremely wary of strangers and never participate in the experiments, while others respond to the initial call quite eagerly. We wanted to understand how a dog might build trust upon a stranger. It has been hypothesized that the wolves underwent a process of self-domestication, following humans for food. A study on shelter and pet dogs had concluded that a brief social reward is less effective than a food reward (Feuerbacher & Wynne, 2012), and another showed that pets prefer food to petting but petting to vocal praise (Feuerbacher & Wynne, 2014). Though it seemed most likely that free-ranging dogs would bond with humans who fed them, our qualitative impression of the dogs seemed to differ from this logical conclusion. We needed to test this, experimentally, to be sure.

We conducted an experiment in which 30 randomly selected adult dogs in different areas were offered two pieces of chicken, one placed on the ground and the other held out in the palm of the hand, held very close to the ground. The experimenter was unknown to the dog before the experiment and was constant across all trials. We recorded the location of the food (the ground or the hand) and the latency to approach. When the dog had made a choice, the experimenter provided the dog a social reward – petting thrice on the head. After a gap of 5–10 s, the test was repeated. This was termed as the one-off test, in which each dog was tested only once using the two trials. The control set consisted of the same experiment, without the social reward.

Another set of 43 adult dogs were subjected to a long-term test. They were tested similarly on Day 0, with the two pieces of chicken, and randomly assigned to one of two reward conditions – food or social reward. The dogs were tested subsequently with increasing gaps between tests, on Days 1, 3, 6, 10, and 15. The experimenter visited the dogs and either provided them with a food reward (a piece of chicken) or a social reward (petting thrice on the head). This was followed by the usual test, as on Day 0.

Most of the 103 dogs preferred to take the piece of chicken from the ground in the first trial. In the one-off test, we did not see an effect of the social reward, as most of the dogs did not change their preference in the second trial, though they showed a reduction in the latency to respond in the second trial. The results of the long the experiments were most fascinating. In the long-term food reward experiment, majority of the dogs (52%) consistently took food from the ground, in spite of being given food by the same experimenter, and very few individuals showed increased socialization with the experimenter toward the end of the month-long experiment. However, in the social reward condition, we observed a change in preference, with more individuals shifting to feeding from the hand as the experiment progressed (Fig. 4.13). This experiment showed that free-ranging dogs build trust on unfamiliar humans when they receive affection and not food (Bhattacharjee et al., 2017c). Though this might appear to be an inconsistent behavior on the part of a scavenging species, this indeed fits into our understanding of free-ranging dogs. Humans often poison dogs to kill them. A dog that trusts a stranger and feeds from their hand may not survive to feed another day. However, someone who shows affection to a dog is less likely to attempt to kill it too. Hence, the tendency to build trust based on a show of affection and not on food rewards would be adaptive for free-ranging dogs in a human-dominated environment in which it has a complex relationship with our species.

We carried out a follow-up experiment with a set of randomly selected adult dogs to understand if petting for a short period of time can influence the tendency of point

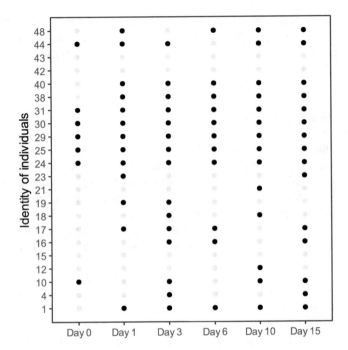

Fig. 4.13 Plot showing the identity of individuals and their preference of obtaining reward at specific day intervals for the long-term social reward condition. The black dots indicate obtaining food from hand, and the gray dots indicate obtaining food from ground. Day 0 responses are naïve, as dogs had no previous exposure to social reward. (Redrawn from Bhattacharjee et al., 2017c)

following in free-ranging dogs. A total of 80 dogs were tested (40 male, 40 female), with 40 in the test category and 40 in the control category. On Day 1, each dog was tested using the dynamic proximal pointing cues for their naïve response to pointing. After recording the naïve response, dogs were randomly assigned to the test and control conditions. Of the 40 dogs in each group, half were further assigned to informative cue condition and the other half to deceptive cue condition.

The test dogs were provided social petting (10 s) by a single experimenter on days 2, 3, and 4. The dogs assigned to the control condition did not receive any petting. On Day 5, the same experimenter tested the dogs for their response to pointing in three consecutive trials. The experimenter pointed either to the bowl containing the food reward (informative cue) or to the bowl that was sham-baited (deceptive cue). The dog was allowed to respond. The dogs that had received petting increased their likelihood of point following from Day 1 (55%) to Day 5 (97.5%) ($z = -3.307$, $p < 0.001$; Fig. 4.14). However, dogs in the control condition exhibited comparable point following tendencies on Day 1 (67.5%) and Day 5 (55%) ($z = 1.185$, $p = 0.63$; Fig. 4.13). Interestingly, the dogs that had received petting did not show negative reinforcement – they followed pointing even when they received a deceptive cue in an earlier trial (Bhattacharjee & Bhadra, 2021).

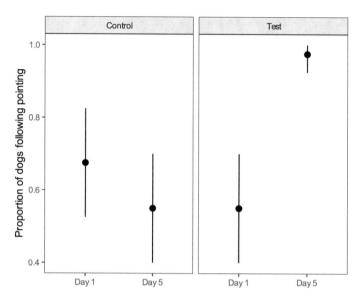

Fig. 4.14 Comparison of dogs following pointing cues without (control) and with petting (test). Dots represent means, and error bars represent between-subjects 95% confidence intervals. (Redrawn from Bhattacharjee & Bhadra, 2021)

This study reinforced our earlier result of the effectiveness of petting over food in helping to develop trust and bonding between dogs and humans. This underlines the impact of immediate experiences with humans in the dogs' behavioral adjustments in a communicative context. While considering the larger picture, such findings support the idea that ontogenic experiences can impact dogs' socio-cognitive skills like human point following (Udell et al., 2010; Udell & Wynne, 2010; Wynne et al., 2008). An ability to understand human reliability and the use of conditional strategies are highly beneficial for free-ranging dogs' successful coexistence in the human-dominated environments.

4.5 Conclusion

Free-ranging dogs in India are ubiquitous in every human-dominated habitat. They have complex social lives, and do not necessarily need us to provide them homes and families. They have a complex love-hate relationship with our species – humans are their primary source of food and the biggest threat to their survival. They have an excellent capacity to understand various social gestures of humans and use them to adjust their own behavior. This gives them the edge over many other species to survive in the human jungle. Our many studies have consistently revealed a high degree of behavioral plasticity in the dogs, and it is very likely that their lifetime experience with humans shape their personalities, leading to dogs in areas of high human flux less anxious and more prone to responding to unfamiliar humans and dogs in areas that have low human flux being more wary of strangers (Bhattacharjee et al., 2020). Whether one is a dog lover or not, humans influence the lives of free-ranging dogs immensely to the extent that humans occupy central positions in the social interaction networks of dogs (Bhattacharjee & Bhadra, 2020). They share the habitat with a large number of species, many of which also scavenge on human-generated resources. However, dogs emerge as the key species in the scavenging community in urban spaces (Biswas et al., n.d.), which suggests that they have a major role to play in energy dynamics of the urban ecosystem.

These dogs have been living around humans for centuries. They have survived urbanization, as we have upgraded from bullock carts to electric cars, and they have learned to cross busy roads, adapted their behavior to remain hidden from humans when required, and wag their tales at friendly people. They have evolved the "puppy eyes" that melt our hearts (Kaminski et al., 2019) and have learned to scavenge rather than hunt. They have adapted to our carbohydrate-rich diets and learned to eat everything from chapatis to curd rice. They are resourceful enough to find dens for their pups near friendly humans and beg for food, especially when they have pups. They have learned to trust people who show them love, rather than those who offer them food, because food can be poisoned, and it often is a means of removing pups from the streets. They are quick-thinking and adaptable, perhaps more so than many pet breeds that we so rigorously maintain and flaunt. We need to understand that we share our habitat with them. Their ancestors have scavenged on the battlefields of our ancestors, given birth in their courtyards and have been fed leftover from their meals. They are a species we share our ecosystems with, like the crows, mynahs, rats, bees, ants, and monkeys. They have been on the streets, in the Indus Valley and Indraprastha, in Kalinga and Kurukshetra, in Banaras and Bengaluru, carving out their own niche and learning to adapt to our changing lifestyles.

References

Altmann, J. (1974). Observational study of behavior: Sampling methods. *Behaviour, 49*(3–4), 227–267. https://doi.org/10.1163/156853974X00534

Axelsson, E., Ratnakumar, A., Arendt, M. L., Maqbool, K., Webster, M. T., Perloski, M., Liberg, O., Arnemo, J. M., Hedhammar, Å., & Lindblad-Toh, K. (2013). The genomic signature of dog domestication reveals adaptation to a starch-rich diet. *Nature, 495*(7441), 360–364. https://doi.org/10.1038/nature11837

Banerjee, A., & Bhadra, A. (2022). Time-activity budget of urban-adapted free-ranging dogs. *Acta Ethologica, 25*(1), 33–42. https://doi.org/10.1007/s10211-021-00379-6

Bekoff, M. (1974). Social play and play-soliciting by infant canids. *American Zoologist, 14*, 323.

Bhadra, A., & Bhadra, A. (2014). Preference for meat is not innate in dogs. *Journal of Ethology, 32*(1), 15–22. https://doi.org/10.1007/s10164-013-0388-7

Bhadra, A., Bhattacharjee, D., Paul, M., Singh, A., Gade, P. R., Shrestha, P., & Bhadra, A. (2016). The meat of the matter: A rule of thumb for scavenging dogs? *Ethology Ecology and Evolution, 28*(4), 427–440. https://doi.org/10.1080/03949370.2015.1076526

Bhattacharjee, D., & Bhadra, A. (2020, August). Humans dominate the social interaction networks of urban free-ranging dogs in India. *Frontiers in Psychology, 11*, 1–11. https://doi.org/10.3389/fpsyg.2020.02153

Bhattacharjee, D., & Bhadra, A. (2021). Adjustment in the point-following behaviour of free-ranging dogs – Roles of social petting and informative-deceptive nature of cues. *Animal Cognition, 25*(3), 571–579. https://doi.org/10.1007/s10071-021-01573-6

Bhattacharjee, D., Dasgupta, S., Biswas, A., Deheria, J., Gupta, S., Nikhil Dev, N., Udell, M., & Bhadra, A. (2017a). Practice makes perfect: Familiarity of task determines success in solvable tasks for free-ranging dogs (Canis lupus familiaris). *Animal Cognition, 20*(4), 771–776. https://doi.org/10.1007/s10071-017-1097-3

Bhattacharjee, D., Nikhil Dev, N., Gupta, S., Sau, S., Sarkar, R., Biswas, A., Banerjee, A., Babu, D., Mehta, D., & Bhadra, A. (2017b). Free-ranging dogs show age related plasticity in their ability to follow human pointing. *PLoS One, 12*(7), 1–17. https://doi.org/10.1371/journal.pone.0180643

Bhattacharjee, D., Sau, S., Das, J., & Bhadra, A. (2017c). Free-ranging dogs prefer petting over food in repeated interactions with unfamiliar humans. *Journal of Experimental Biology, 220*(24), 4654–4660. https://doi.org/10.1242/jeb.166371

Bhattacharjee, D., Sau, S., & Bhadra, A. (2018). Free-ranging dogs understand human intentions and adjust their behavioral responses accordingly. *Frontiers in Ecology and Evolution, 6*, 232. https://doi.org/10.3389/fevo.2018.00232

Bhattacharjee, D., Mandal, S., Shit, P., Varghese George, M., Vishnoi, A., & Bhadra, A. (2019). Free-ranging dogs are capable of utilising complex human pointing cues. *Frontiers in Psychology, 10*, 2818. https://doi.org/10.3389/fpsyg.2019.02818

Bhattacharjee, D., Sarkar, R., Sau, S., & Bhadra, A. (2020). Sociability of Indian free-ranging dogs (Canis lupus familiaris) varies with human movement in urban areas. *Journal of Comparative Psychology*. https://doi.org/10.1037/com0000241

Biswas, S., Bhowmik, T., Ghosh, K., Roy, A., Laheri, A., Sarkar, S., & Bhadra, A (n.d.) Scavengers in the human-dominated landscape – An experimental study. Under review. Preprint at https://doi.org/10.48550/arXiv.2208.05030

Bradshaw, J., & Rooney, N. (1995). Social and communication behaviour of companion dogs. In J. Serpell (Ed.), *The domestic dog: Its evolution, behaviour and interactions with people*. Cambridge University Press.

Bradshaw, J., Pullen, A., & Rooney, N. (2015). Why do adult dogs "play"? *Behavioural Processes, 110*, 82–87. https://doi.org/10.1016/j.beproc.2014.09.023

Burghardt, G. M. (2005). *The genesis of animal play*. MIT Press. https://doi.org/10.7551/mitpress/3229.001.0001

Clutton-Brock, T. (1991). *The evolution of parental care*. Princeton University Press.

Debroy, B. (2008). *Sarama and her children: The dog in Indian myth*. Penguin Books India.

Driscoll, C. A., Macdonald, D. W., & O'Brien, S. J. (2009). From wild animals to domestic pets, an evolutionary view of domestication. *Proceedings of the National Academy of Sciences of the United States of America, 106*(Suppl), 9971–9978. https://doi.org/10.1073/pnas.0901586106

Elgier, A. M., Jakovcevic, A., Mustaca, A. E., & Bentosela, M. (2012). Pointing following in dogs: Are simple or complex cognitive mechanisms involved? *Animal Cognition, 15*(6), 1111–1119. https://doi.org/10.1007/s10071-012-0534-6

Evans, R. M. (1990). The relationship between parental input and investment. *Animal Behaviour, 39*(4), 797–798. https://doi.org/10.1016/S0003-3472(05)80391-4

Festa-Bianchet, M., & Jorgenson, J. (1998). Selfish mothers: Reproductive expenditure and resource availability in bighorn ewes. *Behavioral Ecology, 9*(2), 144–150. https://doi.org/10.1093/beheco/9.2.144

Feuerbacher, E. N., & Wynne, C. D. L. (2012). Relative efficacy of human social interaction and food as reinforcers for domestic dogs and hand-reared wolves. *Journal of the Experimental Analysis of Behavior, 98*(1), 105–129. https://doi.org/10.1901/jeab.2012.98-105

Feuerbacher, E. N., & Wynne, C. D. L. (2014). Most domestic dogs (Canis lupus familiaris) prefer food to petting: Population, context, and schedule effects in concurrent choice. *Journal of the Experimental Analysis of Behavior, 101*(3), 385–405. https://doi.org/10.1002/jeab.81

Fox, M. W., & Stelzner, D. (1966). Approach/withdrawal variables in the development of social behaviour in the dog. *Animal Behaviour, 14*(2–3), 362–366. https://doi.org/10.1016/S0003-3472(66)80098-2

Hare, B., & Tomasello, M. (1999). Domestic dogs (*Canis familiaris*) use human and conspecific social cues to locate hidden food. *Journal of Comparative Psychology, 113*(2), 173–177. https://doi.org/10.1037//0735-7036.113.2.173

Hare, B., & Tomasello, M. (2005). Human-like social skills in dogs? *Trends in Cognitive Sciences, 9*, 439–444. https://doi.org/10.1016/j.tics.2005.07.003

Herr, J., Schley, L., Engel, E., & Roper, T. (2010). Den preferences and denning behaviour in urban stone martens (Martes foina). *Mammalian Biology-Zeitschrift Für ..., 75*, 138.

Kaminski, J., Waller, B. M., Diogo, R., Hartstone-Rose, A., & Burrows, A. M. (2019). Evolution of facial muscle anatomy in dogs. *Proceedings of the National Academy of Sciences of the United States of America, 116*(29), 14677–14681. https://doi.org/10.1073/pnas.1820653116

Lakatos, G., Soproni, K., Dóka, A., & Miklósi, Á. (2009). A comparative approach to dogs' (Canis familiaris) and human infants' comprehension of various forms of pointing gestures. *Animal Cognition, 12*(4), 621–631. https://doi.org/10.1007/s10071-009-0221-4

Miklósi, Á., & Soproni, K. (2006). A comparative analysis of animals' understanding of the human pointing gesture. *Animal Cognition, 9*(2), 81–93. https://doi.org/10.1007/s10071-005-0008-1

Moehlman, P. D. (1979). Jackal helpers and pup survival. *Nature, 277*, 382–383. https://doi.org/10.1038/277382a0

Morey, D. (2010). *Dogs: Domestication and development of a social bond*. Cambridge University Press.

Nunes, S. (2014). Juvenile social play and yearling behavior and reproductive success in female Belding's ground squirrels. *Journal of Ethology, 32*(3), 145–153. https://doi.org/10.1007/s10164-014-0403-7

Oftedal, O. T. (1985). Pregnancy and lactation. In R. G. Hudson & R. J. White (Eds.), *Bioenergetics of wild herbivores*. CRC Press.

Ollivier, M., Tresset, A., Bastian, F., Lagoutte, L., Axelsson, E., Arendt, M. L., Bălăşescu, A., Marshour, M., Sablin, M. V., Salanova, L., & Vigne, J. D. (2016). Amy2B copy number variation reveals starch diet adaptations in ancient European dogs. *Royal Society Open Science, 3*(11). https://doi.org/10.1098/rsos.160449

Pang, J. F., Kluetsch, C., Zou, X. J., Zhang, A. B., Luo, L. Y., Angleby, H., Ardalan, A., Ekström, C., Sköllermo, A., Lundeberg, J., & Matsumura, S. (2009). MtDNA data indicate a single origin for dogs south of yangtze river, less than 16,300 years ago, from numerous wolves. *Molecular Biology and Evolution, 26*(12), 2849–2864. https://doi.org/10.1093/molbev/msp195

Parpola, A. (2015). *The roots of Hinduism: The early Aryans and the Indus civilization*. Oxford University Press.

Paul, M., & Bhadra, A. (2017). Selfish pups: Weaning conflict and milk theft in free-ranging dogs. *PLoS One, 12*(2). https://doi.org/10.1371/journal.pone.0170590

Paul, M., & Bhadra, A. (2018). The great Indian joint families of free-ranging dogs. *PLoS One, 13*(5), 1–18. https://doi.org/10.1371/journal.pone.0197328

Paul, M., Sen, S., Sau, S., Nandi, A. K., & Bhadra, A. (2016). High early life mortality in free-ranging dogs is largely influenced by humans. *Scientific Reports, 6*(19641), 1–8. https://doi.org/10.1038/srep19641

Paul, M., Sau, S., Nandi, A. K., & Bhadra, A. (2017). Clever mothers balance time and effort in parental care: A study on free-ranging dogs. *Royal Society Open Science, 4*, 160583. https://doi.org/10.1098/rsos.160583

Pellegrini, A. D., Dupuis, D., & Smith, P. K. (2007). Play in evolution and development. *Developmental Review, 27*(2), 261–276. https://doi.org/10.1016/j.dr.2006.09.001

Popova, E., & Zlatanova, D. (2018). The grey wolf and its prey – Insights from camera trapping in Osogovo Mtn. In Bulgaria and Macedonia. *Annual of Sofia University "St. Kliment Ohridski", 104*, 266–277. https://doi.org/10.13140/RG.2.2.35256.80647

Reece, J. F. (2007). Rabies in India: An ABC approach to combating the disease in street dogs. *Veterinary Record, 161*(9), 292–293. https://doi.org/10.1136/vr.161.9.292

Riedman, M. L. (1982, December). The evolution of alloparental care and adoption in mammals and birds. *The Quarterly Review of Biology, 57*(4), 405–435.

Roff, D. A. (1992). *The evolution of life histories: Theory and analysis*. Chapman and Hall.

Sarkar, R., Sau, S., & Bhadra, A. (2019, April). Scavengers can be choosers: A study on food preference in free-ranging dogs. *Applied Animal Behaviour Science, 216*, 38–44. https://doi.org/10.1016/j.applanim.2019.04.012

Savolainen, P., Zhang, Y., Luo, J., Lundeberg, J., Leitner, T., Vila, C., et al. (2002). Genetic evidence for an East Asian origin of domestic dogs. *Science (New York, N.Y.), 298*(5598), 1610–1613. https://doi.org/10.1126/science.1073906

Sen Majumder, S., Chatterjee, A., & Bhadra, A. (2014a). A dog's day with humans-time activity budget of free-ranging dogs in India. *Current Science, 106*(6), 874–878.

Sen Majumder, S., Bhadra, A., Ghosh, A., Mitra, S., Bhattacharjee, D., Chatterjee, J., Nandi, A. K., & Bhadra, A. (2014b). To be or not to be social: Foraging associations of free-ranging dogs in an urban ecosystem. *Acta Ethologica, 17*(1), 1–8. https://doi.org/10.1007/s10211-013-0158-0

Sen Majumder, S., Paul, M., Sau, S., & Bhadra, A. (2016, August). Denning habits of free-ranging dogs reveal preference for human proximity. *Scientific Reports, 6*, 1–8. https://doi.org/10.1038/srep32014

Sharma, T. R. S., & Gaur, J. (2000). *Ancient Indian literature – An anthology*. Sahitya Akademi.

Shimada, M., & Sueur, C. (2014). The importance of social play network for infant or juvenile wild chimpanzees at Mahale Mountains National Park, Tanzania. *American Journal of Primatology, 76*(11), 1025–1036. https://doi.org/10.1002/ajp.22289

Smith, P. K. (1982). Does play matter? Functional and evolutionary aspects of animal and human play. *Behavioral and Brain Sciences, 5*(1), 139–155. https://doi.org/10.1017/S0140525X0001092X

Soproni, K., Miklósi, Á., Topál, J., & Csányi, V. (2002). Dogs' (Canis familiaris) responsiveness to human pointing gestures. *Journal of Comparative Psychology, 116*(1), 27–34. https://doi.org/10.1037/0735-7036.116.1.27

Stearns, S. C. (1992). *The evolution of life histories*. Oxford University Press.

Sudarshan, M. K. (2004). *Assessing burden of rabies in India* (WHO sponsored national multi-centric rabies survey) (p. 6). Association of Prevention and Control of Rabies in India.

Thalmann, O., & Perri, A. R. (2019). Paleogenomic inferences of dog domestication. In *Paleogenomics* (pp. 273–306). https://doi.org/10.1007/13836_2018_27

Thiel, R. P., Merrill, S., & Mech, D. L. (1998). Tolerance by Denning Wolves. *Canadian Field-Naturalist, 122*(2), 340–342. Northern Prairie Wildlife Research Center Home Page. http://www.npwrc.usgs.gov/resource/2000/wolftol/wolftol.htm (Version 04AUG2000)

This story of a dog who walked 600 kms with a Sabarimala pilgrim is heart-touching. (2016). *The Indian Express*.

Tomonaga, M., Tanaka, M., Matsuzawa, T., Myowa-Yamakoshi, M., Kosugi, D., Mizuno, Y., Okamoto, S., Yamaguchi, M. K., & Bard, K. A. (2004). Development of social cognition in infant chimpanzees (pan troglodytes): Face recognition, smiling, gaze, and the lack of triadic interactions. *Japanese Psychological Research, 46*(3), 227–235. https://doi.org/10.1111/j.1468-5884.2004.00254.x

Trivers, R. L. (1974). Parent-offspring conflict. *Integrative and Comparative Biology, 14*(1), 249–264.

Udell, M. A. R., & Wynne, C. D. L. (2010). Ontogeny and phylogeny: Both are essential to human-sensitive behaviour in the genus Canis. *Animal Behaviour, 79*(2), e9–e14. https://doi.org/10.1016/j.anbehav.2009.11.033

Udell, M. A. R., Dorey, N. R., & Wynne, C. D. L. (2010). What did domestication do to dogs? A new account of dogs' sensitivity to human actions. *Biological Reviews, 85*(2), 327–345. https://doi.org/10.1111/j.1469-185X.2009.00104.x

Wasserman, S., & Fausk, K. (1994). *Social network analysis: Methods and applications*. Cambridge University Press. https://doi.org/10.4135/9781071812082.n576

Woodroffe, R., & Vincent, A. (1994). Mother's little helpers: Patterns of male care in mammals. *Trends in Ecology & Evolution, 9*(8), 294–297. https://doi.org/10.1016/0169-5347(94)90033-7

Wynne, C. D. L., Udell, M. A. R., & Lord, K. A. (2008). Ontogeny's impacts on human-dog communication. *Animal Behaviour, 76*(4), 1–4. https://doi.org/10.1016/j.anbehav.2008.03.010

Zhou, S., & Mondragón, R. J. (2004). The rich-club phenomenon in the internet topology. *IEEE Communications Letters, 8*(3), 180–182.

Chapter 5
Effects of University-Based AAIs: Conceptual Models Guiding Research on Active Treatment Components of AAIs on Stress-Related Outcomes

Patricia Pendry and Alexa M. Carr

5.1 Introduction and Background

There has been a significant increase in the popularity and implementation of animal-assisted interventions (AAIs), which are unstructured or goal-oriented activities that intentionally incorporate animals into educational, healthcare, legal, and human service settings to enhance human development, health, and well-being. The popularity of AAIs is evidenced by enthusiastic anecdotal accounts of participants, increased demand for AAIs in various settings, and a popular media narrative propagating AAIs as delivering powerful benefits for human health and well-being (Morrison, 2021). Aiming to quantify these proclaimed effects, the last decade has seen a substantial increase in research funding by various stakeholders. The influx of research funding has resulted in enhanced scientific knowledge about AAIs, as well as significant growth in the discipline of anthrozoology, the interdisciplinary field focused on studying the interactions between humans and non-human animals.

While research examining AAIs has proliferated, many important questions remain. We know relatively little about the *causal* impact of AAIs across developmental domains and outcomes and virtually nothing about *for whom* and under *what conditions* AAIs are most effective (Rodriguez et al., 2021). Also, our insight into the pathways that may underlie observed treatment effects is limited, nor do we know much about the key components of AAIs. In part, this is due to limited use of adequately powered experimental designs examining causal pathways, the wide variety of intervention and program types studied, a predominant focus on brief exposures and short-term outcomes, reliance on self-report measures, and few designs that isolate active treatment components using relevant comparison

---

P. Pendry (✉) · A. M. Carr
Department of Human Development, Washington State University, Pullman, WA, USA
e-mail: ppendry@wsu.edu

conditions. On the other hand, several studies have recently been conducted that explicitly considered and addressed these shortcomings. Over the last decade, we – researchers and practitioners – have collectively made tremendous strides and progress as evidenced by increased use of sophisticated research designs and methods, consideration of a wide array of measurement approaches, interdisciplinary and multidisciplinary collaborations, and the pursuit of research questions that push the boundaries of our field.

5.2 Current Chapter

In this chapter, we share results of efficacy trials we conducted to determine effects of AAIs conducted in a specific and unique education setting, the university campus. The rationale for focusing on this setting and population is informed by the attention it has received from researchers, practitioners, and the public in response to what has been referred to as a mental health crisis facing post-secondary students worldwide (Henriques, 2018). Moreover, while university-based mental health centers are trying to respond accordingly, they face overwhelming demand and limited capacity. As a result, we have seen a tremendous increase in the use of AAIs on university campuses, even though knowledge about what constitutes best practice is still underdeveloped. The following studies were designed to contribute that knowledge.

We will examine empirical evidence of a multi-study series of two large efficacy trials we conducted – the Pet Your Stress Away Study (PYSA) and the PETPALS Study – which examined the efficacy of campus-based AAIs aimed at preventing and alleviating stress and distress to mitigate the development of mental health disorders and academic failure in typical and at-risk university students. Throughout, we discuss the strengths and limitations of the featured implementation approaches, as well as interpret the significance of this empirical evidence for an existing theoretical model, future research, and implementation. Last, we provide recommendations for implementation of the practice of campus-based AAIs within a context of increasing need and demand of typical and at-risk populations, limited capacity and resources, and mixed evidence on sound practice. Before we delve into study details, we share contextual factors in which this research is embedded.

5.2.1 Characteristics of University-Based AAIs

It is important to consider that AAI is an interdisciplinary umbrella term that refers to a variety of animal-assisted approaches that include the *treatment* of psychopathology through therapy, as well as the *prevention* of psychopathology through strengthening factors associated with resilience during times of risk. An example of an AAI focused on treatment is animal-assisted *therapy* (AAT), which incorporates animals as part of a goal-directed, personalized treatment plan, conducted by a licensed therapist or psychiatrist, aiming to provide measurable improvements in human physical, social, emotional, or cognitive functioning (International Association for Human Animal Interaction Organizations (IAHAIO), 2014). An example of a prevention-oriented approach is the use of animal-assisted *activities* (AAAs), which are commonly implemented by volunteers or paraprofessionals without therapeutic qualifications. These activities focus on improving individuals' quality of life and well-being by reducing stress or distress, providing social support, increasing motivation, creating a sense of community, and facilitating social interactions, as well as facilitating behavioral change or the acquisition of new skills (IAHAIO, 2014). In this chapter, we focus specifically on university-based AAAs.

University-based AAAs exist in a wide variety of forms. Planned and goal-oriented, most of these programs are animal visitation programs (AVPs), which arrange for animal-handler teams to visit a program site to facilitate informal interactions for as little as 10 min to several hours (Haggerty & Mueller, 2017). AVPs are often conducted in the weeks leading up to students' examinations and at times during exam week. The majority of AVPs conducted on university campuses feature dogs; however, the inclusion of cats and other animals is not unusual. In fact, in a geographically representative survey of university-based AVPs, Haggerty and Mueller (2017) reported 86% of sampled programs featured dogs only, while 5% feature cats and dogs, and 10% involve dogs, cats, and other species, including rabbits, baby goats, and alpacas, among others. Since most AVPs are intended to provide access to large numbers of students in a relatively short period of time, they tend to involve supervised interactions in small group settings rather than one-on-one interactions.

As the popularity of AVPs has grown and implementation become widespread, a trend is emerging with universities and colleges expanding the type and range of activities to include more structured, regular, and programmatic AAIs. This includes regular on campus drop-in programs (Binfet et al., 2017; Carr & Pendry, 2022), semester-long programs that incorporate workshops involving varying levels of psychoeducational content and human-animal interaction (HAI) with registered therapy canines (Pendry et al., 2020a, 2021), and visitation programs in dorms and student organizations (Pendry et al., 2018). Altogether, university-based AAIs are appealing to university administrators because they enjoy tremendous positive public perception and require less training and expertise than traditional therapies, allowing for low-cost implementation by volunteer organizations, which increases access to a greater and wider range of populations. In the next section, we focus on the rationale for the increased popularity, demand, and implementation of universal and targeted campus-based AAIs and their most common purpose, alleviating student stress to prevent or modulate the development of stress-related disorders and associated academic failure.

5.2.2 University Student Mental Health, Well-Being, and Academic Achievement

The demand for campus-based AAIs is a response to university administrators' awareness of high rates of students' mental health problems and universities' limited capacity to provide traditional mental services to address them. Even before the COVID-19 pandemic, 66.4% of students reported feeling "overwhelming anxiety," 46.2% felt "so depressed that it was difficult to function," and 14.4% seriously considered suicide (American College Health Association, 2020). Moreover, academic stress played a huge role in creating high levels of stress; for example, over half (52.7%) of students reported that academic responsibilities were "traumatic or difficult to handle," 85% reported feeling exhausted (not from physical activity), and 88% felt overwhelmed (American College Health Association, 2019). Unfortunately, already serious mental health problems (Eisenberg & Lipson, 2019; Lipson et al., 2019) have been further aggravated by the emergence of COVID-19 pandemic consequences (Son et al., 2020). The Healthy Minds Network and American College Health Association (n.d.) reported increased rates of students' depression (from 35.7% in Fall 2019 to 40.9% in Spring 2020), stable yet high rates of anxiety (31% at both time points), and a decrease in students' feelings of flourishing from 38.1% to 36.6%. Moreover, students reported increased rates of academic impairment due to anxiety (from 27.8% in 2019 to 31.1% in 2020) and depression (from 22.1% to 24.4%). Finally, 81.8% of surveyed undergraduates reported an overall level of moderate or high stress within the last 12 months (The Healthy Minds Network & American College Health Association, n.d.). It is clear that university students are in need of interventions designed to help students manage stress and stress-related symptoms.

5.2.2.1 Risk Factors

Reports also demonstrate that individual risk factors play an important role both in perceiving high levels of stress and the development of clinical disorders. For example, there is a significant gap between the prevalence of symptoms and disorders by gender with significantly higher rates for cis women than for cis men. Depression diagnoses were reported by 25.3% of cis women and 14.1% of cis men; 32.7% of women and 15.4% of men reported an anxiety diagnosis; and 85.7% of women compared to 70.7% of men rated their overall level of stress experienced in the last 12 months as "moderate" or "high" (American College Health Association, 2021). Additionally, mental illness was particularly prevalent among students who identified as transgender or gender non-conforming (50.9% reporting a depression diagnosis, 54.9% an anxiety diagnosis), and 89.5% of transgender or gender non-conforming students reported moderate-to-high levels of overall stress within the last 12 months (American College Health Association, 2021). Furthermore, students belonging to racial and/or ethnic minority groups may experience additional stress, anxiety, and depression related to discrimination and institutional racism (Greer & Cavalhieri, 2019). These data clearly suggest that while prevalence of stress-related disorders is universally high – affecting one out of four students – students who are female, transgender, non-gender conforming, and of color are particularly vulnerable. Given the practice of complementing traditional mental health services with animal-assisted approaches, and the limited capacity to scale up such programs while safeguarding animal well-being, our ability to identify individuals most in need, or most likely to benefit from AAIs, has become paramount.

5.3 The "Pet Your Stress Away" Program

In the next section, we first describe the Pet Your Stress Away (PYSA) *program* and continue with a detailed description of the series of consecutive PYSA research *studies*. The PYSA program was a well-established, highly popular university-based "stress-prevention" program held the week before final exams of Spring and Fall semesters at Washington State University (WSU) in Pullman, Washington. WSU is a land-grant university, located in the Pacific Northwest, which hosts nearly 20,000 students, annually featuring more than 100 fields of study. The approach of the PYSA program is the most prevalent type of university-based AAIs, known as an animal visitation program (AVP).

The aim of the PYSA program was to provide undergraduate students with an opportunity to interact with shelter dogs and cats brought to campus by the local humane society for approximately 10 min in supervised small-group settings (Fig. 5.1). Held in a large gym and usually lasting a total of 2 h, the program did not require prior registration of students, nor were any data collected about the participants and their experiences. Typically, several hundreds of students lined up in the hallways outside the gym where their entry and exit into the program space was actively managed by program staff to safely accommodate the highest number of participants, rather than allowing individual students to determine the length of their engagement. Groups of four to five students engaged with dogs under supervision of an animal handler, while they engaged with cats individually. On average, the program featured approximately 25 animals ($N_{dogs} \approx 10$) per session. Dogs were adult, mostly large breed animals (Labrador terrier mix, American Staffordshire pit bull mix, Labrador pit bull mix, boxer Labrador mix, Alaskan Malamute, and several dogs with unknown breed mixes) from two local shelters. Dogs were seated on pillows and blankets and kept on leash in close proximity of their handler, or at times seated in a large playpen area, which students were allowed to enter. Cats were housed in large cat condos, which facilitated interaction between individual students and cats. Students could freely interact with the animals, which most often centered on petting and stroking the animals while seated on the ground. Students also had opportunities to hold the animal on one's lap or in one's arms depending on its size, species, and temperament.

Fig. 5.1 The Pet Your Stress Away Program. Randomly assigned study participants were met by research assistants who managed entry into the program space

5.3.1 Study Aims of Study 1

The overall goal of the series of PYSA *studies* was to conduct a large-scale, randomized controlled trial to determine the effects of the PYSA program on students' stress-related outcomes. This efficacy trial had to be conducted during a time frame determined by university administrators, independently planned and implemented the PYSA program according to procedures developed and employed over three semesters prior to our team's involvement. While challenging, we proposed an embedded causal research design conducted during real-life implementation, rather than merely conduct a program evaluation examining within-person changes in program participants. The main research aims were to examine whether exposure to 10 min of human animal interaction affected students' moment-to-moment emotion states (e.g., feeling content, anxious, irritable, and depressed). The 10-min dosage and strength of manipulation was decided based on experiences of program implementers, who identified that in prior semesters, students engaged with animals for approximately 10 min.

Our rationale for measuring impacts on students' emotion states was the following. First, at the time we applied for funding, no prior efficacy trials of this size and population had examined impacts of AAIs on momentary emotion in situ. It was, however, well-known that emotion states are indicators of individual differences in appraisal and arousal, which are known to play a major role in overall health and well-being. An individual's momentary emotional state is linked to activation of the hypothalamic pituitary adrenal (HPA) axis, one of the body's physiological stress-response systems associated with the development of psychopathology in response to chronic or extreme stress. Examining changes in moment-to moment emotional states in response to either a stressor or activity intended to *downregulate* emotional and possibly physiological arousal is thus useful as an indicator of individual differences in stress-system activation and development of mental health issues (Adam, 2012). Given strong evidence in the risk and resilience literature that risk and protective factors play role in these processes, we also explored whether treatment effects were moderated by individual differences related to clinical levels of mental health symptoms including students' levels of depression, perceived stress, worry, and anxiety in the weeks preceding the program.

5.3.1.1 Recruitment, Design, and Procedures

In the week before final exams were to take place, the study team visited a wide variety of general education classes to recruit and consent undergraduate students ($N = 233$) representing approximately 33 different majors across all student standings.[1] Given the universal orientation of the planned program, students were not approached based on individual characteristics deemed risk factors but rather based on their enrollment in large general education classes, taught by instructors who had given permission to the research team to conduct recruitment presentations during class time. Given that the planned program dates and times had been determined months in advance and unchangeable, students were asked to confirm that they were available during the PYSA program time. After we described study procedures, interested and available students were consented and completed a screening survey, which included a participant ID number and a randomized treatment condition identifier (meaningless to participants), indicating the treatment condition to which they were randomly assigned ($N_{experimental} = 76$; $N_{control} = 79$; $N_{waitlist} = 78$). The screening survey contained questions pertaining to demographic characteristics (e.g., class standing, gender, age, major); self-report measures assessing mental health symptomatology, including depressive symptomology (BDI: Beck et al., 1996), anxiety (BAI: Beck & Steer, 1993), worry (PSWQ: Meyer et al., 1990), and perceived stress (PSS-10: Cohen et al., 1983); and questions about participation in animal-assisted programming and/or counseling activities. Participants of study 1 were mostly female ($N_{female} = 86\%$), across standings ($N_{freshman} = 25\%$, $N_{sophomore} = 24\%$, $N_{junior} = 31\%$, $N_{senior} = 20\%$; $M_{age} = 20.19$, SD = 1.69).

---

[1] All procedures performed in studies involving human participants were in accordance with the ethical standards of the institutional and/or national research committee and with the 1964 Helsinki declaration and its later amendments or comparable ethical standards. All procedures performed in studies involving animals were in accordance with the ethical standards of the University's Institutional Animal Care and Use Committee.

5.3.1.2 In Situ Data Collection Procedures

Two days after recruitment and screening, participants came to the PYSA program and study site during the 2-h program time frame. Study participants prominently displayed the provided ID label containing their "blind" condition identifier on the outside of their clothing so research assistants could direct them before even entering the building to check-in rooms specific to their randomly assigned study condition to avoid contamination by other conditions or viewing any of the animals or fellow students waiting in line. Participants randomly assigned to the *experimental condition*, the hands-on PYSA program, were directed to a curtained-off program entry area where research assistants carefully managed and documented students' time of entry and exit into the human-animal interaction area, located in the large gym where the PSYA program took place. As such, other than the study's data collection procedures, experimental study participants' program experiences were identical to non-study participants attending the PYSA program as they blended into the regular program space.

Immediately before entering the program area, students in the experimental condition completed a 2-min, 25-item scale rating the extent to which they experienced various positive and negative emotions *at that moment* on a 4-point Likert scale ranging from 0 (*not at all*) through 3 (*very much*), which were later factor analyzed. The measure was based on the experience sampling method (ESM: Csikszentmihalyi & Larson, 1987) and was utilized in several prior studies by the first author. Students then entered the animal interaction area, where they engaged with animals of their choosing for exactly 10 min. After exactly 10 min, study participants were escorted to a curtained-off section where they immediately completed the same 2-min survey reporting on their emotional state following the intervention.

Participants randomly assigned to the *control condition* ($N = 57$) were given instructions before entering the program area. They were to view a 10-min slide presentation containing pictures of the same program animals so they could indicate their preferences for certain animals using a checklist (i.e., rate how much you like to pet this animal, etc.). Unbeknownst to participants, the only purpose for asking students to complete this checklist was to engage students in 10 min of viewing still images of the program animals to facilitate assessment of momentary emotion in response to the control condition, rather than actually informing which animals they would later interact with. This was not done for the purpose of exploring whether viewing a slide presentation would be an effective AAI for future programming but rather to isolate the impact of the component of *hands-on touch* of the animals, separate from the impact of *viewing* animals, since both components are commonly enmeshed during administration of AAIs. Control participants thus completed their pre- and post-intervention ratings of moment-to-moment emotional states immediately before and after the 10-min slide presentation. Upon completion, students entered the program area where they too interacted with program animals for 10 min. Given our choice to conduct an independent groups design rather than a repeated measures approach exposing each participant to each condition, we did not assess their emotion states following these interactions.

Participants assigned to the *waitlist condition* ($N = 57$) were directed to a "waiting" area and instructed to refrain from verbal interaction, cellphone use, and reading materials. Immediately after receiving these instructions, they completed their first pre-intervention measure of momentary emotion. They sat in silence for 10 min, after which they completed their post-intervention measure of momentary emotion. They did not know that they were being assessed in response to non-treatment but were led to believe that completing the checklist was standard procedure for all PYSA participants to gather information about their preferences presumably to facilitate enjoyable interactions later. Following their completion of the research protocol, waitlisted participants also engaged with the program animals for 10 min.[2] Given the independent groups design, their emotion states following the interactions were not assessed.

5.3.1.3 Effects of PYSA on Momentary Emotion States

Results (Pendry et al., 2018) showed that students in the experimental hands-on condition reported significantly higher levels of *feeling content* after the intervention, compared with students in the control and waitlist conditions (Fig. 5.2), suggesting that participation in the PYSA program focused on small-group, hands-on interactions had a positive, significant, and large effect.[3] Participants in the experimental group also reported feeling significantly and substantially *less anxious* and *less irritable* after completing the program than those in the control condition and non-treatment condition. We did not find significant group differences in levels of feeling *depressed* at post-test, although within-group comparisons showed that participants in the experimental group reported significant and moderate decreases in feeling depressed immediately after program participation. Given the lack of main effects of PYSA participation on depressed emotion states, we explored whether participants' levels of clinical depression, perceived stress, worry, and anxiety moderated treatment effects and found no evidence to reject the null hypothesis. In sum, the results of study 1 clearly demonstrated that 10 min of exposure to the PYSA program as implemented featuring 10 min of hands-on petting and interaction in small group settings led to significantly higher levels of positive emotion (i.e., feeling content) and lower levels of negative emotions (e.g., feeling irritable and anxious), compared with viewing still images of animals or being waitlisted, regardless of risk status.

---

[2] All participants were provided extra credit vouchers to be turned into their professors.
[3] Cohen's effects sizes were > 0.5.

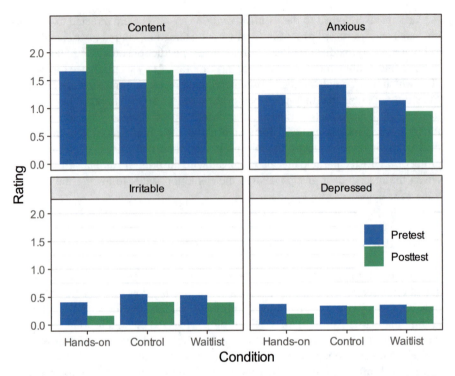

Fig. 5.2 Bar graphs displaying students' average levels of emotion (content, anxious, irritable, depressed) at pre-test and post-test as a function of hands-on, control, or waitlist condition. (Redrawn from Pendry et al., 2018)

5.3.1.4 Considerations for Future Research

Several directions for further future research emerged from this early study. First, during the first round of data collection, several research assistants noticed what appeared to be pronounced individual differences in behavioral responses of program participants. Differences were observed while participants waited in line for their turn, immediately preceding participants entering the interaction space and again immediately following the completion of their 10-min interaction period. While not formally assessed, anecdotal evidence suggested pronounced differences in students' affect with several participants appearing to become progressively more irritated and upset while waiting in line and/or becoming progressively more withdrawn and refraining from social interaction leading up to their participation. Differences in participants' affect seemed more pronounced toward the end of the line close to entry area compared with the general displays of positive affect at the beginning of the line. Similarly, while most participants displayed positive facial expressions upon completion of the program, we noticed a subset of students who left the program area with what can be best described as irritable and/or depressed affect.[4]

Hence, to test whether perceived, unscientifically observed individual difference in affect reflected meaningful difference in perceived emotion states, we set out in study 2 to capture differential effects of this often-overlooked component of AVPs – the experience of waiting in line for an extended period of time while in visible range of animal activities. In addition, we were interested in testing a priori whether the presence of clinical depression moderated the effects of the same PYSA intervention on university students' momentary emotional states for which only main effects were hypothesized and tested in study 1 (e.g., feeling content, anxious, irritable).

5.3.2 Study 2: Moderating Effects of Clinical Depression on Program Effects

A subsequent cohort of participants reported to the study site 2 days after recruitment, which was conducted using identical procedures as those described previously. Participants ($N = 192$) were primarily female ($N_{female} = 81\%$), underclassmen ($N_{freshman} = 32\%$, $N_{sophomore} = 25.5\%$, $N_{junior} = 26\%$, $N_{senior} = 16\%$, $N_{unknown} = 0.5\%$), and $M_{age} = 19$ years, 11 months. We randomly assigned participants to (1) a *hands-on* condition, during which participants could freely pet and stroke cats and dogs in a small group setting for 10 min; (2) an *observation* condition, which constituted observing participants in the hands-on condition while waiting in line for one's turn for 10 min; and (3) a *control* condition, during which participants viewed still images of the same animals while refraining from social interaction for 10 min. We hypothesized that students with clinical levels of depression would exhibit higher levels of negative emotion and lower levels of positive emotion in response to the observation condition compared with non-depressed students.

Participants displayed a condition identifier so research assistants could direct them to check-in stations specific to each condition. Participants in the *hands-on* condition ($N = 73$) were directed to a curtained off program entry area where staff timed students' entry and exit into the program area, which was located in the same large gym featuring similar number and types of animals, handlers, and small group interactions (Fig. 5.3). Participants in the *observation* condition ($N = 62$) were directed to a curtained-off area adjacent to the hands-on condition (Fig. 5.4). Staff managed and timed entry and exit into a roped-off section of the program area where participants could see students, animals, and handlers engage in human

---

[4] Note we are referring not to behavior by study participants but instead describe behavior of non-study participants who were present at the program site and experienced "normal" program conditions including waiting in line for a considerable amount of time.

Fig. 5.3 Illustration of the hands-on condition of Pendry et al. (2018). (**a**) Two smiling students interact with a handler from the human society and pet a large tan dog and a small gray dog. (**b**) A woman reaches through a multilevel condo door to pet an orange short-haired cat eating kibble

Fig. 5.4 Illustration of the observation condition of Pendry et al. (2018). Students in the observation condition observe a handler holding a small dog in front of a curtained off waiting area

animal interaction while awaiting their turn a few feet away from interactions. They were told to refrain from physically interacting with the animals. Participants assigned to the *control* condition ($N = 57$) viewed a 10-min slide presentation containing pictures of the program animals in a separate room during which they indicted their animal preferences while refraining from social interaction (Fig. 5.5). Repeating procedures of study 1, participants in each condition completed the same 2-min, 25-item scale rating the extent to which they experienced various positive and negative emotions *at that moment* on a four-point Likert scale ranging from 0 (*not at all*) through 3 (*very much*) immediately preceding entry and following exit from the program area.

Fig. 5.5 Illustration of the control condition of Pendry et al. (2018). Students assigned to the control condition viewed a slide presentation with still images of program animals during a 10-min time frame in a separate room

5.3.2.1 Effects of Embedded Program Experiences: Waiting in Line

Multivariate regression models showed a significant interaction between clinical depression and treatment condition on *feeling irritable* (Fig. 5.6), suggesting that students experiencing clinical levels of depression felt significantly more irritable than those without clinically relevant symptoms after 10 min of waiting in line (Pendry et al., 2019b). Interestingly, students with clinical levels of depressive symptomology did not differ from students without depressive symptomology when assigned to the hands-on group echoing findings from study 1, suggesting that depressed students experience similar positive effects of 10 min of interacting with cats and dogs as those without clinical depression. Results also showed a significant interaction between clinical depression and treatment group on *feeling depressed* and *feeling anxious*, suggesting that students experiencing depression felt significantly more depressed and anxious than those without clinical symptoms after 10 min of observing other students pet animals. Again, students with clinical depression did not differ from non-depressed students when assigned to the hands-on group, suggesting that 10 min of hands-on petting and interaction with dogs and cats significantly and substantially decreased feelings of depression and anxiety, compared to other comparison conditions. We did not find interaction effects between clinical depression and treatment group on *feeling content*, although students with clinical levels of depression were significantly less content than those not depressed, a main effect that remained significant across conditions. This result is not unexpected, given that anhedonia, or decreased ability to feel pleasure, is a common symptom of depression.

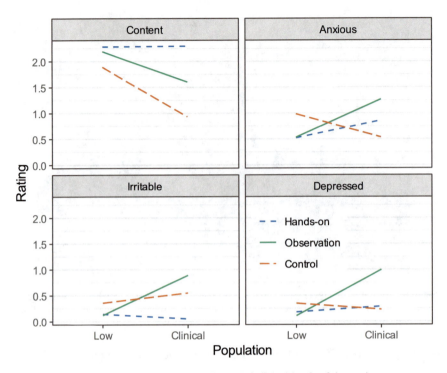

Fig. 5.6 Interactions between treatment condition and clinical levels of depression on mean ratings of momentary emotion for feeling content, anxious, irritable, and depressed. Models predicting *Feeling Irritable*, *Feeling Anxious*, and *Feeling Depressed* were redrawn from Pendry et al. (2019b)

In sum, results revealed that clinically depressed students felt significantly more anxious and irritable after standing in line waiting for their turn. These findings are relevant in that they capture previously unidentified undesirable "program effects" that are specific to at-risk populations. Implementors may want to consider providing more immediate access to clinically depressed students to avoid creating pronounced negative emotion states leading up to participation in response to long waiting periods, which are quite common during these types of programs given their popularity. Given the challenges of identifying at-risk students, it may not be feasible to provide priority entry, and as such, an indicated approach toward prevention may be more appropriate and effective. To meet *indicated* prevention goals, researchers and practitioners could require registration for these types of events so participants' potential vulnerabilities and existing symptoms are ascertained beforehand. Overall, considering previously unexplored effects during program design may enhance uptake of the intervention by individuals most in need who otherwise may experience the period leading up to participation as too stressful. In addition, positive treatment effects may be enhanced by entering the program space with lower negative arousal, although these effects have not yet been evaluated.

5.3.3 Study 3: Effects of PYSA on Momentary Cortisol Levels

Given evidence of causal effects of AVP participation on momentary emotion, and moderation effects by clinical depression for embedded AVP-related experiences – waiting in line – we next turned to examining whether similar effects could be observed in students' salivary cortisol levels, markers of activity of the hypothalamic pituitary adrenal (HPA) Axis. This research aim was also inspired by results from prior research demonstrating effects of an 11-week equine-assisted learning program on adolescent diurnal cortisol levels through repeated downregulation of HPA-axis activity (Pendry et al., 2014). We thus hypothesized that human-canine interaction would affect activation and cessation activity of the HPA axis cascade. We proposed that physical contact associated with hands-on interaction – petting – would increase oxytocin production (Beetz et al., 2012), resulting in subsequent downregulation of cortisol and attenuation of the cascade through attenuation of corticotropin-releasing hormone and adrenocorticotropic hormone production. The rationale informing these research questions and hypotheses are fully conceptualized in the HAI-HPA transactional model we developed (Fig. 5.7) (Pendry & Vandagriff, 2020).

To capture physiological program effects of what is considered the most popular feature of college-based AVPs – freely touching and petting the animal and engaging in physical contact with the animal – the study team thus set out to compare changes in students' salivary cortisol levels in response to 10 min of hands-on petting of cats and dogs, with three comparison conditions. Based on study 2, we again incorporated a comparison condition testing effects of an overlooked component of

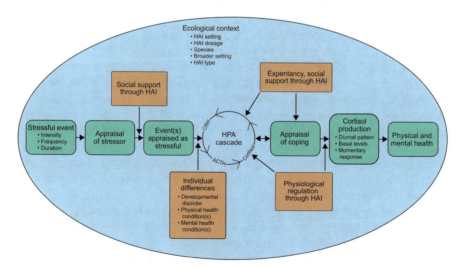

Fig. 5.7 HAI-HPA transactional model. *HAI* human-animal interaction, *HPA* hypothalamic-pituitary-adrenal, *CRH* corticotrophin releasing hormone, *ACTH* adrenocorticotropic hormone. (Redrawn from Pendry & Vandagriff, 2020)

AVPs – the experience of waiting in line in visible and audible range of program animals. Effects of hands-on PYSA participation effects were also compared with effects of 10 min of visual exposure to still images of the same program animals and 10 min of waiting for program access without visual or physical exposure to program animals.

We hypothesized that students in the hands-on condition would experience most significant stress relief as evidenced by most pronounced reductions in salivary cortisol levels compared with those in other conditions. The effects of participation in the comparison conditions were examined to isolate the distinct contributions of the *physical* components of human animal interaction on salivary cortisol levels, separate from contributions incurred by the presence of animals, socializing with peers, aspects of visual exposure, or neither. Since these features are inherently embedded in AVPs, our goal was to understand whether the physical component – touch – during AVPs is a necessary feature of successful stress reduction or whether socialization with peers or viewing animals may be sufficient.

5.3.3.1 Salivary Sampling Procedures

During the recruitment meeting, which took place a few days before the study and program were set to take place, participants were instructed, consented, screened, and randomly assigned ($N_{hands-on} = 73$; $N_{slideshow} = 62$; $N_{observation} = 57$ $N_{waitlist} = 57$) using the same procedures as described above. Participants ($N = 249$) were primarily female ($N_{female} = 208$), underclassmen ($N_{freshman} = 33\%$, $N_{sophomore} = 24\%$, $N_{junior} = 27\%$, $N_{senior} = 15\%$, $N_{unknown} = 0.5\%$), and $M_{age} = 19$ years, 11 months. Participants also observed a salivary sampling demonstration, practiced taking their own sample, and received thorough verbal and written instruction to take a wake-up sample immediately upon waking on program day (e.g., before moving, ingesting anything, or brushing their teeth, etc.) using the passive drool method and thereafter marking their exact sampling time. To accommodate collection of this baseline sample, participants were given a take-home sampling kit containing written saliva sampling instructions, a cryovial, straw, labels containing their study ID number, permanent pen, and a short survey to report physical activity, food and beverage intake, medication use, and exposure to animal interaction. Participants stored their completed sample in the refrigerator until study check-in. Later that day, research staff collected participants' take-home sampling kits and inquired about their sampling compliance. They also reminded participants not to eat or drink until pre- and post-intervention sampling was completed.

To accurately calculate treatment effects on salivary cortisol, we employed a salivary sampling paradigm assessing both indices of diurnal and momentary cortisol activity. The samples collected by participants immediately upon waking were used to calculate basal levels and diurnal slopes toward pre-intervention cortisol levels. Given that cortisol is reflected in saliva 25 min following the onset of an event, participants subsequently provided a sample 15 min after the conclusion of their 10-min condition to reflect cortisol levels at the start of their condition (Gunnar & Adam, 2012; Kirschbaum & Hellhammer, 1994), as well as a sample 25 min after completion to reflect cortisol levels at the end of their 10-min condition, resulting in three samples. Sampling took place in a designated sampling area where participants also completed a checklist to document behavior that day pertinent to sampling (e.g., use of medication, etc.). Saliva samples were stored on ice, recorded, freezer stored, and assayed.

5.3.3.2 Lower Cortisol Levels Through Hands-on Touch

Results indicated that participants in the hands-on condition had significantly lower cortisol levels after the intervention than those in comparison conditions (Fig. 5.8). Post-intervention cortisol levels of participants in the control condition were higher by 27% and higher by 30% for those participants waiting in line. Using multivariate regression analyses, these results considered each participants' sampling time – wakeup time – basal levels and the slope of diurnal pattern for that individual to account for potential dysregulation of HPA-axis activity known to affect momentary reactivity, and total hours awake until the start of the intervention. Given the significance of main effect models, we did not explore moderation effects of students' risk factors beyond those anticipated through clinical levels of depression, which were found not to be significant.

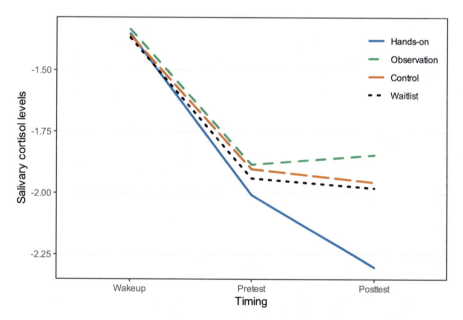

Fig. 5.8 Trajectories of predicted salivary cortisol by condition. Predicted post-test cortisol values are natural log-transformed (µg/dL) and were modeled while controlling sampling time as a covariate. (Redrawn from Pendry & Vandagriff, 2019)

5.3.4 Summary of Results and Considerations for Future Research

Results of these three studies demonstrated that 10 min of petting of cats and dogs increased students' positive emotion and decreased negative emotion (i.e., feeling anxiety, irritability) (Pendry et al., 2018). The findings also showed that students' levels of clinical depression moderated effects of waiting in line, a common yet understudied aspect of many AVPs, on moment-to-moment emotion, suggesting targeted programs for at-risk students may be beneficial (Pendry et al., 2019b). Most exciting were the first *causal* findings showing that hands-on petting led to significantly lower cortisol levels even when students' diurnal cortisol patterns and cortisol levels immediately preceding the program were considered (Pendry & Vandagriff, 2019).

Given these results, it is reasonable to hypothesize that increased frequency, intensity, or duration of HAI exposure would yield even greater positive effects. However, we felt it was important not only to consider whether upscaling of AAAs featuring hands-on exposure would constitute effective stress-prevention but also whether increased exposure would be more effective *over and above* the impact of evidenced-based stress prevention approaches already offered on campus. It is important from an animal well-being perspective to consider whether the infusion of AAIs on university campuses is needed and/or if AAIs are at least as effective as treatment as usual approaches and for which outcomes. Last, given concerns about consequences of increased AAI implementation for animal safety and well-being, we were interested in understanding how much HAI was minimally needed to "outperform" traditional stress-prevention programs already offered at the university. Last, but not the least, since findings revealed a role of risk factors as moderating treatment effects, questions remained about which risk factors to consider and how to assess them to target participants most in need without stigmatizing them.

These questions directly informed the aims of our next research project, the PETPALS study, a 3-year randomized controlled trial to examine the causal effects of incorporating various levels of HAI into a 4-week long, evidence-based, university-based stress prevention program on four cohorts of university students' stress-related outcomes (e.g., mood, mental health problems), executive function, behavioral engagement in academics (e.g., study and learning skills, motivation), and basal, diurnal, and momentary activity of stress-system functioning (e.g., salivary cortisol, alpha-amylase). We designed this program in collaboration with WSU students' health services, our local Pet Partner affiliate, mindfulness specialists, health educators, and research staff. Throughout the implementation of the 4-week program, we collected over 8000 samples of relevant stress hormones such as salivary cortisol and alpha-amylase and conducted assessments in multiple stress-relevant domains at multiple timepoints spanning 12 weeks of the semester. Recognizing that HAI is inherently dynamic and bidirectional, we also video-recorded 38,000 min of interactions and developed coding procedures capturing dyadic and triadic interaction behavior of therapy dogs, their handlers, and student participants, resulting in a reliable ethogram. In the following section, we share our methods and a small selection of relevant results.

5.4 The PETPALS Program

The PETPALS program and curriculum was designed through collaboration between our research team and health educators of WSU's department of health and wellness. We created three program versions with various combinations (0–100%, 50–50% or 100–0%) of HAI and existing evidenced-based academic stress management presentations across four weekly, hour-long sessions. Stress management approaches used a didactive approach including content presentations and guided activities based on workshops regularly conducted at WSU. Activities focused on enhancing self-regulation (e.g., progressive muscle relaxation, deep breathing, meditation, replacing negative self-talk with positive self-talk) and metacognitive skill training (e.g., time management, test taking skills, study planning, prioritization exercises). Each weekly session featured a different theme related to promoting academic success including academic stress management (Week 1), motivation and goal setting (Week 2), benefits of sleep (Week 3), and test anxiety (Week 4). For a complete week-by-week description of program content and activities by theme and condition, see Pendry et al. (2021).

The three program versions constituted three conditions to which participants were randomly assigned. The first condition, referred to as *Academic Stress Management* (ASM), did not include any exposure to animal-assisted activities ($N = 97$; 0% HAI) but focused the entire hour on ASM content and activities.[5] The second program condition – the *Enhanced Human-Animal Interaction program* (HAI-E) – was created by adapting the ASM program to accommodate incorporation of HAI. In this program, students engaged in animal-assisted activities (e.g., petting, relaxation activities, meditation, discussion with peers) for half of the time ($N = 109$; 50% HAI) while engaging equally with didactive content presentations and activities on stress management along the four weekly themes. The third program was the *Human-Animal Interaction Only program* (HAI-O), which featured semi-structured HAI session with therapy dogs, but no didactive presentation or activities effectively providing student with hour long HAI sessions with registered therapy teams.

---

[5] To avoid condition-specific attrition, all participants, including those in the ASM condition, were told they would experience an opportunity to interact with animals, but that the *timing and amount* of HAI would vary, as such blinding them to the expected ratio of HAI. HAI was provided to the ASM group *after* completion of all outcome assessments.

5.4.1 PET Partner Teams and Setting

Participants in the HAI conditions interacted with registered therapy handler-dog teams who were evaluated members of a regional community partner of the Pet Partners national organization. Teams consisted of 16 male dogs and 11 female dogs, M_{age} = 4 years, with a majority of Labrador and golden retrievers and large mixed breeds. On average, dogs had been registered with Pet Partners for 1.95 years and participated in 3.6 h of therapy work per week. Handlers were mostly female (N = 24; M_{age} = 49.67), with 2.34 years of experience. All program sessions occurred in the same large, carpeted conference room, with comfortable seating arranged to form segmented sitting areas. Handler-dog teams were assigned individual sitting areas with blankets, toys, and water bowl, where they engaged with small groups of four to five students.[6] Program sessions were highly structured, and content was presented using memorized scripts. The same facilitators presented across conditions to prevent internal validity threats due to variation in facilitation quality.

5.4.2 Recruitment and Procedures

Given our research aims, we used a screening tool to recruit a sample of university students with an overrepresentation of at-risk students (e.g., students who endorsed having experienced a mental health condition, academic deficiency, learning disability, and/or suicidal ideation[7]) to examine the effects of varying levels HAI with registered therapy dogs and stress management content presentations by risk status. Undergraduate students attended informational meetings promoted through announcements, university publications, and student services. Participants (N = 309; N_{risk} = 121) were primarily female (n = 80.5%), freshmen ($N_{freshman}$ = 52%, $N_{sophomore}$ = 22%, N_{junior} = 14%, N_{senior} = 1%, $N_{unknown}$ = 1%), and M_{age} = 19 years, 2 months. Study participation spanned 12 weeks including baseline assessments (Week 1), 4 consecutive weeks of program sessions (Week 2–5), post-test assessments (Week 6), and follow-up assessments (Week 12).[8] The primary cognitive outcome of interest was executive function assessed with the Behavior Rating Inventory of Executive Function for Adults (BRIEF-A; Roth et al., 2005). This inventory refers to three types of highly, interrelated brain functions including working memory, mental flexibility, and inhibitory control, which underlie a wide variety of cognitive skills relevant to stress exposure, coping, the development of mental health

---

[6] All proceedings were video-recorded via seven different simultaneous camera angles.

[7] These specific risk factors were chosen as they are commonly used by university administrators and agencies to identify students for referral to campus counseling, psychological services, and the university's access center.

[8] Participants received $60 USD for completing assessments, which were prorated at $20 USD per assessment.

issues, and academic success. In addition, we assessed students' learning and study strategies (LASSI; Weinstein & Palmer, 2002) as they capture aspects of engagement in educationally purposeful activities, skills and competencies, persistence, acquisition of desired knowledge, and attainment of educational outcomes, which are synthesized as defining student success. We hypothesized that interventions focused on stress management through relaxation, increased coping, cognitive training, and/or human-animal interaction could contribute to improvements in both these domains, which are relevant to academic success.

5.4.3 Effects of HAI and Risk Status on Cognitive and Behavioral Outcomes

Results immediately following the intervention showed significant improvements in global executive function and metacognition, achieved particularly for at-risk students who exclusively interacted with therapy dogs, compared with at-risk students who received evidence-based academic stress management content or a combination of both (Pendry et al., 2021). Moreover, the effects remained 6 weeks after program completion (Fig. 5.9). The observed improvements in executive function demonstrate that the amount of exposure to HAI embedded in an AAI is of paramount importance *depending* on the target population and their risk status. Although this study did not test mediating mechanisms potentially underlying the effects of HAI on executive function, the robust effects of exclusive HAI exposure on executive function in at-risk students could be attributed to the fact that the interventions

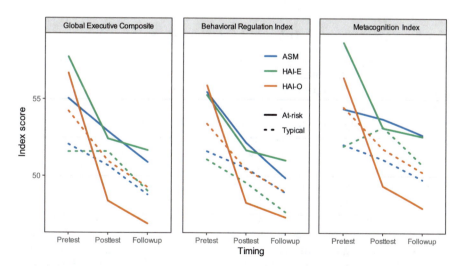

Fig. 5.9 Predicted means of executive function problems by condition and risk status at pre-test, post-test, and follow-up. (Redrawn from Pendry et al., 2021)

featuring HAI distracted these students from potential negative stressful thoughts, whereas attention to stress management strategies may have increased those thoughts. Also, a relaxed, calm state may have supported the development of other adaptive behaviors enhancing executive function skills such as problem-solving, decision-making, and creative and critical thinking, which we know were significantly lower at baseline in at-risk students.

Our findings also illustrated that the impact of risk status varied by outcome and risk factors considered. While students with a history of academic failure, suicidal ideation, mental health problems, and learning issues reported improved levels of executive function and metacognition in the condition featuring 100% HAI, when modeling AAI effects on behavioral domains, we noted significant moderation through *current* mental health symptoms (e.g., depression, anxiety, perceived stress, worry) (Pendry et al., 2020b). Students experiencing higher-than-average levels of these mental health symptoms reported higher levels of study skills and learning strategies related to *will* (i.e., anxiety, attitude, motivation) and *self-regulation* (i.e., concentration, self-testing, study aids, time management) when receiving of HAI either in combination (HAI-E) or exclusively (HAI-O). These findings suggest that designing targeted interventions that incorporate HAI for at-risk students appears to be most beneficial for that population. On the other hand, we showed that typical and at-risk students both experienced lower diurnal cortisol levels in response to experiencing a combination of HAI and evidenced-based content presentations (Pendry et al., 2020b). In sum, given the complexity of underlying pathways likely to inform program effects, further research is needed to replicate these findings and continue to examine these phenomena in real-life settings to avoid making broad generalization about preferred implementation approaches.

5.4.4 *Summary of Results and Considerations for Practice*

While this chapter has mainly focused on summarizing findings presented at the Nebraska Symposium on Motivation, the PETPALS Study has generated several other interesting findings relevant to academic success of university students through AAIs. While this chapter is focused on the two outcomes directly relevant to academic achievement, our data also highlights important components relevant to program implementation and animal well-being. First, while university administrators may design curricula, implement, and evaluate a variety of AAIs, it is essential to evaluate the extent to which students engage in the program and derive benefits from these programs. This can be captured by a construct referred to as responsiveness (e.g., enjoyment, usefulness, recommendation, and behavioral change) (Berkel et al., 2011). Using quantitative and qualitative self-reported survey data, results suggest that combining evidence-based content presentations with HAI was associated with higher levels of student enjoyment, perceived usefulness, and likelihood of recommending the program to others compared to receiving either the content or HAI alone (Pendry et al., 2019a). As such, it raises questions whether it is wise to rely too exclusively on findings from our efficacy trials when applying research findings to curriculum design. Although at-risk students indeed derive most benefits on executive function when traditional stress management information and activities are excluded, if students are less responsive to HAI-only programs, we are better off balancing approaches that are effective with those that encourage uptake, engagement, and completion.

Next, we felt it was important to examine the quality of interactional processes, which may underlie the previously described program effects by examining the dyadic and triadic behaviors between participants, animals, and their handlers. We used video-recorded data captured during each program session, which was open coded, and used to develop an ethogram which was coded for reliability. Based on 150 video-recorded "meet and greet sessions" conducted during 10 min of weekly program sessions, we examined *how* handlers interacted with their dogs before and during student interactions, an important but often overlooked component of program success. We found that handlers displayed consistent combinations of control and warmth behaviors toward their animals in ways reminiscent of models of parenting behavior (Kuzara et al., 2019). Coding behavior of handlers along these two dimensions revealed four distinct handler interaction styles referred to as hands-off, permissive, authoritative, and authoritarian (Kuzara et al., 2019). We noticed that most handlers displayed a hands-off interaction style prior or following student interactions, although each of the four styles were observed. Findings also suggested that handlers adapted their interaction style with their dogs once in the presence of students, commonly shifting from authoritarian to authoritative interactions or permissive to hands-off interactions in the presence of students. Based on these same data, we also analyzed the "meet and greet" behavior of students and occurrences of dog's stress behaviors during the "meet and greet" periods. We also found that while the quality of student greeting and petting behavior influenced dogs' pro-social, postural state and oral behavior, animals did not exhibit overt stress behavior (Pendry et al., 2020c), although we did observe displays of increased arousal.

5.5 Conclusion and Recommendations

We started this chapter by contextualizing the increased demand for campus-based AAIs by highlighting high prevalence of university students' mental health issues associated with academic failure and demographic risk factors. In response to students' overwhelming need for mental health services and limited capacity of universities to provide these services, AAIs can play an important *complementary* role in providing students' much-needed stress relief. An important take-home message is that AVPs and AAIs are especially suitable for implementation on university campuses *if* they are evidence-based and *tailored* to the needs of the intended population. The most relevant recommendation we make is to align the aims and selection approach of prevention programs with the availability and capacity of registered animal handler teams and the nature and prevalence of risk in the student population on campus. For example, offering a universal AVP program that serves the general student population can effectively provide adequate stress relief to many, as indicated by lowering cortisol levels of participants after merely 10 min of hands-on interaction. Similarly, 4 weeks of programming activities with emphasis on HAI and stress management skills and knowledge reduced average cortisol levels over time, which is a promising sign of the ability of AAIs to potentially strengthen adaptive functioning. That said, we must be cautious not to overinterpret the role of the animal during HAI, since interventions that incorporate animals also embed social interactions with peers and handlers. Also, without considering that these effects are moderated by students' risk status, we may inadvertently overlook the possibility that effective stress relief was obtained by low-risk students, who represent the majority in a general sample. It is thus possible that universal AVPs may inadvertently ignore the unique needs of students with significant risk factors or existing mental health problems. Those students may be better served by selected and indicated approaches that provide regular opportunities for more intense or prolonged hands-on interactions. Also, the current evidence suggests that at-risk students' behavioral outcomes appear to improve in response to hands-on interaction combined with didactic content presentations and activities focused on academic stress management. Instead, cognitive outcomes such as executive function appear to be enhanced in at-risk populations through providing hands-on interaction exclusively. In sum, while the most suitable approach is likely informed by the nature of the intervention, the intended population, resources available, and outcomes targeted, each presented approach has utility for implementation and evaluation aims, which can be clarified by further research conducted in real-life settings.

References

Adam, E. K. (2012). Emotion—Cortisol transactions occur over multiple time scales in development: Implications for research on emotion and the development of emotional disorders. *Monographs of the Society for Research in Child Development, 77*(2), 17–27.

American College Health Association. (2019). *American College Health Association-National College Health Assessment III: Undergraduate student reference group executive summary spring 2019*. American College Health Association. https://www.acha.org/documents/ncha/NCHA-III_Fall_2019_Reference_Group_Executive_Summary.pdf

American College Health Association. (2020). *American College Health Association-National College Health Assessment III: Undergraduate student reference group executive summary fall 2019*. American College Health Association. https://www.acha.org/documents/ncha/NCHA-III_Fall_2019_Reference_Group_Executive_Summary.pdf

American College Health Association. (2021). *American College Health Association-National College Health Assessment III: Undergraduate student reference group executive summary spring 2021*. American College Health Association. https://www.acha.org/documents/ncha/NCHA-III_SPRING-2021_UNDERGRADUATE_REFERENCE_GROUP_EXECUTIVE_SUMMARY_updated.pdf

Beck, A. T., & Steer, R. A. (1993). *Beck anxiety inventory: Manual* (2nd ed.). The Psychological Corporation.

Beck, A. T., Steer, R. A., & Brown, G. K. (1996). *Manual for the Beck depression inventory* (2nd ed.). The Psychological Corporation.

Beetz, A., Uvnäs-Moberg, K., Kotschal, K., Kikusui, T., Hart, L. A., & Olbrich, E. (2012). Psychosocial and psychophysiological effects of human-animal interactions: The possible role of oxytocin. *Frontiers in Psychology, 3*, 1–15. https://doi.org/10.3389/fpsyg.2012.00234

Berkel, C., Mauricio, A. M., Schoenfelder, E., & Sandler, I. N. (2011). Putting the pieces together: An integrated model of program implementation. *Prevention Science: The Official Journal of the Society for Prevention Research, 12*(1), 23–33. https://doi.org/10.1007/s11121-010-0186-1

Binfet, J.-T., Passmore, H.-A., Cebry, A., Struik, K., & McKay, C. (2017). Reducing university students' stress through a drop-in canine-therapy program. *Journal of Mental Health*, 1–8. https://doi.org/10.1080/09638237.2017.1417551

Carr, A. M., & Pendry, P. (2022, July). Assessing attendance frequency and duration in a drop-in canine visitation program among first-semester university students separated from their family pets. In *Anthrozoology in translation: Communicating research from and to multiple audiences*. International Society for Anthrozoology (ISAZ), Virtual.

Cohen, S., Kamarck, T., & Mermelstein, R. (1983). A global measure of perceived stress. *Journal of Health and Social Behavior, 24*(4), 385–396. https://doi.org/10.2307/2136404

Csikszentmihalyi, M., & Larson, R. (1987). Validity and reliability of the experience-sampling method. In M. Csikszentmihalyi (Ed.), *Flow and the foundations of positive psychology: The collected works of Mihaly Csikszentmihalyi* (pp. 35–54). Springer. https://doi.org/10.1007/978-94-017-9088-8_3

Eisenberg, D., & Lipson, S. K. (2019). *The healthy minds study 2018–2019 data report*. https://healthymindsnetwork.org/wp-content/uploads/2019/04/HMS_national.pdf

Greer, T. M., & Cavalhieri, K. E. (2019). The role of coping strategies in understanding the effects of institutional racism on mental health outcomes for African American men. *Journal of Black Psychology, 45*(5), 405–433. https://doi.org/10.1177/0095798419868105

Gunnar, M. R., & Adam, E. K. (2012). The hypothalamic–pituitary–adrenocortical system and emotion: Current wisdom and future directions. *Monographs of the Society for Research in Child Development, 77*(2), 109–119.

Haggerty, J. M., & Mueller, M. K. (2017). Animal-assisted stress reduction programs in higher education. *Innovative Higher Education, 42*(5–6), 379–389. https://doi.org/10.1007/s10755-017-9392-0

Henriques, G. (2018, November 18). The college student mental health crisis (update). *Psychology Today*. https://www.psychologytoday.com/us/blog/theory-knowledge/201811/the-college-student-mental-health-crisis-update

IAHAIO. (2014). *The IAHAIO definitions for animal assisted intervention and guidelines for wellness of animals involved*. International Association of Human-Animal Interaction Organizations. https://iahaio.org/best-practice/white-paper-on-animal-assisted-interventions/

Kirschbaum, C., & Hellhammer, D. H. (1994). Salivary cortisol in psychoneuroendocrine research: Recent developments and applications. *Psychoneuroendocrinology, 19*(4), 313–333. https://doi.org/10.1016/0306-4530(94)90013-2

Kuzara, S., Pendry, P., & Gee, N. R. (2019). Exploring the handler-dog connection within a university-based animal-assisted activity. *Animals, 9*(7), 402. https://doi.org/10.3390/ani9070402

Lipson, S. K., Lattie, E. G., & Eisenberg, D. (2019). Increased rates of mental health service utilization by U.S. college students: 10-year population-level trends (2007–2017). *Psychiatric Services, 70*(1), 60–63. https://doi.org/10.1176/appi.ps.201800332

Meyer, T. J., Miller, M. L., Metzger, R. L., & Borkovec, T. D. (1990). Development and validation of the Penn State Worry Questionnaire. *Behaviour Research and Therapy, 28*, 487–495. https://doi.org/10.1016/0005-7967(90)90135-6

Morrison, N. (2021, May 13). The therapeutic tool that works better than a stress management program—A dog. *Forbes*. https://www.forbes.com/sites/nickmorrison/2021/05/13/the-therapeutic-tool-that-works-better-than-a-stress-management-programa-dog/

Pendry, P., & Vandagriff, J. L. (2019). Animal visitation program (AVP) reduces cortisol levels of university students: A randomized controlled trial. *AERA Open, 5*(2), 1–12. https://doi.org/10.1177/2332858419852592

Pendry, P., & Vandagriff, J. L. (2020). Salivary studies of the social neuroscience of human-animal interaction. In D. A. Granger & M. K. Taylor (Eds.), *Salivary bioscience: Foundations of interdisciplinary saliva research and applications*. Springer. https://doi.org/10.1007/978-3-030-35784-9

Pendry, P., Smith, A. N., & Roeter, S. M. (2014). Randomized trial examines effects of equine facilitated learning on adolescents' basal cortisol levels. *Human-Animal Interaction Bulletin, 2*(1), 80–95.

Pendry, P., Carr, A. M., Roeter, S. M., & Vandagriff, J. L. (2018). Experimental trial demonstrates effects of animal-assisted stress prevention program on college students' positive and negative emotion. *Human-Animal Interaction Bulletin, 6*(1), 81–97.

Pendry, P., Kuzara, S., & Gee, N. R. (2019a). Evaluation of undergraduate students' responsiveness to a 4-week university-based animal-assisted stress prevention program. *International Journal of Environmental Research and Public Health, 16*(18), 3331. https://doi.org/10.3390/ijerph16183331

Pendry, P., Vandagriff, J. L., & Carr, A. M. (2019b). Clinical depression moderates effects of animal-assisted stress prevention program on college students' emotion. *Journal of Public Mental Health, 18*(2), 94–101. https://doi.org/10.1108/JPMH-10-2018-0069

Pendry, P., Carr, A. M., Gee, N. R., & Vandagriff, J. L. (2020a). Randomized trial examining effects of animal assisted intervention and stress related symptoms on college students' learning and study skills. *International Journal of Environmental Research and Public Health, 17*(6), 1909. https://doi.org/10.3390/ijerph17061909

Pendry, P., Carr, A. M., Vandagriff, J. L., & Gee, N. R. (2020b). *Randomized controlled trial examining effects of varying levels of human canine interaction on college students' diurnal cortisol*. 29th International Society for Anthrozoology annual conference. One Health One Welfare, Virtual.

Pendry, P., Kuzara, S., & Gee, N. R. (2020c). Characteristics of student–dog interaction during a meet-and-greet activity in a university-based animal visitation program. *Anthrozoös, 33*(1), 53–69. https://doi.org/10.1080/08927936.2020.1694311

Pendry, P., Carr, A. M., Vandagriff, J. L., & Gee, N. R. (2021). Incorporating human–animal interaction into academic stress management programs: Effects on typical and at-risk college students' executive function. *AERA Open, 7*(1), 1–18. https://doi.org/10.1177/23328584211011612

Rodriguez, K. E., Herzog, H., & Gee, N. R. (2021). Variability in human-animal interaction research. *Frontiers in Veterinary Science, 7*, 619600. https://doi.org/10.3389/fvets.2020.619600

Roth, R. M., Isquith, P. K., & Gioia, G. A. (2005). *Behavior rating inventory of executive function – Adult version (BRIEF-A)*. Psychological Assessment Resources.

Son, C., Hegde, S., Smith, A., Wang, X., & Sasangohar, F. (2020). Effects of COVID-19 on college students' mental health in the United States: Interview survey study. *Journal of Medical Internet Research, 22*(9), e21279. https://doi.org/10.2196/21279

The Healthy Minds Network & American College Health Association. (n.d.). *The impact of covid-19 on college student well-being*. Retrieved December 18, 2021, from https://www.acha.org/documents/ncha/Healthy_Minds_NCHA_COVID_Survey_Report_FINAL.pdf

Weinstein, B. J., & Palmer, D. R. (2002). *Learning and study strategies inventory (LASSI): Users manual* (2nd ed.). H & H Publishing.

Chapter 6
Canine-Assisted Interventions: Insights from the B.A.R.K. Program and Future Research Directions

John-Tyler Binfet

Under the overarching umbrella of animal-assisted interventions (AAIs), we find the subfield of canine-assisted interventions (CAIs), and although the broader field of human-animal interactions (HAIs) hardly needs another acronym, a review of recent anthrozoological, psychological, educational, and healthcare publications attests to both the popularity and utility of providing opportunities for varied clients to interact with therapy dogs. CAIs are typically situated within the context of research and are introduced to effect change – to elicit improvements in one or more outcome variables (e.g., self-reports or biomarker indicators of stress, homesickness, social connectedness, etc.). CAIs provide an opportunity for study participants to interact with therapy dogs and for researchers to assess the pre-to-post-test effects of such visits (for illustrations of this research, see Barker et al., 2016; Binfet et al., 2018; Pendry et al., 2018) or to explore participants' perceptions of having spent time with therapy dogs (Lalonde et al., 2020). When informal opportunities (i.e., programs that do not have a corresponding research component) are provided for students to interact with therapy dogs within in the campus context, these interactions are typically referred to as animal visitation programs (AVPs). Both CAIs and AVPs are considered a complimentary or adjunct source of support and not intended to serve as a primary mental health intervention (Nepps et al., 2014) and are often introduced to enhance well-being via client stress reduction. It is posited that reducing stress, especially for post-secondary students struggling with the pressures of college life, helps prevent stress reaching heightened or debilitating levels and perhaps renders these students more open to seeking and making use of the formal mental health resources available to them (Benjet, 2020).

J.-T. Binfet (✉)
Okanagan School of Education, University of British Columbia, Kelowna, BC, Canada
e-mail: johntyler.binfet@ubc.ca

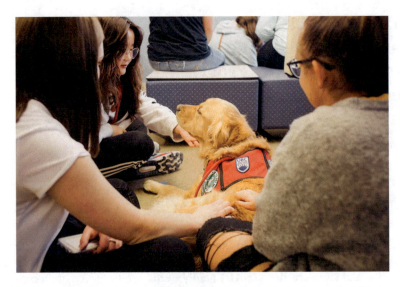

Fig. 6.1 Group of students sitting on the floor petting golden retriever therapy dog. (Photo credit: F. L. L. Green Photography; used with permission)

AVPs in particular are especially popular within the post-secondary context (e.g., Barker et al., 2016; Kivlen et al., 2022), and oftentimes the demand by students to spend time with therapy dogs surpasses programs' capacities to provide enough dog-handler teams to meet the needs of students seeking to reduce their stress. As the founder and director of the University of British Columbia's "Building Academic Retention through K9s" (B.A.R.K.) program, I have learned valuable lessons over the past 10 years, and the aim of this chapter is to share insights related to overseeing CAI programming and research. Established in 2012, B.A.R.K.'s mission is to provide social and emotional support to students seeking to reduce their stress through interactions with therapy dogs (Fig. 6.1). Shared in this chapter are insights learned from overseeing B.A.R.K. and factors undergirding CAI research, including the screening and selection of dog-handler teams, methodological and design considerations, and areas within CAIs requiring additional empirical investigation.

6.1 The Benefits of CAIs

A review of the extant CAI research reveals that providing opportunities to interact with therapy dogs are often introduced to elicit a host of well-being benefits, including both an increase in positive dimensions of well-being and a decrease in negative dimensions of ill-being. On the positive side, we see researchers reporting increases in participants' self-reports of self-esteem (Muckle & Lasikiewicz, 2017) and of both connectedness to campus and satisfaction with life (Binfet & Passmore, 2016). With respect to decreasing negative dimensions of ill-being, we see decreases in participants' self-reports of stress (Barker et al., 2016; Binfet et al., 2018), homesickness (Binfet & Passmore, 2016), and anxiety (Grajfoner et al., 2017). In addition to measuring pre-to-post-test changes in various self-report measures, researchers have also used biomarker indicators to demonstrate the impact spending time with therapy dogs has on participants' stress (Pendry & Vandagriff, 2019; Chap. 5).

6.2 Screening and Selection of Dog-Handler Teams

These claims by researchers that interacting with therapy dogs bolsters well-being are made in light of ample variability in the design of interventions and methodologies used in CAI research. In fact, one merely has to do a cursory review of recent randomized controlled trials to see that there is little consensus around the duration of interventions (i.e., the "dose" in minutes or exposure to dogs varies considerably from one study to the next; see Binfet, 2017, for a comparison of the doses used across varied randomized controlled trials). Although addressing this variability is beyond the scope of this chapter, commentary on the variability in the experience and competency of dog-handler teams warrants discussion, as dog-handler teams are at the center of the CAIs implemented in both programming and research initiatives. The social or interpersonal skills of the dog-handler team hold potential to differentially impact participant engagement and the extent to which interventions are able to effect change (Silas et al., 2019; Rousseau et al., 2020). In the B.A.R.K. program, where we typically have 60 dog-handler teams working in both on-campus and community protocols, we have learned the importance of careful screening of dogs and the formative training of handlers. No research could be identified that has yet examined how dog-handler team skill level or competency impacts participant engagement and participant well-being; however, it stands to reason that the more skilled the team, the more potent or effective the interaction. Not all dog-handler teams are equally proficient, and honing interaction skills is one of the reasons the B.A.R.K. program has teams participant in a semester-long internship that sees program staff provide constructive feedback to teams to guide and strengthen their ability to support students (see Binfet & Kjellstrand Hartwig, 2020, for a comprehensive overview of skill training for dog-handler teams).

6.2.1 Therapy Dogs

It goes without saying that not all dogs are suited for participation in CAIs or AVPs. In B.A.R.K., we undertake a detailed screening and assessment process that helps us determine which dog-handler teams are "well suited," "not yet ready," or "not suited" for our programs (see Hartwig & Binfet, 2019, and Binfet & Kjellstrand Hartwig, 2020). Therapy dogs who are well suited to working in CAIs are dogs who have a strong and keen desire to interact with the public and meet new people. Therapy dogs should be genuinely excited to meet new people. As our sessions see several dogs working concurrently within the same space, dogs must have little interest in socializing with other dogs and remain human- and not dog-focused. We are careful not to position our program as a dog socialization experience that see dogs routinely meet and greet other dogs. Dogs working on behalf of B.A.R.K. programs will invariably cross paths with other dogs, riding the same elevators, for example; however, our intention is not to purposefully have dogs interact. Although we assess inter-dog compatibility, our dogs generally have little interaction with other dog-handler teams as teams are spaced throughout the lab when programs are running. A therapy dog who is seeking to interact with a dog at an adjacent station will convey disinterest to a visiting client. It is how the dog invites engagement with the client that fosters interactions (e.g., a wagging tail or a roll upside down for a belly rub as a greeting).

Therapy dogs must be adaptable both to settling in new environments and to meeting new and varied clients. We use "anchor mats" (i.e., cushioned mats that provide a comfortable place to lay during sessions) that serve as a familiar object in new environments and help establish the working space for dog-handler teams (Fig. 6.2). As part of our assessment practices, we determine dogs' reactions to clients who vary by age, race, and clothing. B.A.R.K. dogs, for example, may support children in learning social and emotional skills (Harris & Binfet, 2022), police constables seeking to reduce their stress in a busy urban precinct (Binfet et al., 2020), or college students seeking support within a virtual context (Binfet et al., 2022b). In this regard, therapy dogs differ from other helping dogs (e.g., guide dogs, PTSD dogs for veterans, etc.) who support but one client.

Fig. 6.2 Students petting therapy dog laying on anchor mat. (Photo credit: F. L. L. Green Photography; used with permission)

6.2.2 Handlers

Often overshadowed by their therapy dog, the handler plays a key and central role within CAIs. Their primary tasks are to safeguard their dog's welfare, create and oversee optimal working conditions for their dog, and facilitate interactions between their dog and the visiting client(s) (Silas et al., 2019). Safeguarding dog welfare involves verifying there are no noxious substances in the working space (note: this is also verified by program personnel prior to introducing dogs), and when on campus, this might mean ensuring there are no staples or food remnants on the floor. Handlers are required to create optimal working conditions for their dogs during the duration of their working session, and this involves (1) ensuring the dog is groomed and toileted prior to entering buildings, always under the direct their supervision, (2) not working longer than the recommended guidelines (i.e., sessions not surpassing 90 min), and (3) not participating in multiple sessions on any given day. In tandem with B.A.R.K. program personnel, handlers are responsible for monitoring their dog for signs of distress (e.g., whale eye, ears back, panting, pawing, etc.; Beerda et al., 1998; Glenk, 2017; Hatch, 2007; Rooney et al., 2007). Therapy dogs in B.A.R.K. who demonstrate any signs of distress, including the inability to settle, are first taken outside for a toilet break. Dogs then return to the session for a second try, and if the dog is unable to settle (i.e., does not want to participate in the session) or shows any signs of distress, a discussion with the handler and B.A.R.K. program personnel occurs, at which point a decision is made to terminate the visit and send the team home. Over 10 years of programming, we have noticed that therapy dogs, on average, take 5–7 min to settle in their new environment, and we recognize that even experienced therapy dogs can have off days when their interest in working is low or they are especially agitated. A constant monitoring of dogs by handlers and program personnel helps ensure that dogs are not subjected to undo stress and that they are not coerced into working, as this runs counter to their best interest and well-being. We recognize as well that dogs who are reluctant to participate in sessions are less likely to effectively engage participants as part of the human-animal interaction experience.

In addition to monitoring and safeguarding the well-being of their dog, handlers play a key role in welcoming and facilitating interactions between their dog and visiting clients. Handlers in the B.A.R.K. program attend an orientation session as well as a series of practice or mock sessions that see them practice how to position their dog and how to welcome and interact with visitors. Handlers can draw from a bank of questions or open-ended prompts to engage student visitors to sessions (e.g., "How has your adjustment to campus been?", "Which class is your favorite?", etc.). Handlers may also share information about their dog as a way of establishing rapport with students. It merits noting that handlers are also responsible for educating clients around optimal interactions, and in B.A.R.K., we might see a handler teach a student with little or no prior experience interacting with dogs how to seek consent from a dog upon approaching a station. This would involve modeling for the student how to approach and subsequently pet their dog.

Once a visitor to a station has obtained consent and is interacting with a therapy dog, handlers volunteering in on-campus programs may encounter students in distress, as students begin to relax, engage in conversation, and share their experiences on campus. College students are known to experience heightened stress (Durand-Bush et al., 2015; Othman et al., 2019), and CAI programs are frequently implemented as a stress-reduction initiative. Though the motivation of students who attend on-campus CAIs has yet to be investigated (to my knowledge), in addition to students who simply have an affinity for dogs, the students who make use of CAIs may be overwhelmed by their coursework or homesickness or struggling with their mental well-being and assume/hope that interacting with dog-handler teams can elicit positive outcomes for them. As we say in B.A.R.K., "There's not much we can guarantee, but we know you'll leave a session feeling better than when you arrived!" In B.A.R.K., handlers are trained to share information regarding the well-being resources on campus that students might use, and we have a protocol in place for handlers to notify program personnel of students who are especially distressed and require additional support. An example of this latter point is a student who discloses to a handler an indication of self-harm.

As outlined above, handlers bear a great deal of responsibility in overseeing the environment within which their dog is working, preparing dogs prior to their beginning their work in a session, monitoring and overseeing the welfare of their dog over the course of a session, and educating visitors and facilitating interactions between their therapy dog and visiting clients. In short, handlers are skilled volunteers whose knowledge, training, and behavior influence and impact the effectiveness of the CAI.

One last characteristic of handlers working in CAIs merits mention. Handlers, certainly those who work in researcher-intensive programs such as UBC's B.A.R.K. program, must embrace an openness and willingness to regularly participate in research. Handlers in the B.A.R.K. program routinely are asked to participate in various studies that see them completing demographic information and surveys to capture their own views of themselves or their dogs (see Rousseau et al., 2020, for an illustration) or provide observations about the participants with whom they have interacted (e.g., see Harris & Binfet, 2022). Despite the important role that handlers play in facilitating CAIs, there is a remarkable dearth of research examining handlers' views or elucidating just what they do as part of facilitating interactions between their therapy dog and visiting participants. We have made inroads in understanding the motivation of handlers to volunteer in CAIs by asking 60 handlers a series of open-ended prompts to capture their views around why they volunteer, what they perceive to be the impact of the CAI on participants, and their perceptions of the impact of CAIs on their dogs (see Rousseau et al., 2020). Our findings revealed that handlers are driven to volunteer, as doing so affords ample social benefits both for themselves and for their dogs. Handlers also reported that helping students was a key factor behind their motivation to volunteer. Last, handlers described themselves as having strong awareness of their dog throughout sessions and when asked to describe their dog after a session, handlers reported that their dogs were relaxed, calm, and respectful. As handlers play a key role within CAIs, researching how their role impacts the efficacy of the CAI is an area requiring additional empirical attention.

6.3 Innovations in CAIs

> There is very little study of just how humans and animals interact and which interactions with or features of the animal are therapeutic. (Fournier, 2019, vii)

The quotation above by HAI researcher Angela Fournier from Bemidji State University succinctly captures what is needed in the field of AAI. Not unique to AAIs or CAIs, but we often see programs or interventions implemented without the requisite scientific evidence to undergird and justify the introduction of such a program. That is, we can see animals introduced to new clients in a new setting as part of a newly created program that is not (yet) supported by empirical evidence. Good practice is driven by strong science, and in applied AAI programming, the creation of programs and their introduction to clients should be supported by or grounded in prior empirical evidence.

What follows next are two recent examples of innovative research we have conducted in the B.A.R.K. lab as we strive to push the subfield of CAIs forward and demystify and elucidate the mechanisms within CAIs that optimally contribute to well-being outcomes in participants.

6.3.1 The Importance of Touch

Study after study attests to the benefits of college students spending time with therapy dogs to reduce their stress and enhance their overall well-being (Crossman et al., 2015; Dell et al., 2015; Pendry & Vandagriff, 2019; Robino et al., 2021; Sokal & Martin, 2021; Ward-Griffin et al., 2018); however, there is scant published research identifying or illuminating just what aspects of interacting with a therapy dog contribute to enhanced well-being. In an effort to better understand how different interactions differentially impact well-being outcome measures, we designed a study to assess the effects of touch and no-touch conditions (Binfet et al., 2022a). We randomly assigned 284 undergraduate students to treatment or control conditions with some students assigned to a direct touch condition that saw them pet and scratch a therapy dog, an indirect condition in which students were in proximity to a therapy dog but not allowed to touch the dog, and a control condition in which only a handler and no dog was present. Pre- and post-test measures of both positive (e.g., flourishing, positive affect, happiness, and social connectedness) and negative (e.g., stress, homesickness, and loneliness) dimensions of well-being and ill-being were administered. The dose intervention for this study was 20 min, and the findings revealed that although participants across all conditions reported significant

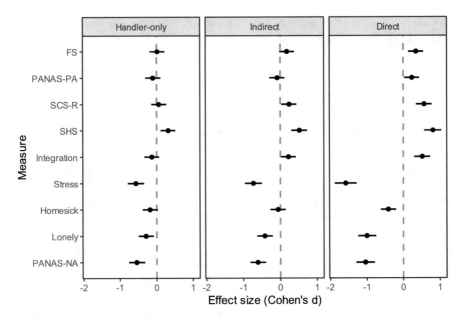

Fig. 6.3 Cohen's d_z for paired t-tests comparing pre-intervention with post-intervention positive and negative measures of well-being across the three treatment conditions. Error bars represent 95% confidence intervals for d_z. (Redrawn from Binfet et al., 2022a)

gains to their well-being, only the participants in the direct touch condition experienced improvements on all the measures administered (Fig. 6.3).

The findings from this study inform our understanding of the nature of the interaction between therapy dogs and visiting students that optimally contributes to students leaving sessions with their mental well-being bolstered. As argued earlier in this chapter, college students who make regular use of CAIs offered on their campus can reduce their stress and help prevent their stress accumulating over time to the point where their mental health and well-being, as well as their peer relationships and their academic standing, are compromised. Also argued earlier, when students reduce their stress, it is thought that they are in a better position to make decisions about their well-being and may be rendered open to seeking additional formal mental health support where warranted.

The findings from this study examining the role of touch within a CAI, in some small way, also help respond to the challenge identified by Fournier (2019) raised at the outset of this subsection. Mixed results have been reported by other researchers examining the role of touch in eliciting well-being benefits. We see studies by Beetz and colleagues (2011) and Pendry and Vandagriff (2019) reporting support for the role of touch in AAIs, whereas recent research by Mueller et al. (2021) found that touch was not an essential aspect of a CAI implemented with adolescents to reduce their anxiety or autonomic reactivity and improve their cognitive performance. The role of touch is an area within CAIs and within HAI more broadly, requiring additional empirical attention and exploration.

6.3.2 Can Therapy Dogs Support Students in a Virtual Context?

Long before COVID-19 forced researchers to explore alternatives to the in-person delivery of well-being interventions, therapists and counselors had long offered remote or virtual options to access mental health support (Kählke et al., 2019; Nguyen-Feng et al., 2017; Ruppel & McKinley, 2015). As COVID-19 prevented the offering of in-person CAIs on our campus, the B.A.R.K. program sought to provide virtual support for students seeking opportunities to reduce their stress. Coined "virtual canine comfort modules," we began by training dog-handler teams to work within a virtual context, both in synchronous (i.e., via Zoom) and asynchronous (i.e., via pre-recorded YouTube videos) formats. This involved creating a script for handlers to follow that would allow them to engage viewers and encourage viewers to reflect upon their stress and how they are feeling. Therapy dogs too required support as they adapted to sitting on raised platforms to optimize their being seen on camera and were familiarized with the technology required to film sessions. Accustomed to greeting and interacting with new and ever-changing visitors to their station, therapy dogs were required to remain in place and respond to the cues or prompts of handlers (e.g., being pet as a handler describes their dog's preferred way to be scratched).

Our initial study consisted of a randomized controlled trial that saw 467 undergraduate students randomly assigned to one of four conditions: (1) Pre-recorded video with a dog and handler; (2) pre-recorded video with only a handler and no dog; (3) live session with a dog and handler; and (4) a live session with only a handler and no dog (Binfet et al., 2022b). Across all conditions, handlers followed the same script, and the same handlers (and dogs where required) participated in both the asynchronous (i.e., pre-recorded) and synchronous (i.e., live Zoom virtual meeting) sessions. The dose duration was 5 min, and participants completed both pre- and post-test self-report measures of connectedness to campus, loneliness, stress, positive and negative affect, anxiety, and a scale asking them to describe their current emotional state.

The findings of this preliminary study revealed that participants, regardless of their assigned condition, reported improvements to their well-being (i.e., increases in their perceived positive emotional state and connectedness to campus) and decreases in ill-being (i.e., decreases in anxiety, stress, loneliness, and negative affect) (Table 6.1). Digging further, we found that participants in the synchronous conditions (i.e., those who participated in live Zoom session either with or without a dog present) had stronger feelings of campus connectedness than did participants in the asynchronous conditions (i.e., participants who watched pre-recorded YouTube videos with or without a dog present). A key finding arising from this study was that undergraduate students in conditions in which a therapy dog was present, when compared to their peers who participated in conditions where no therapy was present, reported greater reductions in self-reports of stress.

Table 6.1 Paired sample *t*-tests of pre-to-post change effects of pre-recorded or live sessions with and without dogs

Variable	t	df	p	d_z
Pre-recorded session, no dog				
Anxiety	9.87	116	<0.001	−0.91
Campus connectedness	9.03	116	<0.001	0.83
Loneliness	5.90	116	<0.001	−0.55
PANAS-NA	9.06	116	<0.001	−0.84
PANAS-PA	0.63	116	0.264	0.06
Stress	10.86	116	<0.001	−1.00
Pre-recorded session, dog				
Anxiety	8.91	118	<0.001	−0.82
Campus connectedness	8.69	117	<0.001	0.80
Loneliness	4.96	117	<0.001	−0.46
PANAS-NA	8.86	116	<0.001	−0.82
PANAS-PA	0.32	116	0.624	−0.03
Stress	10.27	118	<0.001	−0.94
Live virtual session, no dog				
Anxiety	7.42	114	<0.001	−0.69
Campus connectedness	9.83	114	<0.001	0.92
Loneliness	6.71	114	<0.001	−0.63
PANAS-NA	8.45	114	<0.001	−0.79
PANAS-PA	0.71	114	0.762	−0.07
Stress	7.43	114	<0.001	−0.69
Live virtual session, dog				
Anxiety	9.53	115	<0.001	−0.89
Campus connectedness	10.27	115	<0.001	0.95
Loneliness	5.39	115	<0.001	−0.5
PANAS-NA	7.89	115	<0.001	−0.73
PANAS-PA	1.79	115	0.038	0.17
Stress	11.33	115	<0.001	−1.05

Note: *PANAS* positive and negative affect schedule, *NA* negative affect, *PA* positive affect. Data from Binfet et al. (2022b)

The findings of this initial study inform our understanding of the role that virtual CAIs might play in supporting the well-being of college students in virtual or remote contexts. Virtual canine comfort modules afford CAIs to reach students who are hard to reach – those who are in geographically remote locations where access to mental health support is limited or students who are reluctant to seek formal in-person support. Additional research examining the duration of virtual CAIs that are effective in reducing student stress, how best to foster virtual engagement with viewers, and the effects of virtual CAIs on other dimensions of well-being is required.

6.4 Future Directions

As the subfield of CAIs looks ahead, there are areas that require additional empirical attention. These include but are not limited to investigating the effects of dose/duration and the experience of dog-handler teams and incorporating measures of implementation fidelity into study designs.

6.4.1 The Importance of Dose

The dose in minutes of interventions comprising CAIs has varied considerably, and researchers have experimented with providing a wide time range in the opportunities provided to participants to interact with therapy dogs. As part of a randomized controlled trial assessing the effects of a 20-min CAI on college students' perceptions of their stress, homesickness, and affinity to campus, I provided a cursory review of the dose of interventions employed by researchers (see Table 1 in Binfet, 2017). Considerable variability was reported across studies with Crossman and Kazdin (2015) using a 7–10-min intervention and Schuck et al. (2015) using more extensive sessions comprised of 120–150 min.

In an effort to understand how much time interacting with therapy dogs is required to elicit well-being benefits in participants, studies out of the B.A.R.K. lab have examined the effects of 45-min sessions delivered once weekly over 8 weeks to more abbreviated interventions comprised of but 5 min as described below in the description of our new "virtual canine comfort modules." In innovative research conducted over the course of three semesters, we allowed participants to "determine their own dose" – that is, we did not impose a time limit and, rather, allowed the participants to determine the amount of time they felt was sufficient to reduce their stress (see Binfet et al., 2018). In a sample of 1960 participants, it was found that participants stayed, on average, for 35 min, with female participants staying 2 min longer, on average, than their male counterparts.

Related to the dose of the CAI used in studies is the duration of sessions (i.e., the number of CAI sessions offered over time), and here too we see researchers employ varied strategies that range from offering a single session to multiple sessions spanning several weeks. Additional research is required to establish the effects of both dose and duration as researchers continue to investigate just how interacting with therapy dogs impacts various well-being outcomes in participants.

6.4.2 The Importance of Dog-Handler Team Experience

In our research out of the B.A.R.K. lab, as part of our routine reporting of demographic descriptions of our handlers and dogs, we report their mean years of experience volunteering in CAIs. We do this as we recognize that seasoned or experienced dog-handler teams likely engage participants differently than do dog-handler teams just accepted into the program and who have little prior experience. In fact, we typically only recruit veteran dog-handler teams for our randomized controlled trials, recognizing that experienced teams are needed to monitor dog welfare, facilitate participant-animal interactions, and engage participants. Though no empirical research examining the effects of dog-handler team experience on outcome variables has yet been published (to my knowledge), this is an area of research within CAIs requiring exploration.

6.4.3 The Importance of Measuring and Reporting Implementation Fidelity

> It has been demonstrated that the fidelity with which an intervention is implemented affects how well it succeeds. (Carroll et al., 2007, p. 1)

Implementation fidelity refers to the degree to which a program (or intervention) is introduced as it was designed and intended. Within the context of CAI research, there are a number of aspects or dimensions of the intervention that warrant monitoring. Raised above is the notion that there exists ample variability in the dose used by researchers, and the amount of time afforded to participants to interact with animals must be reported when researchers report their procedures as it reveals how much "exposure" to the dog-handler team the client received. Above and beyond reporting the dose, researchers are obliged to provide insights into other factors that impact or potentially impact the efficacy of CAIs on outcome variables. As a starting point, the ratio of participants to each dog-handler team must be reported. In research out of the B.A.R.K. lab, we typically design studies for a ratio of one dog-handler team per three to five participants. Reporting this is important as too many participants at each dog-handler station reduces the likelihood that participants can meaningfully interact with the dog and engage with the handler. This, in turn, impacts the potency of the intervention. Too many participants at each dog-handler station dilutes the effect of the intervention and can compromise canine welfare.

Implementation fidelity is also impacted by the behavior of the handler. Researchers should report whether the handler followed a script (for an example, see Binfet et al., 2022b) or drew from a bank of questions (see Binfet et al., 2022a) or whether handlers were free to discuss and engage with clients as they pleased. Reporting on the behavior of handlers is especially important when interventions are done that see several dog-handler teams work concomitantly within the same space. Researchers want assurances and to establish that participants, regardless, of which dog-handler team they visited, experienced more or less the same handler behavior.

In study designs where the intervention is comprised of multiple sessions (e.g., 20-min dosage delivered once per week over 4 weeks), researchers are required to report the attendance by participants. Did all participants attend all sessions?

Delving further, implementation fidelity might see researchers reporting on the extent to which participants were engaged within and across sessions. Did the participant pet the dog? Did the participant respond to the prompts shared by the handler? The level of engagement (e.g., low, medium, high) by participants is an indication of their participation in the intervention. Researchers might ask participants to self-report their engagement using a Likert-type scale as part of the post-test measures. In our research examining the effects of virtual canine comfort on participants' well-being described above, we examined whether low, medium, or high engagement differentially impacted outcome variables (see Binfet et al., 2022b). We asked participants to reflect upon their engagement in a virtual CAI and respond to the prompt "How engaged were you over the course of the session?" and to indicate on a five-point Likert-type response ranging from "not at all" to "very." In our study assessing the effects of virtual canine comfort modules, across all participants in all sessions, we found the following:

> After controlling for pre-intervention scores, higher engagement was associated with better outcomes for anxiety ($b = -0.04$, $d = -0.26$, $p = 0.006$), campus connectedness ($b = 0.17$, $d = 0.44$, $p < 0.001$), negative affect ($b = -0.04$, $d = -0.28$, $p = 0.003$), positive affect ($b = 0.15$, $d = 0.56$, $p < 0.001$), and stress ($b = -0.14$, $d = -0.35$, $p < 0.001$); as well as a non-significant change in loneliness ($b = -0.05$, $d = -0.12$, $p = 0.19$). (Binfet et al., 2022b, p. 13)

6.4.4 The Importance of CAIs for Diverse Clients and Contexts

After 10 years of CAI programming at the University of British Columbia, we have noticed that, when implemented, CAIs appeal predominantly to women – both with respect to the recruitment of handlers and in the student population drawn to attend sessions. As mentioned earlier, we report demographic information describing our handlers, and we typically have upward of 85% female handlers participating in both studies and routine on-campus and community-based programming. Coinciding with this, we consistently see more female students participate in studies (i.e., >70%) and attend the programs we offer. This gender distribution is not unique to B.A.R.K., and certainly other researchers have reported a similar gender distribution in alignment with our findings (e.g., Pendry and Vandagriff, in 2019, reported 83% of female participants, and Ward-Griffin et al., 2018, reported 78% of female participants in their study). Questions arise from this inspiring additional empirical inquiry: *Why are handlers predominantly women and drawn to engage in CAI volunteerism? How might more male and non-binary/gender fluid handlers be encouraged to participate in CAIs? Correspondingly, might there be barriers perceived by male and non-binary participants that impede or restrict their participation? How might CAIs be designed and delivered through an equity lens so that diverse handler and client populations can be engaged?*

Related to the above discussion around gender, so too do we see a need for CAIs to be reimagined so that they respond more transparently and earnestly to issues of equity, diversity, inclusion, and decolonization. The opportunity to interact with animals more broadly in AAIs and more specifically as part of CAIs should be made available to diverse clients within and across diverse contexts. Driving CAI research we find talented and creative researchers from varied backgrounds and with expertise in varied methodologies who will undoubtedly begin reconfiguring how CAIs may be designed and implemented to meet the needs of varied clients across varied settings.

6.5 Conclusion

The aim of this chapter was to provide insights from overseeing on-campus CAIs over the span of 10 years and to offer commentary on areas within CAIs requiring additional empirical attention. With the surge in popularity of CAIs, especially within the context of post-secondary education, researchers must focus their attention on understanding the mechanisms within interactions between therapy dogs and participants that optimally elicit or foster well-being outcomes. The screening and selection of dog-handler teams is important as they are the driving force undergirding CAIs. Also argued here was the need for greater transparency around describing interventions, especially around the experience of dog-handler teams serving at the core of the intervention itself. Researchers are also called to report indicators of implementation fidelity – to provide evidence that the intervention was delivered as intended and that participants were engaged in sessions comprising the intervention. Last, a virtual iteration of a CAI was described that afforded participants from varied locations to interact remotely with dog-handler teams. Collectively, the insights throughout this chapter are offered to strengthen the empirical evidence being sought, claiming that interacting with therapy dogs provides benefits to humans, and to nudge the field forward as it explores CAIs in varied contexts, in support of varied clients, and through varied platforms of delivery.

References

Barker, S. B., Barker, R. T., McCain, N. L., & Schubert, C. M. (2016). A randomized cross-over exploratory study of the effect of visiting therapy dogs on college student stress before final exams. *Anthrozoös, 29*, 35–46. https://doi.org/10.1080/08927936.2015.1069988

Beetz, A., Kotrschal, K., Turner, D. C., Hediger, K., Uvnäs-Moberg, K., & Julius, H. (2011). The effect of a real dog, toy dog and friendly person on insecurely attached children during a stressful task: An exploratory study. *Anthrozoös, 24*(4), 349–368. https://doi.org/10.2752/175303711X13159027359746

Beerda, B., Schilder, M. B., van Hooff, J. A. R. A. M., de Vries, H. W., & Mol, J. A. (1998). Behavioural, saliva cortisol and heart rate responses to different types of stimuli in dogs. *Applied Animal Behaviour Science, 58*, 365–381.

Benjet, C. (2020). Stress management interventions for college students in the context of the Covid-19 pandemic. *Clinical Psychology: Science and Practice*, e12353. https://doi.org/10.1111/cpsp.12353

Binfet, J. T. (2017). The effects of group-administered canine therapy on first-year university students' well-being: A randomized controlled trial. *Anthrozoös, 30*(3), 397–414. https://doi.org/10.1080/08927936.2017.1335097

Binfet, J. T., & Kjellstrand Hartwig, E. (2020). *Canine-assisted interventions: A comprehensive guide to credentialing therapy dog teams.* Routledge. https://doi.org/10.4324/9780429436055

Binfet, J. T., & Passmore, H. A. (2016). Hounds and homesickness: The effects of an animal-assisted therapeutic intervention for first-year university students. *Anthrozoös, 29*(3), 441–545. https://doi.org/10.1080/08927936.2016.1181364

Binfet, J. T., Draper, Z. A., & Green, F. L. L. (2020). Stress reduction in law enforcement officers and staff through a canine-assisted intervention. *Human–Animal Interaction Bulletin, 8*(2), 34–52. https://doi.org/10.1079/hai.2020.0011

Binfet, J. T., Passmore, H. A., Cebry, A., Struik, K., & McKay, C. (2018). Reducing university students' stress through a drop-in canine-therapy program. *Journal of Mental Health, 3*, 197–204. https://doi.org/10.1080/09638237.2017.1417551

Binfet, J. T., Green, F. L. L., & Draper, Z. A. (2022a). The importance of client-canine contact in canine-assisted interventions: A randomized controlled trial. *Anthrozoös, 35*(1), 1–22. https://doi.org/10.1080/08927936.2021.1944558

Binfet, J. T., Tardif-Williams, C., Draper, Z. A., Green, F. L. L., Singal, A., Rousseau, C. X., & Roma, R. (2022b). Virtual canine comfort: A randomized controlled trial of the effects of a canine-assisted intervention supporting undergraduate wellbeing. *Anthrozoös.* https://doi.org/10.1080/08927936.2022.2062866

Carroll, C., Patterson, M., Wood, S., Booth, A., Rick, J., & Balain, S. (2007). A conceptual framework for implementation fidelity. *Implementation Science, 2*(40). https://doi.org/10.1186/1748-5908-2-40

Crossman, M. K., & Kazdin, A. E. (2015). Animal visitation programs in colleges and universities: An efficient model for reducing student stress. In A. H. Fine (Ed.), *Handbook on animal-assisted therapy: Foundations and guidelines for animalassisted interventions* (pp. 333–337). Elsevier.

Crossman, M. K., Kazdin, A. E., & Knudson, K. (2015). Brief unstructured interaction with a dog reduces distress. *Anthrozoös, 28*(4), 649–659. https://doi.org/10.1080/08927936.2015

Dell, C. A., Chalmers, D., Gillett, J., Rohr, B., Nickel, C., et al. (2015). PAWSing student stress: A pilot evaluation of the St. John Ambulance therapy dog program on three university campuses in Canada. *Canadian Journal of Counselling and Psychotherapy, 49*(4), 332–359. https://cjc-rcc.ucalgary.ca/article/views/61079

Durand-Bush, N., McNeill, K., Harding, M., & Dobransky, J. (2015). Investigating stress, psychological well-being, mental health functioning, and self-regulation among university undergraduate students: Is this population optimally functioning? *Canadian Journal of Counselling and Psychotherapy, 49*(3), 253–274. https://cjc-rcc.ucalgary.ca/article/view/61066

Fournier, A. (2019). *Animal-assisted intervention.* Palgrave Macmillan.

Glenk, L. M. (2017). Current perspectives on therapy dog welfare in animal-assisted interventions. *Animals, 7*(2), 7. https://doi.org/10.3390/ani7020007

Grajfoner, D., Harte, E., Potter, L., & McGuigan, N. (2017). The effect of dog assisted intervention on student well-being, mood and anxiety. *International Journal of Environmental Research and Public Health, 14*(5), 483. https://doi.org/10.3390/ijerph14050483

Harris, N. M., & Binfet, J. T. (2022). Exploring children's perceptions of an after-school canine-assisted social and emotional learning program: A case study. *Journal of Research in Childhood Education, 36*(1), 78–95. https://doi.org/10.1080/025685543.2020.1846643

Hartwig, E., & Binfet, J. T. (2019). What's important in canine-assisted intervention teams? An investigation of canine-assisted intervention program online screening tools. *Journal of Veterinary Behavior: Clinical Applications & Research, 29*, 53–60.

Hatch, A. (2007). The view from all fours: A look at an animal-assisted activity program from the animals' perspective. *Anthrozoös, 20*(1), 37–50. https://doi.org/10.2752/089279307780216632

Kählke, F., Berger, T., Schulz, A., Baumeister, H., Berking, M., Auerbach, R. P., Bruffaerts, R., Kessler, R. C., Cuijpers, P., & Ebert, D. D. (2019). Efficacy of an unguided internet-based self-help intervention for social anxiety disorder in university students: A randomized controlled trial. *International Journal of Methods in Psychiatric Research, 28*(2), e1766. https://doi.org/10.1002/mpr.1766

Kivlen, C., Winston, K., Mills, D., DiZazzo-Miller, R., Davenport, R., & Binfet, J. T. (2022). Steadying the stethoscope: A randomized controlled trial of a canine-assisted intervention on the well-being of health science graduate students. *American Journal of Occupational Therapy, 76*(6), 7606205120. https://doi.org/10.5014/ajot.2022.049508

Lalonde, R., Dell, C., & Claypool, T. (2020). PAWS your stress: The student experience of therapy dog programming. *Canadian Journal for New Scholars in Education, 11*(2), 78–90.

Muckle, J., & Lasikiewicz, N. (2017). An exploration of the benefits of animal-assisted activities in undergraduate students in Singapore. *Asian Journal of Social Psychology, 20*(2), 75–84. https://doi.org/10.1111/ajsp.12166

Mueller, M. K., Anderson, E. C., King, E. K., & Urry, H. L. (2021). Null effects of therapy dog interaction on adolescent anxiety during a laboratory-based social evaluative stressor. *Anxiety, Stress, & Coping*. https://doi.org/10.1080/10615806.2021.1892084

Nepps, P., Stewart, C. N., & Bruckno, S. R. (2014). Animal-assisted activity: Effects of a complementary intervention program on psychological and physiological variables. *Journal of Evidence-Based Complementary & Alternative Medicine, 19*(3), 211–215. https://doi.org/10.1177/2156587214533570

Nguyen-Feng, V. N., Greer, C. S., & Frazier, P. (2017). Using online interventions to deliver college student mental health resources: Evidence from randomized clinical trials. *Psychological Services, 14*(4), 481–489. https://doi.org/10.1037/ser0000154

Othman, N., Ahmad, F., El Morr, C., & Ritvo, P. (2019). Perceived impact of contextual determinants on depression, anxiety and stress: A survey with university students. *International Journal of Mental Health Systems, 13*(1), 17. https://doi.org/10.1186/s13033-019-0275-x

Pendry, P., & Vandagriff, J. L. (2019). Animal visitation program (AVP) reduces cortisol levels of university students: A randomized controlled trial. *AERA Open, 5*(2), 1–12. https://doi.org/10.1177/2332858419852592

Pendry, P., Carr, A. M., Roeter, S. M., & Vandagriff, J. L. (2018). Experimental trial demonstrates effects of animal-assisted stress prevention program on college students' positive and negative emotion. *Human-Animal Interaction Bulletin, 6*(1), 81–97.

Robino, A. E., Corrigan, V. K., Anderson, B., Werre, S., Farley, J. P., Marmagas, S. W., & Buechner-Maxwell, V. (2021). College student mental health in an animal-assisted intervention program: A preliminary study. *Journal of Creativity in Mental Health, 16*(1), 49–58. https://doi.org/10.1080/15401383.2020.1757002

Rooney, N. J., Gaines, S. A., & Bradshaw, J. W. S. (2007). Behavioural and glucocorticoid responses in dogs (Canis familiaris) to kenneling: Investigation mitigation of stress by prior habituation. *Physiology & Behavior, 92*(5), 847–854. https://doi.org/10.1016/j.physbeh.2007.06.011

Rousseau, C. X., Binfet, J. T., Green, F. L. L., Tardif-Williams, C., Draper, Z., & Maynard, A. (2020). Up the leash: An investigation of handler well-being and perceptions of volunteering in canine-assisted interventions. *Pet Behavior Science, 10*, 15–35. https://doi.org/10.2107/pbs.vi10.12598I

Ruppel, E., & McKinley, C. (2015). Social support and social anxiety in use and perceptions of online mental health resources: Exploring social compensation and enhancement. *Cyberpsychology, Behavior and Social Networking, 18*(8), 462–467. https://doi.org/10.1089/cyber.2014.0652

Schuck, S. E., Emmerson, N. A., Fine, A. H., & Lakes, K. D. (2015). Canine-assisted therapy for children with ADHD: Preliminary findings from the positive assertive cooperative kids study. *Journal of Attention Disorders, 19*, 125–137. https://doi.org/10.1177/1087054713502080

Silas, H. J., Binfet, J. T., & Ford, A. (2019). Therapeutic for all? Observational assessments of therapy canine stress in an on-campus stress reduction program. *Journal of Veterinary Behavior: Clinical Applications and Research, 32*, 6–13. https://doi.org/10.1016/j.jveb.2019.03.009

Sokal, L., & Martin, T. (2021). Post-secondary paw patrol: Effects of animal-assisted activities on students' stress, happiness, and well-being. *International Journal of Contemporary Education, 4*(1) Early online edition. http://ijce.redfame.com

Ward-Griffin, E., Klaiber, P., Collins, H. K., Owens, R. L., Coren, S., & Chen, F. S. (2018). Petting away pre-exam stress: The effect of therapy dog sessions on student well-being. *Stress and Health, 34*(3), 468–473. https://doi.org/10.1002/smi.2804

Correction to: Canine Cognition and the Human Bond

Jeffrey R. Stevens

Correction to:
J. R. Stevens (ed.), ***Canine Cognition and the Human Bond,***
Nebraska Symposium on Motivation 69,
https://doi.org/10.1007/978-3-031-29789-2

The book was inadvertently published without a properly created index for the book in the back matter. This has now been updated in the book.

The updated original version of the book can be found at
https://doi.org/10.1007/978-3-031-29789-2

© The Author(s), under exclusive license to Springer Nature
Switzerland AG 2023
J. R. Stevens (ed.), *Canine Cognition and the Human Bond*, Nebraska
Symposium on Motivation 69, https://doi.org/10.1007/978-3-031-29789-2_7

Index

A
Academic deficiency, 8, 110
Academic success, 109, 111, 112
Accidents, 66, 74
Activation patterns, 48, 50, 54, 55
Activity patterns, 64, 65
Adolescent, 105, 124
Adrenal glands, 17
Adrenocorticotropic hormone (ACTH), 14, 16, 105
Age, 7, 17, 41, 44, 46, 64, 66, 67, 70–76, 97, 120
Aggression, 13, 48, 65
Aggressive, 12–14, 27, 48, 65, 68
Aggressiveness, 64
Allomothers, 7, 74–77
Allonursing, 74, 76
Alloparental care, 74, 76
Alpacas, 93
Alpha-amylase, 108
Amygdala, 49–52
Anhedonia, 103
Animal-assisted activities (AAAs), 93, 108, 109
Animal-assisted interventions (AAIs), 7, 8, 45, 46, 91–114, 117
Animal-assisted therapy (AAT), 93
Animal visitation programs (AVPs), 7, 8, 93, 95, 101, 105, 106, 108, 113, 114, 117–119
Anterior cingulate cortex, 51
Anterior superior temporal gyrus, 52
Anterior temporal pole, 51
Anthrozoology, 7, 91, 117

Anxiety, 94, 95, 97, 99, 103, 108, 109, 112, 119, 124–126, 129
Approach, 2, 6, 11–28, 39, 49–52, 54, 55, 80–83, 92, 93, 95, 97, 98, 104, 108, 109, 112–114, 121
Arousal, 17, 48, 96, 97, 104, 113
Artificial selection, 11–13, 63
Assistance dogs, 4–6
At-risk populations, 92, 104, 114
Attachment bond, 13, 26, 46
Attachment style, 44–46
Attachment theory, 37
Attendance, 128
Attentional cues, 40
Attentional state, 41
Auditory, 7, 48
Austria, 17
Aversion, 51

B
Bark, 64
Barking, 12, 65
Beating, 66, 81
Begging, 78, 80
Behavioral change, 13, 93, 112
Behavioral regulation, 52
Behavior Rating Inventory of Executive Function for Adults (BRIEF-A), 110
Belyaev, D., 13
Biomarker, 117, 119
Births, 7, 65–70, 74, 86
Bite, 64
Body contact, 25, 27

Bottom-up processing, 50
Brain activity, 7, 47
Brainstem, 16
Breed differences, 41
Breed dogs, 63
Breeding, 5, 12–14, 63, 68, 70
"Building Academic Retention through K9s" (B.A.R.K.), 8, 117–130

C
Canine-assisted interventions (CAIs), 117–130
Canine Behavioral Assessment and Research Questionnaire (C-BARQ), 46, 54
Carbohydrates, 63, 78–80, 86
Caretaker, 13, 42, 44, 54
Catecholaminergic, 14
Cats, 93, 95, 101–103, 105, 108
Caudate, 47–50
Causal pathways, 91
Chase, 64
Chickens, 14, 15, 78–81, 83
Client, 117, 120–123, 128–130
Climatic factors, 66
Coats, 11, 64
Co-evolution, 2, 3
Cognition, 1–3, 6–8, 49, 50, 53
Cognitive abilities, 78
Cognitive mentalization, 50–53
Cognitive representations, 52
Cognitive training, 111
Commands, 22
Commensal scavenger hypothesis, 12
Communication, 1, 7, 11, 53
Communicative interactions, 38
Companion dogs, 4–5, 40, 44–46, 54
Comparative studies, 12, 15, 17, 28
Compatibility, 120
Compliance, 28, 106
Connectedness, 117, 118, 123, 125, 126, 129
Connectivity networks, 49
Conspecifics, 1, 15–17, 48, 52, 53
Contact, 3, 6, 15–17, 19, 20, 23–28, 40, 44, 45, 76, 80, 105
Contact-seeking behavior, 15, 27
Content, 50, 93, 96, 99–101, 103, 104, 109–112, 114
Cooperation, 1, 27
Coping, 110, 111
Corticotropin-releasing hormone (CRH), 16, 17, 105
Cortisol, 8, 22, 105–108, 112, 114
COVID-19, 5, 8, 94, 125
Creative, 112, 130

Critical thinking, 112
Cross-species adoption hypothesis, 12

D
Darwin, C., 1
Deaths, 7, 65–68, 81
Decision-making, 112
Decolonization, 130
Deep breathing, 109
Defecate, 64
Deferential behavior hypothesis, 27, 28
Dens, 7, 65, 67–71, 76, 86
Depression, 94, 95, 97, 99, 101–105, 107, 108, 112
Detection dogs, 5
Disabilities, 6, 37, 110
Disease, 5, 66
Distress, 24, 42, 44, 92, 93, 121, 122
Diversity, 6, 63, 130
Docility, 13
Dog face area (DFA), 49
Dog-handler teams, 8, 118–123, 125, 127–128, 130
Dog-human attachment, 37–55
Dog-human relationship, 37, 46, 49
Domestication, 1–3, 6, 11–19, 21, 23, 25–28, 38, 40, 63, 77, 81, 82
Domestication syndrome, 11, 28
Dopaminergic reward circuit, 15
Dorsal putamen, 52
Dorsolateral prefrontal cortex, 52
Dose, 119, 123, 125, 127, 128
Ducks, 14
Dyadic social interaction test, 23

E
Ears, 11, 121
Efficacy, 8, 92, 96, 113, 123, 128
Emotional bond, v, 12
Emotional mentalization, 50, 51, 53
Emotional reactivity hypothesis, 13–15, 22
Emotional regulation, 52
Emotional support, 6, 118
Emotional support dogs, 6
Emotional valence, 48, 50
Emotions, 3, 49, 50, 96, 98–102, 104, 105, 108
Endocrine, 13–14, 17, 28
Engagement, 22, 95, 108, 111, 113, 119, 120, 126, 129
Enjoyment, 112
Enzymes, 63
Equine-assisted learning program, 105

Index

Equity, 129, 130
Ethogram, 64, 65, 109, 113
Evolution, 1–2, 11–28, 38, 64
Executive function, 108, 110–112, 114
Expectation, 48–50, 52
Experience, 6–8, 16–21, 23, 25–28, 40–42, 44–46, 52, 81, 82, 85, 94–96, 98, 101–106, 109, 110, 112, 119–122, 124, 127–128, 130
Experience sampling, 98
Exploring, 2, 7, 20, 22, 26, 98
Exposure, 16, 17, 84, 91, 96, 99, 106, 108–111, 119, 128
Eye contact, 3, 40, 80
Eye-tracking, 49

F

Face processing, 48, 49
Faces, 3, 21, 27, 48–50, 53, 75, 81, 92
Facial stimuli, 48, 50
Facility dogs, 6
Familiarity, 40, 47, 48, 50
Fear, 11–16, 24, 27, 51
Feeding, 12, 81, 83
Fidelity, 8, 127–130
Fight-or-flight, 51
Fights, 66, 77
Finches, 14
Flourishing, 94, 123
Foraging efficiency, 79
Foster dogs, 46
Fox, 13–15
Free-ranging dogs, 4, 6, 7, 18–21, 26–28, 63–66, 68, 70, 78–86
Frontal cortex, 48
Functional magnetic resonance imaging (fMRI), 7, 38, 47–50, 52–55
Fusiform face area, 49
Fusiform gyrus, 52, 53

G

Garbage, 7, 64, 69, 79
Gaze, 45, 80
Gaze alteration behaviors, 41
Gender, 64, 94, 97, 129, 130
Gender non-conforming, 94
Gene expression, 13
Generalists, 65
Genes, 13, 63, 78
Genetic diversity, 63
Genetics, 2, 3, 11, 13, 15–17, 41, 63
Genetic variability, 41

Genome, 15
Gestures, 14, 38–41, 46, 80–82, 85
Glancing, 38
Global South, 4, 63
Glucocorticoids (GC), 14–17, 21–23, 25, 26
Glutaminergic, 14
Goats, 15, 93
Golden retrievers, 110, 118
Grooming, 68, 76
Guarding, 5, 12, 68
Guide dogs, 44, 120
Guinea pigs, 14

H

Handler, 8, 44, 95, 101, 102, 108, 110, 113, 114, 119, 121–123, 125, 127–129
Hand signals, 47, 48
Happiness, 123
Head and body shaking, 24
Healthy Minds Network and American College Health Association, 94
Heart rate, 44
Herding, 5
Hippocampus, 50–52
Homeostasis, 14
Homesickness, 117, 119, 122, 123, 127
Hormones, 3, 6, 13, 14, 16, 17, 105, 108
Horses, 15
Human-animal interactions (HAIs), 7, 17, 93, 96, 98, 105, 106, 108–114, 117, 121, 123, 124
Human-canine interaction, 105
Human development, 91
Human-directed gazing, 41
Human-dog interactions, 15
Humane society, 95
Human face area (HFA), 49
Human social cues, 80, 82
Hunter-gatherer societies, 12
Hunting, 5, 12, 77
Hyper-sociability hypothesis, 13, 16, 20, 24, 27
Hypothalamic pituitary adrenal (HPA) axis, 96, 105
Hypothalamo-pituitary-adrenal (HPA) axis, 6, 14–17
Hypothalamus, 16, 17, 49, 52
Hypothalamus-pituitary-adrenal axis, 51

I

IISER-Kolkata, 64
Ill-being, 118, 123, 125

Images, 49, 50, 52, 53, 68, 98, 99, 101, 103, 106
Inclusion, 22, 93, 130
India, 7, 63, 64, 78, 85
Indian Institute of Science, 64
Individual differences, 8, 53, 96, 97, 100, 101
Infant-mother relationship, 37
Inhibitory control, 110
Injury, 66
Insecure attachment styles, 44, 45
Insula, 49, 51
Interaction styles, 27, 113
Intervention, 7, 8, 45, 46, 91, 94, 98, 99, 101, 104, 107, 111, 112, 114, 117–130
Intonations, 48

K
Kennel, 40, 54

L
Labrador, 95, 110
Lactation, 67, 74
Lateral orbitofrontal cortex, 52
Learning and study strategies (LASSI), 111
Learning disability, 110
Leftovers, 12, 63, 78, 86
Lexical-intonation effects, 48
Lexington Attachment to Pets Scale, 46, 54
Life experience, 6, 16–21, 23, 25–27, 44, 46, 82
Life history strategies, 67
Lifetime reproductive fitness (LRS), 67
Lip licking, 22, 24
Livestock guarding, 5
Loneliness, 123, 125, 126

M
Malnutrition, 66
Marker, 17, 28, 40, 105
Maternal care, 7, 65, 67, 68, 70–72, 74, 75, 78
Mating season, 65
Meat, 12, 78–80
Medial orbitofrontal cortex, 52
Medial prefrontal cortex, 52
Meditation, 109
Mental flexibility, 110
Mental health, 5–8, 92, 94–95, 97, 108, 110, 112–114, 117, 124–126
Mental health disorders, 92
Mental state representation, 52
Metabolism, 13

Metacognition, 111, 112
Milk, 67, 72, 76
Mindfulness, 108
Minks, 14
Model system, 64
Morocco, 18, 19
Mortality, 7, 66, 75, 81
Mortality rate, 7, 66
Mother-offspring bonding, 15
Mothers, 3, 7, 13, 37, 52, 53, 67–77, 81
Motivation, 6, 15, 16, 19, 21, 26, 27, 41, 93, 108, 109, 112, 122
Multimodal approaches, 49, 50, 54, 55
Mutations, 63

N
Name calling, 40
Natural history, 7
Natural selection, 12
Negative emotions, 17, 98, 99, 101, 102, 104, 108
Neotenic, 77
Neural crest, 11
Neuropeptide, 3, 15
Neuroscience, 6, 7
Neurotransmitter systems, 14
Noradrenaline, 16
Nursing, 7, 67, 68, 72–73, 75–77

O
Object-choice task, 7, 38–41, 46
Olfactory stimuli, 48
Ontogenetic effects, 16, 26
Organizational-activational hypothesis, 13
Owners, 3, 5, 6, 16, 18, 19, 23–25, 27, 37, 40, 42–45, 49, 54, 68
Oxygenated blood, 47
Oxytocin (OT), 3, 15–17, 23–27, 52, 105

P
Pacing, 22
Packs, 17, 23, 24, 78
Pair-bonding, 15
Panting, 22, 121
Paraventricular nucleus (PVN), 16, 17
Parental care, 7, 66, 67, 71, 73, 74
Parental investment, 7, 67
Parental investment theory, 67
Parenting behavior, 113
Parent-offspring conflict, 7
Parent-offspring conflict theory, 72

Index

Pawing, 121
Persistence, 41, 111
Perspective-taking abilities, 53
Pet, 2–7, 12, 16, 18–21, 23, 25–28, 46, 54, 63, 64, 68, 71, 80, 83, 86, 95–110, 121, 123, 125, 129
Pet dogs, 5, 6, 16, 18–21, 23–28, 63, 64, 68, 80–82
Pet-keeping hypothesis, 12
Pet parents, 2, 5
Pet Partner, 108, 110
Pet Your Stress Away (PYSA) program, 92, 95–99, 101, 105–107
PETPALS program, 109–113
Petting, 7, 81, 83–85, 95, 99, 103, 105, 108, 109, 113, 118, 120
Philopatry, 75
Phylogenetic, 16
Pigs, 14, 15
Pile sleeping, 75, 76
Play, 1, 2, 7, 43, 75–78, 82, 86, 94, 96, 97, 113, 121–123, 126
Pointing, 14, 38, 80, 81, 84, 85
Pointing gestures, 14, 80, 81
Poisoning, 66
Police, 37, 120
Polymorphic structural variants, 15
Positive affect, 100, 123, 126, 129
Positive emotion, 99, 101, 108, 125
Positively reinforced training, 21
Posterior cingulate cortex, 52
Posterior superior temporal sulcus, 52
Praising, 48, 49
Precuneus, 52
Predation, 66
Primary auditory cortex, 48
Primates, 45
Prioritization, 109
Problem-solving, 112
Protection, 5, 7, 67, 75, 76
Protective factors, 97
Protein, 12, 78–80
Proto-dogs, 12
Proximity-seeking behaviors, 37, 42
Psychiatrist, 93
Puppy eyes, 86
Puppy-dog eyes, 3
Pups, 7, 12, 65–81, 86

R
Rabbits, 93
Racial and/or ethnic minority groups, 94
Racism, 95
Randomized controlled trials, 96, 108, 119, 125, 127, 128
Rats, 14, 15, 86
Reactivity, 13–15, 22, 23, 25–28, 107, 124
Rearing history, 40, 41
Regurgitate, 75
Reinforcement, 80, 81, 84
Relaxation, 109, 111
Remembering, 52
Reproduction, 13, 67
Resilience, 92, 97
Responsiveness, 112
Reward expectancy, 47
Rich clubs, 78
Rig Veda, 64
Risk, 92, 97, 99, 104, 108, 110–114
Risk factors, 94–95, 97, 107, 108, 110, 112–114
Rostral dorsal cingulate gyrus, 49

S
Salience, 48
Saliva, 106, 107
Salivary, 22, 105–108
Satisfaction, 118
Scavenging, 12, 63, 69, 78–80, 83, 86
Screening, 97, 98, 110, 118–123, 130
Script, 110, 125, 128
Search and rescue, 5, 37, 45
Secure, 37, 42–46, 54
Secure base test, 45–46, 54
Selection for tameness hypothesis, 13
Selective breeding experiments, 14
Selective pressures, 13
Self-domestication hypothesis, 12
Self-esteem, 118
Self-harm, 122
Self-regulation, 109, 112
Self-report measures, 91, 97, 119, 125
Self-talk, 109
Sentinels, 12
Separation, 42, 44
Serotonergic, 14
Service dogs, 6
Sex, 44, 46, 65, 74
Shelter dogs, 40, 44, 46, 54, 95
Sheltering, 68
Siblings, 71, 72, 74, 76
Sled pulling, 5
Sleep, 76, 109
Sleeping, 75, 76
Snouts, 11
Sociability, 13, 15–16, 20, 23–28

Social bonding, 3
Social bonds, 15, 16, 76, 77, 82
Social cognition, 3, 50, 53
Social connectedness, 117, 123
Social contact, 6, 15, 16, 19, 20, 23–26
Social interactions, 22–26, 28, 49, 81, 86, 93, 100–102, 114
Social learning, 1
Social network analysis, 78
Social partners, 12, 15, 27, 28
Social plasticity, 15
Social proximity, 20
Social relationships, 1, 78
Social support, 17, 37, 93
Socialization, 3, 16, 21, 26–28, 44, 83, 106, 120
Socializing, 106, 120
Socio-cognitive abilities, 7, 38, 40–42, 46, 78
Socio-cognitive measures, 38–42
Socio-cognitive skills, 14, 85
Strange situation test, 42–46, 49, 50
Stress, 7, 8, 12, 14–17, 21, 22, 25, 26, 91–114, 117–118, 120–127
Stress-buffering effect, 17
Stress cascade, 17
Stress management, 109–114
Stressor, 97
Stress response, 12, 14, 16, 17, 26, 97
Students, 7, 8, 64, 65, 79, 92–114, 117–127, 129
Study planning, 109
Submissive, 65
Substantia nigra, 48, 52, 53
Suckling, 72, 73, 76, 77
Suicide, 94
Superior temporal sulcus, 49, 52

T
Tameness, 13
Temperament, 14, 44, 46, 48, 95
Temporal lobe, 48
Temporo-parietal junction, 52
Test taking skills, 109
Thalamus, 48, 52
Theft, 76
Theory of mind, 52, 53
Therapist, 93, 125
Therapy dogs, 6, 8, 108–111, 117–126, 130
Therapy handler-dog teams, 110
Threat, 51, 80–82, 85, 110
Time management, 109, 112
Top-down, intentional processing, 52

Touch, 8, 17, 98, 106, 107, 123–124
Trainers, 21, 23, 54
Training, 5, 6, 8, 21, 23, 26, 40, 41, 44–47, 53, 77, 93, 109, 111, 119, 122, 125
Training experience, 41, 44, 45
Transgender, 94, 95
Trivers, R.L., 67, 72
Trust, 82, 83, 85, 86
Tucked tail, 22

U
University, 7, 8, 91–114, 118, 123, 129
University campuses, 7, 92, 93, 108, 113
Unsolvable task, 7, 39–42, 50
Urban habitats, 65
Urinate, 64
Urine, 23
Usefulness, 112

V
Ventral striatum, 52
Ventral tegmental area, 48, 52, 53
Ventromedial prefrontal/orbitofrontal cortex, 52
Vienna, 18
Village dogs, 4, 63
Virtual, 8, 120, 125–127, 129, 130
Vocalizations, 48

W
Waitlist, 99, 100
Walk, 23, 64
Washington State University (WSU), 95, 108, 109
Water rescue, 45
Welfare, 5, 8, 121, 122, 128
Well-being, 2, 5, 7, 8, 17, 91, 93–96, 108, 112, 117–119, 121–126, 129, 130
Whale eye, 121
Will, 112
Williams-Beuren syndrome, 15
Wolf Science Center (WSC), 17–28
Wolves, 2, 3, 6, 12–28, 40, 41, 63, 74, 78, 82
Working dogs, 4, 5, 54
Working memory, 110
Worry, 97, 99, 112

Y
Yawning, 24